希望 奧莫克 看見

Tzu Chi Village of Hope

薩馬島

奧莫克 ————

奧莫克簡介
Brief Introduction of Ormoc

萊特島

菲律賓

宿霧

保和島

位置
Location
菲律賓東米沙鄢地區萊特省西北部港口城市，臨奧莫克灣，為重要避風港。

The port city of North Western Leyte, in the East Visayas region of the Philippines, is adjacent to Ormoc Bay and is an important harbor.

歷史
History
興建於一八三四年二月二十六日。城市名稱源於 Ogmok，指窪地和地勢低的平原。

Built on February 26, 1834, the city name is derived from "Ogmok", which refers to the low-lying ground and low-terrain plains.

地形
Topography
以平原為主。

The topography is dominated by terrain plains.

氣候
Climate
熱帶海洋性氣候，終年有雨，平均溫度攝氏三十三至三十九度。

Tropical maritime climate, rainfall all year round, with an average temperature of 33 to 39 degrees Celsius.

人口
Population
約二十一萬五千

The population is about 215,000

語言 Language	萊特島語 Lineyte-Samarnon
宗教 Religion	天主教 Catholicism
交通 Transportation	沿岸航運便捷，有環島公路和航空站。 Coastal shipping is convenient, with round-the-island roads and air stations.
經濟 Economy	是萊特省西部的經濟、文化、商業和交通樞紐。工業以糧食加工為主，出口大米、椰乾和糖。 the economic, cultural, commercial and transportation hub of the western province of Leyte. The industry is mainly engaged in grain processing and exports rice, copra and sugar.

奧莫克慈濟大愛村

二〇一三年海燕風災後，由前奧莫克市長艾德華・寇迪拉捐地，慈濟籌資援建。

面積五十公頃，共一千五百八十五戶、六千多人，其中慈濟會員四千多人，老人與兒童兩千多人。

Tzu Chi Great Love Village, Ormoc

After the Typhoon Haiyan in 2013, the former Mayor of Ormoc, Edward Codilla donated the land and Tzu Chi funded the construction.

It covers an area of 50 hectares, with a total of 1,585 households and more than 6,000 people, including more than 4,000 volunteers and more than 2,000 elderly folks and children.

目錄 Contents

第一章　綿延不絕一如春光暖陽
Unceasing Warmth from the Spring's Sunshine

第二章　等待著我們溫柔的梳理
Waiting for Our Gentle Touch

第三章　夜再黑永遠有光的線索
Light at the End of the Tunnel

【推薦序】迎向燦爛未來

謝金龍

　　望著落日，被渲染的彩霞，如此豔麗，似幻若夢，又如此恬靜⋯⋯

　　習習海風，陣陣濤聲，如此規律，使人醺醉。

　　噓，可千萬不要喚醒我，就讓我，這樣地沈沈睡去⋯⋯

　　若非團員的點醒，幾乎忘了這是在海燕風災的重災區！大自然可賦予大塊文章，也可窮洪荒之力，摧枯所有人為的一切！沿途皆是傾頹的牆壁，被拔了根的大樹，沒有屋頂的建築，卷曲如麻花的鋼架⋯⋯

　　有人驚慌逃離，有人卻逆勢整裝進入。失了魂魄的災民，漸漸被喚醒。自己的家園，自己救！精神來了，眼睛也亮了！沒有被困境擊倒的，再次翻轉自己的人生！

　　一波波的藍天白雲志工，如潮水般，信實地，不歇地湧入。一批批的萊特島志工，擦乾眼淚，堅定地，踏實地，不斷地湧出！一個要被放棄的鬼島，終將擦亮，傲然放光！

　　有一地主慨然捐出五十公頃土地，要讓慈濟蓋大愛村，讓流離失所鄉民有棲身之地。從此，一千五百多戶的大愛屋，在這片愛的土地上，壯闊展開！

　　為什麼神父會說，「這從天上掉下來的恩典，是證嚴法師讓慈濟志工李偉嵩送來的」？是誰願意掏錢來購置交通車，只因不捨大愛村孩子們的迢迢上學路？

　　菲律賓慈濟志工裏有位鼎鼎有名的 Alfredo Li（李偉嵩）！

By Chin-Lung Hsieh

Gazing at the sunset, I see the clouds are tainted with colours. Such beauty seems to exist only in dreams. There is just so much peace....

The gentle gust of the sea breeze, the sound of the crashing waves—these pleasant rhythms just makes it so easy to lose oneself in that moment.

"Shh...Don't ever wake me up. Just allow me to sleep peacefully."

If not for a fellow volunteer who woke me up, I would have almost forgotten that this is one of the most devastated areas of the Typhoon Haiyan disaster. Mother Earth possesses great beauty of nature. However, its power can also destroy everything man has ever built. On the way to the disaster site, we saw collapsed walls, uprooted trees, roofless buildings and severely twisted steel bars.

Many had left their village, panic-stricken while others packed up to go in instead. Traumatized survivors were gradually enlightened. "We have to save our own hometown!" They were inspired! Those who were not knocked down by the tragedy stood up to transform their lives anew!

Batch after batch, volunteers clad in blue and white enter the disaster site with firm committed steps. Wiping away their tears, groups after groups of survivors in Leyte province stood up steadily to join the ranks of volunteers. An abandoned ghost town was finally cleared...beaming brightly with pride.

A kind donor donated fifty hectares of his land, allowing Tzu Chi to build a Great Love village for the homeless survivors. Since then 1,585 houses have been built in this land filled with love.

現在又多了讓人嘖嘖稱奇的 Alfreda（艾菲達）！為什麼稱奇？因為牠是一隻會跪拜的母牛！

為何從一位虔誠的天主教受災戶，轉而變成慈濟志工？不只自己做，又帶動了全家人。他說：「慈濟好比是一個『金屋』。」他的金屋不是金錢，竟是證嚴法師給他的法。不只給了他生命的方向，更有力量幫助自己的同胞。

曾經因斜視，從小被人指指點點，而封閉自己。刻意留著瀏海來掩飾天生帶來的缺陷，不敢敞開胸懷接納男孩的愛意。就在因緣下遇到了眼科醫師史美勝，掃除了自卑，並昂首闊步，發揮自己的社工所長，幫助了更多不幸的人。

一群正如朝陽的青少年，充滿著活力與尋找自我定位。為何會在不同的宗教裏，找到了方向，放棄感官的享受，茹素、環保，一起學著助人的快樂？

許多的動人樂章，就在您翻閱芳霈藥師用著浸潤過生命歷練的筆，將更了然於胸。您可以跟著笑，當然，更可以跟著掉眼淚……

時間回到二〇一三年海燕風災，獨魯萬的興華中學。就在臺灣醫療團結束義診，拍完團體照，要上車之前，蔡昇航跑來說：「師伯抱抱～」在熊抱之後，發覺本來就瘦的他更瘦了！皮膚也被晒得更黑了！一下子，不知該說什麼，只能說：「加油！加油！」

但環顧四周，這麼巨大的創傷，該如何重建？

我們醫療團，時間到了，離開了。而他與菲律賓的慈濟人則是義無反顧地，陪伴著這些鄉民走出傷痛。這是何等巨大的

How come a Catholic priest says: "This is a grace from heaven, and Dharma Master Cheng Yen sent Tzu Chi volunteer Alfredo Li to bring it to them"? Who then is willing to contribute by purchasing a vehicle, just because he cannot bear to see children in the Great Love village taking a long walk to school?

Alfredo Li is famous among volunteers in the Philippines! And now we have an amazing "Alfreda"! Why is she amazing? Because she is a carabao who kneels down to pay respect.

How did a devout Catholic disaster survivor became a Tzu Chi volunteer? Not only does he actively participate in volunteer activities but he also leads his entire family to take part in it as well. He explained, "Tzu Chi is like a golden house." But the gold that he talks about has nothing to do with money. It is the Buddha Dharma that he had learned from Master Cheng Yen. Not only did the Dharma gave him a direction in life, it also gave him strength to help his fellowmen.

Having a crossed eye, a girl isolates herself from others since young because people poked fun at her. Keeping her bangs was how she concealed her flaw. She could not even open herself up to accept boys' affection. Yet, in a twist of fate, she met Dr. Antonio Say, who freed her from her insecurity, allowing her to walk confidently, and bring out her best in helping more unfortunate people as a social worker.

A group of young people, who were like the morning sun beaming with radiant energy, seeks to discover their purpose. How come in an environment of different religion, they were able to find their direction in life, leaving behind sensual pleasures, and choosing to be vegetarian, to do recycling and to experience the joy of helping others?

You will be all the more enlightened as you flip through the many touching stories written by Susu and inked with her pen full of life's

任務啊！一個以華人為主，又是佛教徒的團體，這要如何去完成啊？

然而，這不可能的任務，就在年輕的昇航、解放、紅紅、亮亮等，資深的萬擂、偉嵩、國英、青山等，與無數的當地志工，無間斷地長期陪伴，一步步地走出悲情，迎向燦爛的未來。

原來，「安邦定國」，證嚴法師曾對菲律賓慈濟人的期許，如是地展開與落實……

（本文作者為慈濟北區人醫會副召集人、金龍牙醫診所負責人）

experiences. The stories will make you laugh. Of course, it will also make you weep as you go along the pages.

Looking back to the year 2013 at the Leyte Progressive High School when Taiwan's medical team was done with our free clinic service during the Typhoon Haiyan disaster response, and was about to board the van after taking our group picture, Tzu Chi volunteer Michael Siao came up to me and asked; "Uncle, may I hug you?" After we embraced, I noticed he is even skinnier than before! Even his complexion is darker! At that moment, I was speechless as I try to hold back my tears. All I could tell him was: "Keep up the good works!"

However, as I looked around, I saw the whole place is so devastated. How can this be possibly rebuilt?

When the time is up, our medical team would have to leave. But Michael and other local volunteers in the Philippines have to stay behind to accompany the survivors to walk out of their misery. This is such an enormous task! Comprised mostly by Chinese volunteers, and moreover being a Buddhist organization, how would they accomplish such mission?

Yet such impossible feat was accomplished by the young Michael, Chieh Fang Caroline, Carolina, among others, together with senior volunteers Manuel, Alfredo, Henry, James, and many other local volunteers. They endlessly provided long term attention to survivors, helping them to walk out of their pain one step at a time and welcome the bright future ahead.

Finally, we get to realize that the expectation of Master Cheng Yen to the volunteers in the Philippines, which is to "bring peace and stability to the nation", is already gradually being carried out.

(This article was written by TIMA Northern Taiwan Deputy Coordinator, also proprietor of Chin Lung Dental Clinic; Translated by Gloria Chou)

李偉嵩

> 希望是生命的靈魂
> 像是稻田裏的水
> 像是天地萬物的陽光

一位朋友去醫院做身體檢查，檢查結果說是得了肺癌。他整個人立刻精神崩潰，消極、無精打采，對人生感到無奈。

幸好他又再到臺灣慈濟醫院檢查，醫師診斷他沒有肺癌。我們再見面時，他情緒一百八十度轉變，眼神發光、臉孔燦爛、說話有力、走路有風。

搬進菲律賓奧莫克大愛村的一千五百八十五戶居民，是海燕颱風的受災戶，是社會弱勢的族群。他們生活的來源，大多靠的是做農工、三輪車夫、建築工人、保安、小攤販、洗衣幫傭等。

村民經濟收入微薄，又子女眾多，通常只能讓孩子讀到中學，就無法再繼續升學。這些失學的孩子失去社會的競爭力，大部分也只能打零工幫父母養其他手足。

村裏的孩子都不敢有夢想，如父親是三輪車夫，孩子長大了也是三輪車夫；如媽媽是洗衣婦，女兒也就跟著當洗衣婦，貧窮代代相傳。這讓我看了很不捨，總想結合眾人的力量，一起來創造奇蹟與希望。

而證嚴法師的三大願：「淨化人心，祥和社會，天下無災

Foreword Hope Saves All

By Alfredo Li

Hope is the soul of life
Like the water to rice paddies
Like sun to every creature

I have a friend who went to get his health checkup at a hospital. The checkup result showed that he had lung cancer. He went to pieces, became passive, felt listless, and hopeless after he heard this bad news. Fortunately, he went to the Tzu Chi Hospital in Taiwan to get a second opinion. The doctor claimed that there were no signs of lung cancer. When we met again, he was really different. His eyes were brightly shining, his face was glowing, he could speak loudly, and he was walking on air.

The 1,585 households who moved to the Philippines Ormoc Great Love Village were victims of Typhoon Haiyan. They were among the less privilege in society and earned their living as farmers, pedicab drivers, construction site workers, security guards, vendors, and laundry ladies among many other occupations. These villagers earned a meager salary yet they raise many children at home. Most of these children could only finish their high school education. After that their parents could no longer afford to continue sending them to school. Deprived of good education, these young adults could not compete for opportunities in society. Most of them could only take part-time jobs in order to help their parents raise their younger siblings.

The village children could not dare to dream. If a father was a pedicab driver, his child would most likely become a pedicab driver when he grew up. If the mother is a laundry lady, her daughter would be a laundry lady too. The cycle of poverty is passed down to generations. I could not bear to stand and watch the cycle continue for generations more. I dream of gathering everyone's power to create a miracle and bring hope to these families. In this poverty-

難。」在這貧苦之地，該怎樣去實現呢？

藉著施行法師的教法和教誨，讓村民了解家庭、社會的動盪不安，源於身心的不淨，所以我們在奧莫克大愛村持續提倡「三好」與「三不」。

三好就是：「口說好話，心想好意，身行好事。」這是做人成功的祕訣；三不就是：「不抽菸，不喝酒，不賭博。」因為這三種壞習慣，是貧窮的根。

慈濟志工不斷為村民愛灑，分享法，講故事，啟發眾人發揮愛與關懷。村民開始認同證嚴法師的理念，不僅僅改變壞習慣，也逐漸對家庭負起責任，想做子女的好榜樣。

秉持著證嚴法師的智慧：「父母的希望在孩子，孩子的希望在教育。」我們把願意上進的孩子納入助學對象，幫助他們上專科學校和大學，圓他們的夢想。但並非無償資助，我們有條件，條件是希望學生利用週末和假期來做志工，做環保、關懷村裏的老人、參與慈青活動等。期盼藉由親身參與，讓他們在做中學、學中覺。

慈濟志工們最感欣慰的，就是看到村民棄惡行善，孩子在良好的環境下成長，經過一番努力，如今已看到大愛村升起希望的曙光。

在慈濟的人醫年會、大型義診、國際賑災行動中，常遇見來自臺灣、很有愛心的藥師蘇芳霈，她是慈濟委員，也是資深人醫會志工。我對她的印象則是感情豐富，後來才發現她是創作許多圖文書籍的作家。

所以這本有關奧莫克大愛村的專書，就邀請她來為我們書

stricken land, how do we achieve Master Cheng Yen's three great vows: to purify people's minds, harmonize society and free the world from disasters? Utilizing the Master's principles and teachings, we helped the villagers understand that a turbulent family and society originated from unpurified minds. Therefore we promoted "Three Goods" and "Three Don'ts" at Ormoc Great Love Village.

The "Three Goods" are: speak good words, have good thoughts, and do good deeds. These are the secrets to become a successful person. The Three Don'ts: No smoking, No drinking of alcohol and No gambling are three bad habits that are also the roots of poverty. Tzu Chi volunteers constantly held gatherings to share the Buddha dharma and tell stories to inspire villagers to spreading love and care. Many villagers started to understand Master Cheng Yen's ideals and they quit their bad habits and became more responsible members of their families and society. They also wanted to be good role models to their children.

We also helped uphold Master Cheng Yen's wisdom which is: the parents' hopes lie in their children while the children's hope lies in education. We willingly support students who strive to reach their dreams by sending them to colleges and universities. However, the scholarship grant requires the students to volunteer on weekends and school holidays. They do recycling, care for the elderly villagers, join the Tzu Chi Collegiate Association, among other activities. Through volunteer work, we hope that these youths will learn by doing and awaken to the truths of life.

The most fulfilling part for the volunteers are to see the villagers finally turn their backs on their bad habits to practice good deeds and raise their children in a positive environment. After putting in a lot of effort and hard work, hope is rising in Great Love Village.

Tzu Chi International Medical Association, or TIMA, holds large-scale medical outreaches and international relief projects. In these activities, we

寫，圓一個夢，寫大愛村這五年來，它的美麗與哀愁，它的努力與希望。

志工潘信成曾經在萊特島的帕洛，協助大愛村興建長達八個月，他對萊特島民有相當程度的熟悉與情感。他是一位思想敏捷、善解又聰慧慈悲的年輕人，在奧莫克與蘇芳霈搭檔，負責攝影，他的付出常令我動容。

他們兩人來奧莫克參與了大愛村的活動，朝山、浴佛、學校動土；他們採訪了村民、志工、慈青、神父、人醫會醫師和社會菁英等，面對不同對象都能掌握方向與分寸，應對得體。

在採訪的過程中，奧莫克慈濟團隊感受到作者的用心、悲心與細心。每位受訪者吐露的真情，感人的一舉一動，蘇芳霈都不放過，而且總是陪著受訪者一起流淚。

而潘信成甚至為讓大愛村辦公室與廚房有更好的通風，還親自去商場購置設備來組裝，他那種細心、體貼，感動了這裏所有志工，深受志工喜愛。

這本書不僅重於文學也重於感情，這本書充滿村民的奮鬥血淚，翻轉人生的勝利與希望。作者把點點滴滴的故事，經過深刻感受後寫出——《看見希望》。

祈願永遠，在奧莫克大愛村，看到希望。

（本文作者為前慈濟菲律賓分會執行長，現任副執行長）

always see the pharmacist and TIMA senior volunteer Fang Pei Su, who is also a Tzu Chi commissioner. My impression of her was that she is a sentimental person. Later, I found out that she is an illustrator of many books. We invited her to write this book about the Ormoc Great Love Village. To complete this book was a dream come true. It is a record of what the Great Love Village had been through in its first five years, describing its beauty, sorrow, hard work and hopes.

Volunteer Apollo Pan helped build the Great Love Village in Palo, Leyte for eight months. He got to know the local people well and formed a deep bond with them. He is a clever, understanding, wise and compassionate young man. He partnered with Fang Pei Su to tell the story of the Great Love Village using photography. His dedication moved me very much. They both joined in the activities held in the village such as the bowing pilgrimage, the Buddha Day and the groundbreaking ceremony for the Tzu Chi elementary and high school building. Together, they interviewed villagers, volunteers, Tzu Chings, fathers, TIMA doctors and the elites of society. Both of them could properly interact with different interviewees.

During the interviews, Ormoc Tzu Chi team could feel how mindful the author of this book is. Fang Pei Su never missed a detail of what their interviewees had said. She also empathized when the interviewees become emotional.

This book is not only a piece of literature but is also about relationships. This book contains stories of villagers who struggled for their families, turned their lives around and gained victories and hope. The author collected every bit of the villagers' touching stories and presented them in this book, "Tzu Chi Village with Hope". May Ormoc Great Love Village always see hope!

(This article was written by Deputy CEO Tzu Chi Foundation Philippines, Former CEO 2008-2016; Translated by Gloria Chou)

蘇芳霈

　　年初始，寒冷依舊，然我已進行今年新書，寫臺灣島上一些地理環境，它們猶如自己能呼吸、自有存在的生命哲學。

　　「生命」的定義在我來看，並非特定動植物而已，更多是能給予鮮活而正向的能量處。某些人所處的環境與生命哲學有著同等波長，進而傳達更多共振的善良與美麗，解讀同樣具有生命傳承與壯闊胸襟、善護他人生命的態度與地誌。

　　比如臺中清水西側大甲溪出海口，時序入冬，兩岸遍開黃澄澄的油菜花，木棧道的木麻黃樹與海床上的保育植物雲林莞草，遠望風力發電的高聳大風扇，排排站立於海上防坡堤，不斷緩緩旋轉那搖樂。

　　我舒適地靜坐木棧道上，身邊的年輕人一圈圈相偕出遊的身影，聒噪的喧嘩聲漸漸被杜絕於眼尾耳際，消翳入天際；傾聽大海與風的呼吸，壯闊的橘黃暮色，太陽刺眼的金黃只剩一小點，柔美溫暖著大地萬物，當它落在地平線上更展現漫天寬大的存在……

　　那一刻，我明白了一些道理，也深深意識到自己是多麼微不足道的存在！

　　某日，在朱宗慶打擊樂隊裏擔任老師的姪女對我說：「姑姑，應該去一趟南投法治村的武界，看枯水期的濁水溪上游，遍野是五顏六色的彩藻……」

　　我抽空去了，清晨四點多，玄墨籠罩四周，獨自走上陌生

Warm Anecdotes in Cold Days .

By Fang-Pei Su

At the beginning of the year, it was still chilly, but I have already started on this year's new book, writing about the geographical environment on the island of Taiwan. The geographical environment is a philosophy of life that seemed to be breathing on its own and existing freely.

I think "life" does not only refers to animals or plants but also to something that gives a fresh and positive energy. Some people's conditions and life philosophies are in the same wavelength, making it easy for them to resonate kindness and beauty, leave a significant legacy altogether as well as keep an aspiration that safeguards other people's life.

For example, entering into winter, both sides of the river banks at the seaport of Dajia River in the west side of Qingshui, Taichung are blooming with bright yellow canola flowers, horsetail trees along the wooden walkway. Bolboschoenus planiculmis grass are floating on the seabed. Up ahead, lined in rows at the offshore breakwater, towers the wind power generators, its paddles slowly and continuously rotating.

I sat quietly and comfortably on the wooden walkway as young couples, one after another, strolled past me. The noise of people chatting gradually fell into a hush, fading into the sky. I listened to the breathing of the vast sea and the wind, and watched the magnificent orange twilight. The sun's golden glare lingered briefly over the horizon, its gentle warmth still soothing everything on Earth. When it finally set, it showed even more the vastness of the open sky... In that moment, I understood how insignificant my existence is!

One day, my niece, who is the teacher-in-charge of Ju Percussion Group, told me: "Auntie, you should make a trip to Vogai in the Fazhi Village in Nantou county to see the upstream of Zhuoshui River in the dry season, all covered with multi-colored algae...."

路途，找到搭往法治村的公車。準時五點發車，那是一日中唯一一班往返武界的車子，駕駛安靜地開著車，乘客只我一人！

　　靜悄悄的時空，車行過隧道，回頭張望，隧洞透出圓光，彷如墨色中的一輪月亮，雪白的雲海流瀉在山路四周，我彷彿變成動畫片龍貓公車上的主角小月，沁涼地飛翔在天空，再一次體會──在這個世界上，我渺小如微塵，如浮雲一朵。

　　「我思故我在」，暗自告訴自己，行走人間路，該秉著悄然、超脫、不攀附的修為在每一件、每一次人生的試探裏，用心。

　　三月，菲律賓慈濟志工李偉嵩邀約寫一本書！他說，經過了五年，奧莫克大愛村有太多感人的故事發生，「出版這本書，我沒什麼想法，只希望奧莫克的故事能啟發人人的愛心。」

　　權衡輕重，此書是記錄整個村子的翻轉與善良，是收割一畝田，揉合了許許多多人的血汗，才能點亮這六千人的瑰麗人生路，我決定先把私書暫擱。

　　一行人飛到彼岸，我們不懂當地米沙鄢方言，靠著李偉嵩與李劍蘭時而英文、時而福建話交雜著翻譯，錄音帶回來。每寫一篇文稿，都請本土志工翻譯過，再與自己的翻譯核對，就擔心紀錄不詳實或有所遺漏，因此每寫一篇步步維艱。

　　時間有限，記人的本事又差，靠的都是潘信成拍攝或李偉嵩提供的照片來回想這些人那些事，有時覺得翻譯有出入，事件發生時間拿不定，還得追溯慈濟相關報導，來來回回再確認。

　　總共去了三趟，其中兩趟要轉菲律賓國內飛機通三關，再搭車繞山路到奧莫克，最後一次直飛宿霧轉搭船直達奧莫克，前後約一個月時間，從燠熱的夏天跨過溽暑的雨季。

I spared time to go there. At four o'clock in the morning, the place was embraced with total darkness. I walked alone on the unfamiliar path and boarded the bus going to the Fazhi Village. Leaving at five o'clock sharp, it is the only daily means of transportation to and from Vogai. The bus was driven quietly and I was its sole passenger!

In the serenity of time and space, the bus passed through a tunnel. As I looked back, the tunnel revealed a round light, like a moon in the dark, the white clouds lingering around the mountain road. I felt like the protagonist Little Moon on the animated film of the Chinchilla bus, flying above the sky in desolation. Once again, I realized that in this world, I am as minutiae as the sand dust, like the floating cloud.

"In deep contemplation," I murmured. Walking on the path in the living world, I must uphold stillness, transcendence; and with unattached moral cultivation, be mindful every second of life.

In March, Tzu Chi Philippines volunteer Alfredo Li invited me to write a book. He said, after five years, Ormoc Great Love Village is teeming with touching stories. "I do not have any idea how to publish this book. My only wish is that Ormoc's stories will inspire everyone's loving kindness," he said.

And so this book came to be. It serves to record the transformation and goodness of the entire village.

Like harvesting a rice field, only with many people's painstaking efforts is it possible to bring to light the magnificent life of the six thousand people who live in this village, so I decided to put on hold working on my own book.

A group of people flew over to the other shore. We could not understand the local dialect, which is Visayan, so we relied on Alfredo Li and Lana Li to translate using mixed English and the Fujian dialects, and make sure that it was voice recorded. Every time I wrote the manuscript, I asked the local volunteers to translate again, then countercheck with my own translation. I was worried that the recording might not be

二〇一八年五月赴獨魯萬義診，由於前兩日患者不多，及至第三日，雖有安排讓義診者能赴奧莫克大愛村巡禮，然估計當日患者量必大，為了讓藥局作業順暢，我並未前往，但意料之外的，訪奧莫克竟是為了出版書籍而來。此外也為朝山活動、慈濟中小學動土典禮與浴佛兩大典，寫下兩則新聞稿處女作。

　　為此書的誕生，我與潘信成不間斷地採訪與多方融入大愛村，從訪談到相處、攜手拜訪大愛村民與醫療案例、聽李偉嵩熟悉地一一如數家珍，聊他心中的大愛村與可貴的翻轉生命故事，回到旅店寂靜下來記錄時，總感覺自己努力要在一夕之間，由幼童變成高大堅強、有志有為的大人一般困難。

　　第二次赴奧莫克時，我與潘信成接引的海地醫師傑里（Jery Esperance）自高雄醫學院進修熱帶醫學課程畢業，卻因海地內亂無法回家，於是邀他同行。希望傑里親眼目睹大愛村樣貌，以後可把經驗帶回海地；他同時也能回饋熱帶醫學常識給奧莫克本土志工。

　　潘信成是慈青大學長，二〇一三年海燕風災發生後，於萊特島的帕洛待了八個月，陪伴本土志工組合簡易屋。他機敏手巧，鏡頭下捕捉許多美好瞬間，還幫我扛著打穀機、擔米籮、帶鐮刀、提茶水……自己還背著相機、三腳架。

　　每晚慈濟辦公室廚房的安琪莉（Angelique Tizon）與米拉（Myra Pepito）為我們準備熱騰騰的飯菜，菲利士（Felix Cascara）載我們來去飯店不誤時。

　　我們在奧莫克大愛村最遠走到希望之橋，由於橫跨河流，下雨時孩子走在淤泥上容易滑倒。李偉嵩很想將奧莫克大愛村

accurate or have missing parts, so every chapter was tough to write. With the limited time and my poor ability to remember faces, I relied on Apollo Pan's videos and Alfredo Li's photographs to recall the names of these people. At times I felt that the translations have some discrepancies. The time of the incidents were uncertain so I have to trace back to the relevant Tzu Chi news report to confirm over and over again.

To complete this book, we made a total of three trips to Ormoc. Two were on board the Philippine domestic aircrafts, then we travelled by van through the mountain road of Ormoc. The final trip was a direct flight to Cebu, then we took a boat to our destination. From beginning to end, it took us about a month of going back and forth - from the sultry summer to the damp rainy season.

The second time I went to Ormoc, Apollo Pan and I were joined by a medical physician from Haiti, Dr. Jery Esperance. After graduating from Kaohsiung Medical University with a degree in tropical medicine, Dr. Esperance could not return home yet due to the civil war in Haiti so we invited him to come along. We had hoped that he would personally witness the many stories that are unfolding at the Great Love Village, so that when he gets a chance to return to Haiti someday, he will have beautiful memories to take home. At the same time, he could also share his knowledge on Tropical Medicine with the local volunteers of Ormoc.

Apollo Pan is a Tzu Ching alumnus. In 2013, after the Typhoon Haiyan disaster, he stayed in Leyte for eight months to support the construction of the prefabricated houses for the victims. He is both wise and smart, using his camera to capture many beautiful moments. He even helped me carry the threshing machine, the rice buckets, the bell knife and my water jug, all the while carrying on his back his own camera and the tripod.

Every night, Angelique Tizon and Myra Pepito would help prepare hot meals for us in Tzu Chi office's kitchen, while Felix Cascara provided us transport to and from the hotel without delay.

In Ormoc Great Love Village, we walked as far as the bridge of hope as it

建設得更完整，有小教堂、有一所醫院、有許多運動場地，有各種學習科目，讓大愛村的父老孩童都能遠離憂慮，從學習中找到自我長才。然而因緣未能具足，離理想還有一段距離。

一個人最大的修養是知人不評人，最大的愛是付出不求回收，可我今年卻幸福地收割了一畝如此大的福田！

回想十九歲那年的慘澹歲月，「我只能送你到這兒了，剩下的路你要自己走，不要回頭。」父親離世時說的話，在我寫書此時，一再響自沈睡已久的夢田。那些孩子的希望、村民的未來，讓我想到當年的自己，潮起潮落刷過一篇又一篇。

最後一次赴菲勘查奧莫克五十公頃土地利用時，正值慈濟於奧莫克市區舉辦義診，所有慈青與幹部、奧莫克團隊，甚至做大事業亦兼顧慈善的顏長偉也來當志工。他總說：「常年做生意，偶爾也要放下手上工作回饋社會。」

當我們自奧莫克大愛村勘查回來，到學校義診點，安琪莉已備好晚餐，顏長偉走來親自為我盛一碗地瓜粥，望著他酷似韓劇男主角朴新陽的臉龐時，忽然想起他請李偉嵩喝地瓜粥那往事，終於明白他的地瓜粥其實就是他的「莫忘那一年、那一人、那一念」；因為地瓜粥揉合了他艱辛的歲月及至成為富商而識慈濟到付出，種種感恩的甘甜滋味……我腦海又不斷湧現大愛村那些可親又讓人不捨的臉孔。

此書收割不易，收穀攤在「稻埕」上曝粟，先篩穀又去稻芒、草莖，穀粒堆在地上，用粟耙將穀粒一再翻轉堆成山稜狀，讓陽光晒成粒粒金黃。時值秋收，風鼓騰騰滾過粒粒金黃，就等放入笟櫥冬藏了！

crosses over the river. When it rains, the children walking on the sludge could easily slip. Alfredo Li wanted very much to build the Ormoc Great Love Village perfect for the villagers with a small church, a hospital, facilities for sports, recreational and educational activities so that both adults and young villagers will find peace and even develop themselves with new learning. However, karmic affinities have not yet fully developed. The Great Love Village is still a distance away from the ideal.

A person with great self-cultivation understands without judgments. The greatest manifestation of loving kindness is to give unconditionally. I am glad to say that this year, I have the privilege to harvest such a large field of blessings!

"I can only stay with you up to here. You have to walk the rest of the road by yourself. Don't look back." These were the words that my father said to me before he passed away when I was only 19 years old. It was a miserable year. When I was writing this book, I remember his words as if they were echoes from a long-forgotten dream. The hopes of those children and the future of the villagers reminded me of myself during those years as tides brushed over one chapter after another.

This book was not easy to harvest. Spread across the threshing floor, the grains were exposed to the sun. First, their husks were sieved, their rice awns and grass stalks removed. Rice grains were then piled on the ground. Using a hoe, they were turned over repeatedly until they piled up in the shape of a mountain ridge. The sun shines upon them until they turn golden. And then autumn comes. The wind rolls over the golden grains, which are waiting to be reaped and stored in the winter cupboard!

(Translated by Si Ho Ooi)

I. 綿延不絕一如春光暖陽

Unceasing Warmth from the Spring's Sunshine

寇迪拉夫婦 Mr. and Mrs. Codilla

奉獻大地

Billionaire of the Earth

二〇一五年三月，奧莫克大愛村簡易屋完成，前菲律賓分會執行長李偉嵩象徵性移交鑰匙給前市長寇迪拉夫婦。

In March of 2015, the construction of Tzu Chi Ormoc Great Love houses were completed. The former CEO of Tzu Chi branch in the Philippines Alfredo Li handed over the symbolic key to the then mayor Mr. and Mrs. Codilla.

二〇一九年五月，我跟隨團隊來到菲律賓奧莫克大愛村，記錄發生在其中的兩件盛事，一是朝山活動與慈濟中小學預定地動土儀式，一是浴佛典禮。

菲律賓擁有三個鮮明季節，雨季從五月中旬到十一月，此外還有兩個乾季，乾冷季從十二月到隔年二月，乾熱季則是三到五月。熱帶氣旋通常在六到十二月期間襲擊各群島，主要影響地區包含呂宋島、比科爾島和東米沙鄢島（薩馬島、萊特島）。在臺灣正陷入燠熱季節的此刻，菲律賓萊特島相對涼爽一些。

奧莫克是萊特島上兩大城市之一，另一個是獨魯萬。二〇一三年底的海燕風災造成萊特島重大毀滅性創傷，當地政府束手無策，準備棄島，當時慈濟菲律賓分會執行長李偉嵩帶領蔡昇航等志工，從首都馬尼拉買了單程機票到獨魯萬，一心要與

In May 2019, together with a team of Tzu Chi volunteers, I visited the Ormoc Great Love Village in the Philippines. Recorded here are two main events that have happened: one, is the 3 steps 1 bow pilgrimage and ground breaking ceremony for Elementary and High School, and two, is the Buddha Bathing Ceremony.

The Philippines has three seasons. The rainy season is experienced from May to November while the other half of the year is divided into the hot dry season and the cold dry season. The hot dry season starts from March and ends in May, while the cold dry season begins in December and lasts until February.

Tropical Cyclone normally affects the Philippine islands from June to December. The areas which are often on its path includes the Luzon island and East Visayas island. When Taiwan experiences extremely hot weather, the Philippines' Leyte province is the complete opposite wherein it is pleasantly cool.

受災鄉親同在。

　　他們利用「以工代賑」方式，帶動倖存鄉民清理自家環境，三天內使得死城復活；志工楊國英調動五十臺山貓、大卡車等重機械，不到兩個月讓萊特島恢復清淨。

　　這次死傷慘重僅次於南亞海嘯的災難，讓菲律賓政府看到一個佛教組織，不計宗教、語言、膚色之別，用大愛的精神、慈悲的身影陪伴至今，為了鄉民心靈的依歸，甚至不惜重金重建聖嬰教堂。

　　已經揮別近六年的那些記憶，依然有人記得。

　　當我們出入食堂，總有人來問：「先生，我們可以幫您付錢嗎？」李偉嵩問：「為什麼？」那人說：「我們在海燕風災時得到慈濟的救助，所以我們還能在此安心而快樂地生活……」

　　李偉嵩婉拒了好意，另一戶人家也站起來表示感謝，他們家如今已有一個女孩當醫師了，李偉嵩邀請她來加入人醫會，一起造福鄉民。

　　海燕風災的發生，改變了許多人的生命價值觀。其間有政府首長受到感召，捐出五十公頃土地興建大愛村安置受災鄉民。這位善心人士即是奧莫克市前市長艾德華・寇迪拉（Edward Codilla）及其夫人薇歐莉（Violy Codilla）。

　　五十公頃土地究竟有多大？對數字一向混沌的我，上網查了一下，發現奧莫克大愛村的大小，約是七十個足球場大。

　　那是很大一塊平疇綠野，一千五百八十五戶純白色大愛屋如 U 字形整齊蓋在綠絨絨的大地上，像一隻白色大雁棲在舒適的窩裏。村民實在太幸福了！他們擁有大量綠地可以耕種、自力更

Ormoc is one of the two biggest cities in Leyte. The other one is Tacloban. On November 8, 2013, Typhoon Haiyan left significant devastation and trauma to the people of Leyte. The destruction was so extensive that there were suggestions to abandon the city. This is when Tzu Chi Philippines' volunteers bought one-way tickets from Manila to Tacloban, promising Master Cheng Yen not to return to Manila until they had cleaned up the city.

The Cash-for-Relief Program was launched to buoy up the spirit of the residents and encourage them to clean up their own homes and communities. This program, along with the deployment of heavy equipment, such as dump trucks, pay loaders and backhoes, cleaned up the city in 19 days.

Because of the success of the Cash-for-Relief Program, which provided direct financial assistance to the typhoon survivors and revived the economy of Tacloban, Buddhist Tzu Chi Foundation was recognized by the government and hailed by the calamity survivors. Master Cheng Yen even extended financial assistance for the repair and reconstruction of the oldest church in Leyte, the Sto. Niño Church. This is her advocacy: to teach that Great Love goes beyond the borders of religion, nationalities and creed.

Six years have already passed, but the people of Leyte still remember the relief efforts of Tzu Chi. The goodness they have shown are engraved in the people's hearts. In many instances, these people have expressed their gratitude by offering to pay for the volunteer's food whenever they come across them in restaurants as well as through their smiles of gratitude whenever they see Tzu Chi volunteers.

Typhoon Haiyan had changed the life values and perspective of many of its survivors. Former Mayor Edward Codilla and his wife, Engr. Violy Codilla, donated 50 hectares of their own land to build a housing community for Ormocanons.

Why were the Codillas willing to donate such a big piece of land? They

生。村子的形狀正好像一隻耳朵，耳廓處是一條河流包圍住大愛村，村外不遠處盡是綠色的丘陵，只有一小部分與其他平原相接壤。

這麼大一片土地，寇迪拉夫婦為何捨得捐出？他們說：「比起慈濟在萊特島所付出的一切，我們捐出的這塊土地還太渺小了。」「這塊地是上天賜予，而我們只是轉出使用權而已，只有這樣，這塊地才能發揮最好的功能——大愛屋的興建讓受災鄉民不愁住處；有慈濟陪伴補助獎學金，學子們能受教育，五年來，大學畢業的孩子成為社會菁英。只要聽說是慈濟陪伴出來的青年，公司都喜歡錄用，因為慈濟人文教導孩子要用愛與慈悲關懷別人，以誠正信實的觀念為處世依歸。」

住在奧莫克大愛村的鄉民，百分之八十已經完全不抽菸、喝酒、賭博，去除舊有惡習，大家在房子周圍種樹種花，變成桃花源般惹人喜愛的住家。這些人如果沒有受教育而改變，會繼續惡性輪迴，幸虧在愛的陪伴下，他們變成有責任心、勤奮、有希望的家庭，這對整個社會都是正面的轉變。

寇迪拉夫人薇歐莉出生貧困家庭，她小時候常陪父親去捕魚，賣剩的魚才給家人吃。吃不完的魚，沒有冰箱儲存，薇歐莉就隨父親乘夜發送給鄉鄰。曾經驚擾到狗兒而被咬，為此注射了三次抗狂犬病的針劑，但她並不害怕，即便那傷痕還留在身上，但是父親給她的身教比起傷口實在寶貴太多了。

慈悲又慷慨的父親往生時，許多鄉人都前來悼念，那個情景告訴她，即使再貧困也要付出。

海燕風災造成的死傷至今無法估計，慈濟的救助與付出，

answered: Our donation is a little gesture of goodness compared to what Tzu Chi had given to the province of Leyte. This land is God's. We are only its temporary owners. Through Tzu Chi Foundation, more than a thousand shelters for the typhoon victims were built in this land, giving them a safe place to call their own. The young typhoon survivors also received scholarship grants so they can have a brighter future and become sturdy pillars of society.

After five years of living in Tzu Chi Ormoc's Great Love Village, many of the residents had adopted the teachings of Master Cheng Yen. They learned to avoid the three Nos (No smoking, No drinking and No gambling), which is the root of poverty. Most comforting to know is that they planted vegetables in their back and front yard for their own consumption as well as flowers to bring out the beauty of their surroundings. Tzu Chi's Ormoc Team accompanied them, step by step, on this journey of transformation.

Engr. Violy Codilla grew up in a poor family. Her father was a fisherman and she used to accompany him to work. They would sell as many fish as they could and then eat or share the remaining with their neighbors. Her father is not only a good parent but is also a generous person. His kind deeds were witnessed by his daughter and the seeds of kindness also took root in her heart.

There was a time, she recalled, when she was bitten by a dog while delivering fish to their neighbor. It left scars that, to this day, are still visible on her body. For Engineer Codilla, the scars remind her of her father's teachings. When her father died, so many people came to pay respect in his wake.

The devastation wrought by Typhoon Haiyan led Engr. Violy to admire Buddhism. In the disaster's aftermath, she witnessed the dedication of the Tzu Chi volunteers in holding relief operations. She fell in love with the kindness and compassion that Master Cheng Yen embodies.

Violy shared: "When my husband and I went to Hualien to visit the Master, I found that the Master walks with light footsteps that she seems to be

她全看在眼裏，她恨不得自己也是一位佛教徒，她愛上了證嚴法師。她說：「我與先生到臺灣花蓮見法師時，發現法師走路好輕，帶著藝術，像是飄浮一般；法師話聲輕柔，卻充滿了意志與人生智慧。」薇歐莉還想在奧莫克大愛村蓋一間小醫院。

在臺灣，艾德華看見慈濟志工在自家頂樓種蔬菜，興起了他的兒時回憶。他來自一個貧困的家庭，讀小學時，利用休息時間，賣冰棒給同學，這是他掙得零用錢的方式。讀高中時，一直想當神父，但母親不允許，他內心有一處很澄明的想望，相信未來可以用不同的方式實現。

兒時，父親與他一起種蔬菜，把賣冰棒與蔬菜賺來的錢都存在銀行，然後買了一部三輪車。有一天，他到一個私人的沙灘，放眼一望無際的海洋，他坐在那兒沈思，他想若未來能擁有一個私人沙灘，他要把沙灘分享，如今他實現了。

有人建議他把海邊變成一個度假村，薇歐莉立刻拒絕說：「不，我先生要免費供人使用。」艾德華與薇歐莉兩人總是在生活的各方面，相互支持彼此的處事理念。

學建築的薇歐莉，曾經自己操作機械蓋機場。夫家原是做建築硬件，她嫁進來後，把家族事業發揮得淋漓盡致，帶到最高峰。與艾德華結婚十五年後，艾德華的父親選上奧莫克市長。

回想他們夫妻離開家族事業，從零開始打拚時，用房子向銀行貸款做生意，歷經許多艱辛歲月，艾德華每天都會去教堂祈禱，從自己虔誠的信仰裏得到堅定與安心，夫妻倆的生意愈做愈好，繼父親之後，艾德華也當選奧莫克市長。

我們不了解節氣，但有時候是可以感受的，當節氣與生活

floating on air and her every movement is an art. Her voice is soft but full of compassion and wisdom." Engr. Violy is hoping to build a small hospital to safeguard the villagers' health.

In Taiwan, Edward saw the volunteers planting vegetables on the roofs of their homes. This sight brought back memories from his childhood.

He also came from a poor family. In grade school, he spent his break time selling popsicles to his classmates. In high school, Edward considered the path of priesthood. However, his mother objected to the idea. Although he followed his mother's wish back then, he continued to nurse a clear picture of this dream in his mind and held on to the possibility of achieving this later in life.

When he was a child, Edward helped his father plant vegetables. The profit they had made they saved in the bank. Sometime later, his father bought Edward a tricycle. He recalls going to a private beach one day. As he sat meditating, watching the endless ocean, he wished he could own a private beach. For if he does, he would share it with everybody. This is when his dream was created.

Someone suggested that he open a resort at the beach but Violy rejected that idea right away, declaring: "No, my husband will offer it for free."

In all aspects of life, Edward and Violy supported each other's ideas. Violy studied civil engineering and once operated the heavy equipment necessary to build an airport. Her husband's family was in the construction hardware business, and after they were married, Violy helped take the family's business to new heights.

Fifteen years after Edward and Violy were married, Edward's father was elected mayor of Ormoc City.

產生連結的時候。政治圈生態亦是如此，艾德華市長任內，對政治的分裂感到疲憊，因此不再續任。

他們懂得知足常樂，認為這許多的幸福都是上天賜予，因此艾德華也能以同理心看待那些因受災而失去所有的鄉民。他願意分享他的土地，也樂意看見那些跟他同樣經歷貧困的孩子們，能安心住，能受教育，能有翻轉自己人生的機會。

從貧苦到富足，他始終懷抱一顆赤子之心，慷慨地分享他所擁有。不當市長的他，如今也學臺灣志工在自家屋頂種菜，用一箱箱廢棄的箱子，環保再利用裝土，種植了很多蔬菜。他對平實的生活很滿足，也從慈濟學習到愛地球的理念。

他為人樸實，穿著不講究，只要舒適乾淨就好，雖然寡言，但該說話的時候，卻字字珠璣，毫無贅言，親和充滿笑顏，就像鄰家的爸爸般慈祥。他總是尊重妻子的發言，因為他知道薇歐莉言行端正得體，是他一生不可或缺的良伴。

提起李偉嵩，薇歐莉說：「他就像大愛村所有孩子的爺爺，村民都好喜歡他。他很富有，但完全沒有架子，即使下雨天也還在大愛村的泥濘地上工作。他的家族捐助興建慈濟中學，他一直給孩子們孝順的觀念，因為他自己的父母在一場火災中雙亡，來不及孝順的他，把證嚴法師當成母親，把法師的願望當成自己的願望，他做到了，就像回饋了自己雙親，盡了孝道！」

「我們都是被他感動，被他影響的。」說著說著，薇歐莉開心地笑了！「沒有一個團體像慈濟，直到現在仍在此陪伴並且支持需要幫助的人，這就是為什麼我們非常感謝慈濟，感謝法師給我們這麼美好的靈感，讓我們捐出這塊地，讓它有價值，

Thinking back to the time when they went on their own, the couple started their business from scratch. They financed their home and faced many hard times. Edward went to pray at the church almost every day. From his devout faith, he gained firmness and peace of mind. Their business became better and better. Following his father's retirement from politics, Edward was elected Mayor of Ormoc.

During Edward's tenure as mayor, he got tired of the discord in politics. Unable to resolve it, he opted not to run again.

Knowing that happiness comes from contentment and the belief that our blessings come from God, Edward chose to share his land. Most of his people had lost everything because of the disaster. It also made him happy to see children from poor families and who also experienced the same hardships as he had get an opportunity for a much better life.

From the poor boy who sold vegetables and popsicles to the person that he is today, Edward managed to maintain the purity of his heart and his generosity.

After he stepped down as the city mayor, Edward learned from the Taiwanese volunteers how to plant vegetables on his roof. He collected discarded boxes, filled them with soil and planted many vegetables. He is satisfied with his ordinary life and had learned the concept of loving the earth from Tzu Chi.

Edward is very simple and does not put too much effort into what he wears. As long as his clothes are comfortable and clean, Edward is content. He is a man of few words and always respects whatever his wife says. On the other hand, Violy carefully chooses her words. Violy is an indispensable partner while Edward is like the father of the neighborhood.

Once, while talking about Alfredo Li, Violy remarked, "He is the

也讓我們此生值得。」

　　興建大愛村時，艾德華夫婦不只捐出土地，還貢獻了許多填滿土地、軌道的填充材料，而且不收取任何費用。

　　當你發現自己哭點變低，那表示你真的受過傷了。他們充分體解到災難帶給鄉民的傷痛，而分享就是一種愛。

　　在奧莫克大愛村散步時，夫婦倆很享受那些麻雀在陽臺上小小跳步，左右張望的可愛模樣，牛隻在綠野吃青草，孩子們朗朗的讀書聲，他們還會繼續分享他們所擁有的一切。

二〇一九年四月，寇迪拉夫婦（著紅上衣與白上衣者）受邀參與奧莫克慈濟中小學動土典禮。
In April 2019, the Codilla couple (wearing red and white shirts) were invited to attend the groundbreaking ceremony of Tzu Chi high and elementary schools.

grandpa of the children at the Great Love Village. The villagers like him so much. He is well-off in life, but very humble. He works on the muddy land even through the rain. His family is donating to build the Tzu Chi High School in the village."

"We are all touched by his example," Violy said, laughing with joy. "I know of no other organization like Tzu Chi that continues to accompany the people who are in need long after the disaster. That is why we appreciate all their efforts and are deeply grateful to Master Cheng Yen, who gave us such wonderful inspiration. Because of this, we donated our land and was able to help so many. Through this, we feel that our lives have become more meaningful."

While building the Great Love Village, the Codillas not only donated their land but also contributed much of the needed materials and equipment without asking for any compensation.

When you find yourself crying less and less, it means you were deeply hurt!

The Codillas fully comprehend the suffering of their people. Sharing is one kind of love.

When the couple was walking around the village, they take their time and enjoyed themselves in watching the sparrows hop as they scavenge for food. They watched the cows peacefully graze the green fields. They heard the merry sound of children at play. In their hearts, the Codilla couple knew that they would continue sharing what they have.

(Translated by Celia Chang)

看見美善效應

Religion without Borders

二○一九年十月,菲律賓分會第二四三次大型義診在奧莫克中央小學舉行,伊薩卡尼神父與慈濟志工帶動病患一起為天下災難祈福。
Father Isagani P. Petilos and the volunteers led the patients to offer a prayer for a world to be free of disasters.

橘紅金黃的晚霞流瀉時,墨色漸漸從四面八方緩緩包圍,我保持一個距離望著伊薩卡尼(Isagani P. Petilos)神父。他以莊重的步伐慢慢繞過主持臺,在預備位置就座,黑色衣衫閃著頸部一小片白領,黑色眼鏡後的眼睛清亮,靜默中篤定。

近年閱讀《達文西密碼》時,書裏對宗教的探討與了解,讓我明白「神父獨身回應基督之愛」有如佛教的僧侶,他們都是執行天職去愛世人。

這讓我憶起十九歲失去父親時,胸臆裏充塞的某些想法,我想跟隨父親愛的腳步過這一輩子。父親為了救人失去寶貴生命,永遠地消失在我們的視線裏,這件事雖然每每想起,依舊讓人心碎,卻也為父親珍愛別人如己的作為,感到無比驕傲。

餘暉中,迷蝶撲飛在漸漸發黃的草地,一個小女孩坐在我

As the sun sets and the daylight glow fades, I watched Father Isagani P. Petilos from a distance. He stepped solemnly toward the stage and got ready to sit down. Under the gathering darkness, he wore a black robe with a white collar. He sat silently and confidently. His eyes were clear and firm behind his eye glasses.

I read the "Da Vinci Code" in recent years. Based on the book's exploration and interpretation of religion, I realized that a priest's vow of chastity in response to the love of Christ is similar to the mission of Buddhist monastics, which is to love people.

This reminded me of the time I lost my father when I was 19 years old. I thought of following in his footsteps. To save others' lives, he was forever lost in ours. It still breaks my heart every time I think of this. But for my father's act of selfless love, I am immensely proud of him.

斜後方，張大眼睛與我對望，我微笑著向她輕輕揮手，她緊緊抱著手裏的水瓶，很憂慮地小聲喃喃自語，我思忖著她的表情與她說的米沙鄢方言是什麼意思？但沒有人為我翻譯。

我曾經也有過她那麼可愛的年紀，常常窩在父親的書房看佛書，了解父親的信仰——佛教，教義講的是覺有情：「上求佛道以自覺，下化眾生以覺他」，宗旨就是「大愛」。如今的我深知，慈濟人與神父或其他宗教都有共同的靈犀。

伊薩卡尼神父上臺演說了：「慈濟改變了奧莫克的居民，使整個城市充滿了愛，不只是住在大愛村的人，還有住在好房子裏未受災的人們。為了這片土地上所有人，慈濟人慈悲地付出，這股力量就是我們如此感恩慈濟志工與證嚴法師的原因。」

神父也有過童年，他的成長與願，雖無法有機緣得知，他的濃眉與眉下的魚尾紋，卻充分顯示他常微笑，有溫暖的善心。

二〇一三年海燕風災發生時，所經之處的建築與植物幾乎滅絕，唯有椰子樹與堅固的教堂留下部分殘跡。獨魯萬的聖嬰教堂是當地人心靈的倚靠，伊薩卡尼神父當時任職聖嬰教堂，他目睹獨魯萬如何被政府放棄，而慈濟人如何把一灘死城變成活泉，又是如何修復聖嬰教堂，讓島民的心靈有所寄託……

海燕風災發生兩年後，伊薩卡尼神父調任奧莫克市，更深入接觸慈濟志工。他很驚訝在慈濟志工帶動下，當時的奧莫克市長艾德華夫婦捐出五十公頃土地，許多受災戶及當地居民胼手胝足開墾，快速建造了一千五百八十五戶大愛屋。啟用時，神父前去灑淨，祝福災民們得以安居！

海燕風災發生後的頭一年，來自國際的救援組織給予救濟

As the light fades before the sun sets and the disoriented butterfly flew by the yellowing grass land, a little girl who sits behind me opened her eyes widely and stared at me. I smiled and waved at her. She was tightly embracing a water bottle while anxiously murmuring in the Visayan dialect. I tried to make out what she wanted to say from her gestures and facial expressions but I failed. No one was around to translate it for me, either.

When I was in the same age as that little girl, I often laid in my father's study room, reading books on Buddhism. From those books, I learned about my father's Buddhist faith, which teaches enlightened love, seeking the Buddha's way to attain self-enlightenment and transforming sentient beings to enlighten others, as well as its guiding principle of "Great Love". Now I understand that Tzu Chi volunteers, like the Catholic priests and other religious leaders uphold the same spirit.

Father Isagani went up the stage and said: "Tzu Chi transformed the people of Ormoc, filling the city with love. They influenced not only the residents of the Great Love Village but also those living outside the village. Tzu Chi volunteers give with compassion, and this is the reason why we are very grateful to them and to Master Cheng Yen."

The cleric also had his childhood years. We may not have the affinity to hear about his upbringing and his vow, but his thick eyebrows and fishtail wrinkles tell us he often smiles, and possesses a warm loving heart.

In 2013, typhoon Haiyan swept across Leyte, destroying almost all structures and plants, leaving only coconut trees and the remnants of the sturdy church standing. The Sto. Niño Church of Tacloban City is the spiritual refuge of the local people. At that time, Father Isagani was one of its parish priests. He witnessed how the government almost gave up on Tacloban City, how Tzu Chi volunteers revived the dying city and rehabilitated the Sto. Niño Church knowing that in such trying time, the victims need their spiritual sanctuary.

物品，災民們倖免飢餓，但之後國際組織相繼離開，海鹽泡過的土地無法耕作，人們沒有永久性的工作只能受苦。伊薩卡尼神父觀察到慈濟沒有離開，依然持續陪伴，如今不僅奧莫克，帕洛（Palo）也有相當規模的大愛屋。

慈濟陪伴災民至今已五年，神父在想，或許還有另一個五年，又或者慈濟永遠都會在。他深刻明白慈濟為人們帶來希望，而且是一種堅定的承諾，是觸摸得到、感受得到的幸福與愛！

最重要的是，民眾不是等著被救濟，透過慈濟，帶動出一個希望的方向；透過奉獻、勸募、資源回收、教育助學金、一技之長的培養……神父看見整個村子從老到小都懂得了生活的紀律，安定、努力工作、誠實，擺脫酗酒、賭博諸多惡習！

他用菲律賓俚語來形容奧莫克大愛村的「希望」：「當你去奧莫克大愛村時，無論再貧窮，至少都還能找到一隻公雞！」

他深深感覺奧莫克大愛村居民的轉變，實際生活中，村民已自心底滋養出愛的能力，他們不僅能自力更生，並且與慈濟志工們同心協力，投入許多善良的活動，活出信心。

在伊薩卡尼神父的思維裏，沒有紀律的延伸，便看不見翻轉人生的希望。紀律實際上是一種倍增效應，當你種下一顆愛的種子，慈悲的善根將永續散播奉獻的精神，從貧民的身上，感染了整個社會，各階層人士無不感受到夢是可以變成希望，夢能成真，因而紛紛投入慈善行列。

百分之九十信仰天主教的奧莫克大愛村居民，早已沒有宗教的隔閡，神父認為，只要心中有愛，任何宗教團體都能一起為人們的利益合作，去充實他們的生活，找到生命的價值！

Two years after the typhoon disaster, Father Isagani was transferred to head the oldest church in Ormoc City. There, he developed a deeper bond with Alfredo Li and other Tzu Chi volunteers. He was amazed with the way Tzu Chi volunteers inspired the then city mayor Edward Codilla and his family to donate their 50 hectare land. Later, with the collective effort of the disaster survivors and local residents, Tzu Chi built 1,585 units of Great Love houses in this land. During the moving in ceremony, Father Isagani, among other priests, came to bless the houses.

One year after the Haiyan disaster, many international relief organizations provided material aid which kept the survivors from starving. But these groups eventually left. Soaked with the salty sea water, the farmlands could no longer be planted with root crops and other produce. Without a regular job, the people suffered. Father Isagani noted that Tzu Chi had not left. Rather, they continued with their programs to help the victims fully recover. Aside from Ormoc, Tzu Chi also built a Great Love Village in the municipality of Palo.

Tzu Chi has been accompanying the disaster survivors for five years already. Father Isagani thought, "Will there be another five years?" or, "Will Tzu Chi always be here?" He is convinced that Tzu Chi brings hope to the people. It is the volunteers' firm commitment. It is happiness and love that you can truly feel.

But most importantly, the disaster victims are no longer just waiting for aid. Through Tzu Chi, they are guided towards a path of hope. Through dedication, fund raising, recycling, educational support, livelihood trainings… Father Isagani saw that the residents of the Ormoc Great Love Village, young and old alike, dutifully observe the rules and regulations of the village, persevere for their families and are honest in all their pursuits. Above all, they are staying away from the bad habits of smoking, drinking and gambling.

Father Isagani used the local dialect Pangandoy to describe the Ormoc

夕陽西下，落在遍生綠樹的山坡後面。奧莫克大愛村的 LED 燈亮了起來，四周歌聲溫暖又整齊，似乎在證明這裏的每件事情都具有它的意義。

　　伊薩卡尼神父很喜歡觀賞慈青們比手語，認為那是溝通、拉近彼此距離，相互鼓舞與團結的一種力量：「慈濟不談宗教，只奉獻一切美好，並且謙卑地給予。如今我也受到這分美好的洗禮，九十度鞠躬為一切眾生祝福啊……」

　　奧莫克大愛村將興建中小學和一座小教堂，伊薩卡尼神父已經能想像，幾年之後的奧莫克大愛村將是一片林蔭大道。

　　他想起證嚴法師曾經說：「我想真正改變這個地方，讓人們永久安居，一代又一代；也許這一代人由於教育水平與習慣不那麼容易改變，但年輕一代，我們可以改變這一點。」

　　伊薩卡尼神父關注著萊特島居民普遍沒有正確的生活價值觀，很多人只想在島上工作，和朋友一起享受，而不考慮未來。他看著許多父母是蔗田工人，收入微薄，他們的孩子根本沒有機會受教育；無法與別人平起平坐的傷口難以磨滅，貧困的循環，是萊特島居民普遍的噩夢。過去五十年無法改變的事，卻在慈濟志工帶動下，三年內全改變了。

　　他認為，這從天上掉下來的恩典，是證嚴法師讓慈濟志工送來的！

　　慈濟已經讓五位年輕人到馬尼拉學中文。他們早上在工廠工作賺錢，能有津貼寄給家人，自己也有生活費，漸漸綻放出自信心。下午上中文課，將來能到臺灣繼續學習，再把知識帶回到奧莫克大愛村，分享給同胞和下一代。

Tzu Chi Great Love Village. He said, "When you visit Ormoc Great Love Village, no matter how poor people are, you will still a find a rooster with them." He has seen and felt the transformation of the residents. In their daily life, residents project an aura of goodness. Not only are they self-sufficient, they are also participating in Tzu Chi's many charity works, living a life filled with confidence.

Father Isagani knew that without discipline, it is impossible to see life's transformation toward hope. Discipline has an exponential effect. Whenever you sow a good seed, roots filled with compassion extend far. Starting from the poor people, it will gradually spread to society. Everyone will feel that dreams can translate to hope and become reality, convincing many to join Tzu Chi's charity works.

Over 90% of the residents of Ormoc Great Love Village are Catholics but they have transcended the religious divide. Father Isagani believes that all religions can work together to benefit mankind and give everyone a chance to find their life's purpose.

The sun sets at the back of the mountains. Ormoc Great Love Village was lit up with the street lights and the sound of singing from a distance was soothing, as if attesting that everything that happens here has its meaning.

Father Isagani likes to watch the Tzu Chi Youths practice the sign language. He thinks that it is a form of communication that bridges the gaps between people and encourages unity. He said that in Tzu Chi, religious barriers do not exist. Instead, everyone dedicates their best and gives with humility. Everyone in Tzu Chi knows the art of respect and bows 90 degrees to express it.

Tzu Chi is going to build an elementary school, a high school as well as a chapel in Ormoc Great Love Village. Father Isagani can already picture a boulevard here in a few years time.

晚風在背後輕輕推著伊薩卡尼神父，他慢慢走過一盞又一盞 LED 燈下，每盞都像是小小的太陽。奧莫克大愛村的居民都想成為給人溫暖與力量的人。

神父的眼神突然亮了起來，他看見年輕人的希望藍圖；他們看待事物的眼光放遠了，也敢於夢想！

這分美善的感動，不需要傳揚教義，光從慈濟志工的美好身行與大愛謙卑的儀禮、教育與人文培植，萊特島民都明白了——佛陀愛的方式。

慈濟五十二周年慶暨浴佛典禮中，前菲律賓分會執行長李偉嵩頒發感謝狀給伊薩卡尼神父。
Tzu Chi volunteers presented the certificate of gratitude to Father Isagani P. Petilos during Tzu Chi's 52nd anniversary celebration and Buddha Day Ceremony.

He remembered that Master Cheng Yen had said that she wanted to transform this land so that generations of people can permanently live here. It may not be easy to change this generation because of their different educational backgrounds and acquired habits but Master Cheng Yen is hopeful that Tzu Chi can achieve this in the younger ones, with the help of proper education.

Father Isagani is concerned that the locals of Leyte province do not have a proper perspective in life. Many of them prefers to work in Leyte, have a good time with friends without thought for the future. Many parents are sugarcane farmers with meagre income, which affected their children's chances to receive a good education. As a result, these children cannot keep up with the developments in society, and so goes their cycle of poverty. These were the nightmares of most people in Leyte. These haven't changed in the past fifty years. But with Tzu Chi's guidance, total transformation was seen within three years.

Father Isagani believes that the grace that came from the Heaven was brought by Tzu Chi volunteers as instructed by Master Cheng Yen. A slight evening breeze caressed the back of Father Isagani. He walked slowly, passing one light post after another. Every LED light seems like a little sun. The residents of Ormoc Great Love Village want to bring warmth and strength to people. Father Isagani's eyes brightened up when he heard about Tzu Chi's plans for the younger generation. The youth can now dream and hope for a better future.

This beauty and goodness do not need deliberate propagation of dogmas. By simply observing the goodness in Tzu Chi volunteers' works and the humility in their decorum, their nurturing of education and humanistic values, people of Leyte knew – this is the Great Love taught by the Buddha.

(Translated by Danny Tam)

為使命奔走天涯

Fulfilling His Life's Mission

二〇一一年，輕颱瓦西重創菲律賓南部，慈濟志工於卡加延德奧羅市發放大米，顏長偉自馬尼拉前往協助。

In 2011, Typhoon Washi damaged the southern part of the Philippines. Volunteers distributed rice in Cagayan de Oro. Eric Ngan flew there to help the victims.

起風的晴日午後，菲律賓市區一條美麗的街，兩側有高聳的鳳凰木，秋分了，部分仍盛放一樹火紅。灌木欖毛果玉心花，一簇簇白了整條街，桃紅色的緬梔，樹葉被雨水洗得亮亮的，落葉隨風翻飛，有時繞過我身旋轉，有時繞著別人。

顏長偉（Eric Ngan）從馬尼拉南端驅車前來，他已在清晨走入深山，採來五顆大釋迦。釋迦的種子來自臺灣，種在深山裏，要花兩個半小時車程才能抵達那山上。

我不禁想像，釋迦是他心裏的一個祕密，兩個半小時山路，像是迷宮隧道，隧道外的釋迦園有著雲霧繚繞，空靈的美景。

出生於中國大陸的顏長偉，七歲就開始了小買賣。父親用鐵鍋炒熱沙翻炒花生，翻沙的花生炒熟了就自動會脫膜，再切一節竹子當量筒，把花生倒入藤籃裏，再拌海鹽，他就這樣提

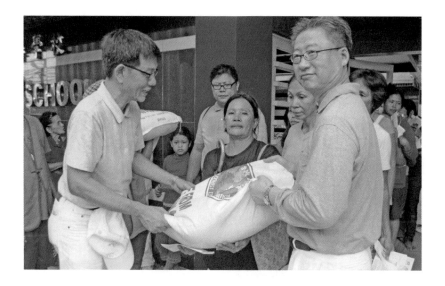

Coming from the south of Metro Manila, Eric Ngan had already gone to the deep parts of the mountains in the early morning to bring us five pieces of big custard apple. Its seeds came from Taiwan, and were planted in the mountains. It will take two and a half hours drive to reach that site. Mr. Eric Ngan is a successful businessman in the Philippines. His is a rag to riches story that can easily qualify for a TV series that will surely become a hit. But more inspiring is his generosity towards his employees and to the less-privileged of society.

Eric Ngan was born in mainland China. He started selling peanuts in the streets when he was only seven years old. He learned the technique of sand-frying peanuts with an iron pot from his father. Many times while selling peanuts, the young Eric had experienced extreme fatigue that he longed to go home and rest. Other times, the weather was so cold and the rain poured so there were very few customers. Yet, knowing that his family needed the money, Eric would shrug off these challenges and carry on selling peanuts.

著藤籃沿街叫賣。

顏長偉的母親是他生母的姊姊，家教十分嚴格，但顏長偉反而覺得嚴格是好的，他懂得不違逆就是孝順，再苦都當成是人生的試煉。

七歲正是快樂嬉鬧的年紀，顏長偉上街賣花生，遇到下雨或酷寒的日子，萬物都想休息，那小小的身影依舊漫步街頭，對於匆匆而去、沒有停下腳步的人群，他沒有戀戀不捨，咬著嘴唇，直到售罄才回家。

堅毅的心志在那麼小的年紀，便已在他心底滋長，春夏秋冬，反覆於求學與買賣中度過。他必須為家掙錢，七歲的心裏溫度是幾分？只有他自己知道。

顏長偉九歲那年，生父把他委託同鄉從鄉下偷渡到香港。同批偷渡的有三艘船，只有顏長偉中間那艘船偷渡成功，前後兩艘船由於大風浪強渡海，大部分的人都遇難，生還的都給香港警察抓走、遣配回大陸。

由於農村生活困苦，兄弟姊妹多，奶奶好不容易蓄夠了路費，讓父親去菲律賓找出路。母親為了每年可以和父親團聚，就和奶奶、姊姊一起到香港定居。

顏長偉從小離開生母，像還學不會飛的鳥，不得不離巢，離了巢還要去覓食……我思忖著他的心受過傷，但無法定位那傷的稱謂。

在香港，他和母親、姊姊、妹妹住在一間小房間。因為在大陸鄉下沒讀過英文，學校要他重讀一年級。他的學習成績都在前茅，一直到小學四年級，書本、簿子都是免費的。

Eric was taken in by his mother's sister. His adoptive mother was very strict, especially when it comes to his education. However, Eric never resented her. He believes that his mother's strict upbringing was for his own good, while not resenting her is filial piety. When it gets difficult, he chose to see it as mere life's challenges.

When he was 9, Eric was smuggled by his father to Hong Kong. The smugglers had prepared three boats to transport the passengers. Unfortunately, two boats sank during the voyage, killing many of its passengers. Those who survived were captured by the Hong Kong police, while the corpses were sent back to China. Only the boat where Eric had boarded managed to reach Hong Kong. Seeing how difficult life was in the farm and Eric's father had many children to support, Eric's grandmother saved up some money to allow his father to venture for greener pasture. Later on, his mother, together with his grandmother and sister joined Eric in settling down in Hong Kong. At a young age, Eric was separated from his mother. He was like a bird that had not fully learned how to fly yet was forced to leave his nest... I wanted to ask if he was ever hurt, but I could not be sure how to properly ask it.

In Hong Kong, Eric lived in a small room with his adoptive mother and sisters. Because he did not learn English in China, the school in Hong Kong made him redo the first grade. Up to his fourth grade, Eric received free books for being one of the students with exemplary academic performance. Every day after class, he and his sister and adoptive mother would work on some handcrafts to augment their daily needs. In fifth grade, Eric began to work part-time. After his class, he would carry his school bag to the factory where he worked. He usually worked there until the factory closed for the day. Even then, he would pick up more work that he could continue to do at home with his mother.

The most difficult time of the year was winter. While other families warmed themselves with cotton quilts, Eric recalled having to work well into the night so he could make money for the family. In the early morning, he

一年級到四年級放學後，他和姊姊、母親一起做手工賺取幫補家庭生活的費用。五年級開始半工半讀，下了課背著書包，就到和學校同一條街的工廠做工；為了賺更多錢，他總是做到工廠關門後，還拿手工回家和母親一起做。

　　最難受的是冬天，別戶人家一早就鑽進棉被取暖睡覺，他和母親還趕著把拿回家的手工做完，隔天一早上學前交回工廠，發薪水就一分不少交給母親做家費。

　　四口人住的小房間擺有上下鋪，每當他一身疲累回到家，就拿出一張屬於他的床板，一頭搭著床邊、一頭在地上。十二月刺骨冷風打房子的隙縫四面八方穿進來，冷得他直打哆嗦，那日子極為艱辛刻苦，但一家四口相親相愛，相互照顧、相互關心，感情很好，想起那段日子，雖然生活困難，但也過得很溫馨的。

　　父親一人在菲律賓打拚，每月寄回四百港幣供一家子生活。但因為外婆早逝，留下出生不久的小舅舅及年幼的雙胞胎舅舅，母親從小就長姊如母照顧弟妹，結了婚也是把大半的錢寄回大陸娘家。

　　當時寄物品到大陸都是用布包，繫成一個果子結……顏長偉似乎生長在古代，泛黃的相片裏，述說著當時情景。想像他的眷戀與信仰，有著從容的美麗，詩情滿溢卻苦澀的心境，看似日常，卻暗藏著時光的推移。

　　一九七八年，他二十四歲，去了菲律賓，用父親勤儉積蓄的一點小本錢做生意，店名就叫「三分錢（Three cents）」。問他為何取了這麼有趣、令人一見難忘的店名？

would take the works he had completed to the factory. He gave all his salary to his adoptive mother. The small room where the family of four lived was very crowded. Decembers were bitterly cold. The wind hit the house from all directions and penetrated their home. Although they had a difficult life, the family loved each other and cared for one another.

Eric's father stayed in the Philippines by himself to work. He sent 400 Hong Kong dollars monthly to his family. In 1978, at the age of twenty-four, Eric came to the Philippines to start a business using the small amount of capital money that his father had saved. He named his store "Three Cents".

I asked him why he chose such an interesting name. He said, "At that time, I had considered many possible good names but they had all been registered. Then I remembered my adoptive mother saying, 'Three cents business can start a shop'. This means that a business with partners is difficult to start. You only need a small amount of money to open a business. So I thought of the name "Three Cents." From a one-person company, his business now has nearly 5,000 employees with sales spanning across the country. Eric Ngan has been a successful entrepreneur for over 50 years.

When his employee broke a kid's leg in a car accident, the employee ran away. The family of the victim demanded a compensation of 186,000 pesos. Eric not only shouldered the responsibility but he also offered to take care of the kid's education. There was another time when an employee broke his leg. Eric personally went to the hospital to pay for his medical expenses. The employee was grateful, and after he recovered, he worked hard to pay Eric back. He is now the manager of the company. Eric never boast about his good deeds, but people see his sincerity and how he cared for them.

Eric's company makes all kinds of items from clocks, clothes, and small appliances to the current motorcycle factory to retail. Eric credits his success to his adoptive mother who taught him to treat others kindly and to keep a sincere heart as the cornerstone of his life's philosophy.

他說：「當時找了很多好店名，但是都已經有人登記，後來想起母親說過『三分生意都要擺一攤』，意思是合夥做生意難，小小本錢都要自己做，不要與人合夥，於是就想到『Three cents』這名字！」

從一人公司發展到如今四千八百多人的規模，銷售區域遍及世界與全國各地，顏長偉邁入工作五十年，儼然已是事業有成的大企業家。

曾經在他公司工作了七個月的員工，騎摩托車送物品途中，把別人家的孩子撞斷腿，卻肇事逃逸了。對方要求十八萬六千披索的代價，他不但一肩扛起，還主動幫對方的孩子負擔教育費用，這分善意與心胸氣度特別讓人感動。

另一次是員工不慎折斷腿，他去醫院為員工付了醫藥費。那員工心底感激，復原後以賣力工作來回饋，如今已是他公司的經理。顏長偉做好事不張揚，但總有人看見他的真誠與愛護。

他的公司代理各樣物品，時鐘、衣服，乃至小家電到現在的摩托車工廠到零售。顏長偉的成功，除了歸功母親嚴格教導待人接物，善良、殷實的心地，更是他成功的基石。

從前菲律賓進口物品需要「遠東公證」，令很多廠商止步不前，他卻一點也不害怕，認為嚴格的簽證代表物品實在且有保證。他原本就是自我要求嚴格的人，自然對代理的物品也信心十足。

做生意雖然也有挫折、傷心的時候，但當時間過去，他退後一點再看，有如爬上圍牆遠望，發現那些都是讓他更理解待人接物的過程，也讓他更加樸實與善解他人，很多時候必須歷

But it was not always sunshine and rainbows for Eric's business. The company also went through setbacks and sad times. After it has passed, Eric would analyze and reflect on the cause of the problem. This helps him to better understand their shortcomings and learn how to treat people right. He refuses to take all the credit for his company's achievements. Instead, he recognizes the role that his employees have played for its success. He respects each and every one of them from the cleaner to the general manager. All these and many other lessons are what he learned from his adoptive mother, including: "The little things should be done well in order to achieve greater things later."

Eric has a deep-rooted love for the Chinese culture. He insisted on doing business the Chinese way. Being Chinese is his greatest pride and he takes pride in its history, its philosophy, its contribution to humanity. He also distinctly remembers his life in Hong Kong. He remembers the neighbor who is a polio victim and who loved to read and share stories to everyone. In his mind, he can still hear the Chinese songs that were so popular back then.

When Typhoon Haiyan struck the provinces of Leyte and Samar, Eric saw on television the massive devastation it left on thousands of lives and properties. The scenes that touched him the most were the images of people crying helplessly. Eric immediately contacted Tzu Chi. Taking his eldest daughter, who just came home from studying in Australia, he joined the relief efforts.

Together with Manuel Siao, James Chua and other volunteers, they boarded a ship from Cebu to Ormoc. During the boat ride, Manuel Siao handed him a pull-up cart that carried an iron box. In turn, he handed the cart to his daughter who asked what was inside. He told her that it contained Jing Si Aphorisms by the Master Cheng Yen. It will be given to the calamity victims.

In fact, Eric secretly guarded the iron box, which contained a large amount of relief money. When they went ashore, they successfully delivered

經破繭才得新生。

他對自己的成就並不居功，反而歸功於所有員工的努力付出。他尊重每一位員工，小到清潔工，上至總經理，認為每項工作都有受人尊重處。在這世界上，也許那就是功課，而每個人所分配到的功課不同，但你不能用世俗的眼光來評價這份工作的貴賤。

外在世界與內心宇宙的縫線處，他放得極寬極廣，寬亮得只剩下一小點黑，廣到地平面上只剩一條線。

記得兒時，母親嚴格的教導，比如抹桌子，抹完桌面一定再抹桌子的四個邊；掃地要向內掃，每個角落都要掃乾淨。母親說小事要腳踏實地做好，以後才能成就大事。

顏長偉對中國文化根深蒂固的愛很難轉彎，他堅持在華人圈做生意，但對象不一定非華人不可，身為中國人，是他最大的驕傲。

五十幾年的歲月如白雲蒼狗，時光溜走的聲音已無法辨識，但他永遠記得香港住家隔鄰，有個小兒麻痹的孩子很愛讀書，常講故事給大家聽。

有回，那孩子講到故事某處，舌頭「抵、抵、抵……」抵了個半天抵不出來，把大夥兒都緊張得笑翻了！還常有人唱黃梅調、劉三姊的歌，是人生幾番消長後，愈是深刻的生活印象。

海燕風災發生時，在電視裏看到萊特島災區一片狼藉、滿目瘡痍的畫面，多少人在那兒無助地哭泣……他心如刀絞，馬上聯絡慈濟，帶了剛從澳洲求學歸來的大女兒，在第一時間與蔡萬擂、蔡青山等人從宿霧上船。

the money to Tacloban City, which was the ground zero of Typhoon Haiyan. He jokingly said: "It was the riskiest mission that I have ever taken in my entire life."

After many years of interactions with Tzu Chi volunteers, Eric began to recognize and appreciate the mission of the foundation. He never hesitated to support its projects financially and to participate personally.

He made fun of Alfredo Li, "He is well-known as the volunteer who cries when sharing Tzu Chi stories. But his tears can open our hearts and our pockets, too." Alfredo Li was not to be outdone. He said: "Once, we visited him in his office. He invited us for lunch. We thought it will be a sumptuous lunch, but he served us a bowl of sweet potato porridge."

This is how the two men admired and respected each other. This also shows the kind of person Eric is. A man of means who still leads a frugal life.

Eric came from a poor family. His journey toward success was long and arduous. But though he eventually reached the top, he did not let it take away his enjoyment of the simple things in life and of helping those in suffering.

Eric lives very simply. He does not wallow in luxury. He worries about the next generations for they will inherit the future. He generously supports Tzu Chi's scholarship programs in Ormoc and Bohol. And when he heard that the children of Ormoc Great Love Village have to walk several kilometers to attend classes, he immediately wrote a check for a vehicle to transport them to school. Little did he know, that vehicle will not only be used to take the students to school. Today, village volunteers are also using it for their recycling activities, relief operations, and even serves as an ambulance, a funerals hearse, among others.

You have to feel life instead of filling it with complains for its many shortcoming. If we cannot have what we desire, then let it go. Every individual

在船上，蔡萬擂交了一臺載著鐵箱的拉車給他，他又轉交給女兒負責。女兒問裏面裝的是什麼？他回答是證嚴法師的著作《靜思語》，要發送給災民的。

　　其實他暗中護著那鐵箱，裏面是一大筆賑災款。上岸時，女兒在前面拉，他在後面推，順利把錢帶到獨魯萬，那是一次膽大心細又危險的行動。顏長偉做到了，以非慈濟人的身分，做了很多慈濟人做不到的事！

　　經過這幾年的接觸，顏長偉除了深愛慈濟，也調侃李偉嵩：「他只要流眼淚，就能打開別人的心門！」李偉嵩不服氣，也說：「有一次我去他辦公室，他請我吃午齋，一碗地瓜粥！」這是兩位相互欣賞的男人褒獎彼此的方式。

　　顏長偉出身清寒，走過漫漫艱辛路途，他的心中擁有一顆解救苦難人的悲心與使命。他看淡生活，不追求奢侈，重視下一代人的前途，不僅捐獎助學金給奧莫克大愛村的孩子們，一聽孩子們要走遠路上學，馬上又捐一輛大卡車，可以一次容納所有上學的孩子，路途往返不讓家長擔憂。可是他並不知道，這大卡車在奧莫克大愛村可說是萬用啊！

　　生命是去感覺它，不是去計較它。如果很多希望期盼不了，就護它安好。每個人都像一顆種子，它們樣子都不同，但卻沒有分別，都在等待合適的季節發芽，然後開出一朵朵美麗的花。

　　顏長偉偶爾山上走著，停下腳步，抬頭仰望天空，有時烏雲密布像重重圍障，彷彿裏面藏著他內心一個一個小小的心願，那時世界似乎距離他很遙遠，但他懂，烏雲會散去。山風吹來，帶著淡淡的香氣，他要懷抱使命奔走天涯！

is like a seed. They may vary in appearance, but they are all just waiting for the right season to germinate, and later bloom into beautiful flowers.

There are times when Eric would retreat to the mountains, away from the troubles of the world. He would look at the far distance, watching the dark clouds pass by. Deep within him is a tiny wish. The world he dreams of may still be far away, but he knows that the dark cloud will soon disperse. Taking a deep breath of the fresh mountain air, he knows he has his life's mission to fulfill.

(Translated by Audrey Cheng)

顏長偉得知奧莫克大愛村的孩子要走好遠的路去上課，立刻購置一輛大卡車，由村民志工載孩子們一起上下學。

When Eric Ngan learned that the kids in the Ormoc Great Love Village had to walk a long distance to reach the school, he immediately purchased a truck that the village volunteers can use to drive the children to school.

一念舞春花

A Cheerful Thought Makes Flowers Dance

王香圃（中）透過好友唐榮謀（右）了解奧莫克大愛村孩童需要助學金，立刻捐助一百五十萬披索。

As soon as Victor Siasat (middle) learned that the children in Ormoc Great Love Village needed education grants through his best friend Julian Tong (right), he immediately donated 1.5 million pesos.

潔淨的大玻璃門內，牆上一幅舞蹈的紅百合花，翠綠細長的葉子深淺有致，鮮紅鮮橘的花熱情綻放其中，顯示餐館的大度與迎賓之氣。高高低低臺階，一群又一群寒暄的面孔，薩克斯風吹奏著熟悉的英文曲子，落地窗外的花與樹，都因這大片的紅綠而變得模糊不清，失去焦距。

王香圃（Victor Siasat）笑出兩顆虎牙，一身黑衣，象徵獨立自主的信任感，他是一個認為每天都不可能重新彩排的人，生活態度十分嚴謹。

小時候，王香圃常跟著母親去買菜，看到街上有人乞討，就心起憐憫向母親要錢布施。雖然家裏窮，但母親知道他有善念，還是給了錢，讓他跑去拿給乞丐。母親操勞家務，但每晚都會騰出時間念《二十四孝的故事》給他聽，王香圃很喜歡。

As we peered inside through the large clear glass door, we glimpsed a painting hanging on the wall. The picture was of dancing red lilies intertwined between the deep and shallow shades of green slender leaves. These bright red and fresh orange-colored flowers were blooming vigorously, exposing the restaurant's magnanimous and warm ambience.

The high and low staircases, group after group of cold faces, saxophones playing familiar English melodies, the flowers and trees outside the floor-to-ceiling windows, all had become blurred and lost in focus caused by this large patch of bright red and fresh orange colors.

Mr. Victor Siasat came in with his gentle and unassuming smile. Dressed in black, he exuded an aura of confidence and yet he remained casual in his manner.

Victor believes that life is something that cannot be rehearsed; which

每年年底，王香圃才有一雙新鞋子，母親總是買大一號，認為小孩子「一暝大一寸」，大一點的鞋子隔年還能穿。

　　從前的年代大都是「嚴父慈母」，王香圃看到父親時總是戰戰兢兢，更別提和父親說句話了！父親的兄弟們生活都過得好，唯獨父親不得志，目睹父母被親戚瞧不起，他小小的心靈很受傷，立志將來要賺大錢，讓父母顏面有光。

　　舊時的菲律賓很排華，華人來此受盡輕視。當地人看到華人皮膚白淨，總要諷言一句「嘸咖」，華人則反譏菲律賓人「番仔」，相互仇怨。華人重視教育，在菲律賓辦校，老師多數來自臺灣，中華文化的薰陶，帶給學子不同一般的思維。

　　孩子不像大人有那麼多偏見，孩提時玩在一起，河邊釣魚抓蝦，不論華人或菲律賓人都是好朋友。孩子的心稚真，如遼遠天際清澈寬闊，像平原野草上的白鷺鷥，恣意飛翔，沒有隔夜的怨仇。

　　菲律賓人天性樂觀、愛享受，沒有儲蓄的觀念，華人懂得儲蓄，因此富商多半是華人。王香圃向親戚借錢做生意，菲律賓員工總是高興就來、不高興就見不著人影，他常常一個人「校長掃地兼撞鐘」，凡事親力親為，埋首苦撐！但若是培養好的員工想出去闖天下，王香圃總會祝福他們成功。

　　他培養出來的員工，其他公司都想聘請，因為各個都具備勤快、認真的條件。假使出去找工作，沒能比在王香圃公司待遇好，大半員工也都會再回來。有些舊部屬會回來找王香圃，找他代理新公司的產品。正因為王香圃栽培員工沒有保留，對員工去留自在慷慨，因此獨立出去的員工都回頭找他代理生意，

is why he is extremely strict with his living etiquette. When he was a child, Victor Siasat often accompanied his mother to buy vegetables in the market. Whenever he saw beggars on the street, he would be filled with empathy and would ask his mother for money to do charitable deeds. Although theirs was not a wealthy family, his mother knows that he has a kind heart so she would give him the money. Victor would rush to give it to the beggars.

Growing up, Victor's mother had strongly influenced him. Day in and day out, she was very busy with the household chores. Still, every night, she managed to spare time to recite the "Stories of Twenty-four Methods of Filial Piety" to Victor. The young Victor enjoyed it very much. He also shared his mother's practicality and wisdom. At the end of each year, he would receive a new pair of shoes. His mother always bought them one size bigger so that he could still wear them the following year.

There is a Chinese saying about parents: "Strict father and kind mother." Victor's parents really lived up to this saying. The mere presence of his father is enough to make Victor feel uneasy. What more is a conversation with him?

Victor's paternal relatives did well financially. However, Victor's father did not. In his younger years, he had witnessed the cruel way other people treated his parents. It broke his heart but it also motivated him to someday earn a lot of money so that his parents can walk with pride on their faces.

In the early 20th century, China was in constant civil wars. Many Chinese immigrated to the Philippines from the province of Fookien. Mostly uneducated and unversed in the local language, they were discriminated. However, understanding the importance of education, they set up schools in the Philippines. Most of their teachers came from Taiwan, who nurtured the students with the Chinese culture and introduced a different kind of mentality in general.

Innocent children have no prejudices, unlike adults. In his childhood,

他所代理的商品愈來愈多，Vans Shoes 也是其中之一。

創業的歲月，彷若將自己安置在波折的時光旅程裏，成為隱隱的漩渦，載浮載沈於商場，單打獨鬥好不孤單！他形容做生意有如騎腳踏車，一開始也許不得法，但吃力地踩上去後，就一路順暢了。

王香圃成功賺了一些錢，慢慢還清債務，讓父母親能享受晚年生活，也讓自己的孩子得到良好的教育。

有一回他拿錢給母親，發現母親不用，都拿去助人。他問母親為何？母親說這樣做，她的心很歡喜！聽母親這樣說，他便經常給母親錢，讓她去助人，希望母親能一直歡喜生活。

待人和氣，不輕視他人、沒有貧賤分別心的王香圃，員工就如他的兄弟。如今員工情義回饋，就如心中有愛，便能善解另一對眼睛，他歷練出沈穩的腳步，說話低沈篤定，而音階又如飛鳥輕快不拘束。

做生意有賺有賠，他認為是天經地義，算一算自己做生意四十幾年，有十幾年在失敗中慘澹度過。成功的這三十年，銀行往往會來問他要不要借錢？年少時看盡別人臉色，如今人家主動要送錢讓他經營生意，對於社會的冷暖點滴，做生意吃盡苦頭的王香圃，早已是打落牙齒和血吞、打斷手骨顛倒勇，不但不需要那些有條件的借錢，還想無求地捐助給社會！

自己年少時苦過，別人生活困難，一旦他知道了而不去幫助，心裏會很難過。有時，他會策畫一些節目來捐錢，但母親提醒他，「你捐了錢究竟用在哪兒，你並不知道，那就失去捐助的意義。」母親喜歡收看大愛電視臺，受慈濟影響頗深。王

Victor played with his Filipino friends. They went fishing and caught prawns in the riverside. Regardless of their nationality, young Chinese and Filipinos became good friends.

Filipinos naturally possess a happy-go-lucky outlook in life. They love to have fun and lead a carefree life. On the other hand, the Chinese know the importance of savings, thus many of them became wealthy businessmen.

Victor started his business from the money he had borrowed from his relatives. In its early years, the business was short on manpower so Victor had to do most of the work. He was the "principal who has to teach and at the same time, the janitor who has to ring the bell". And when an employee, after undergoing training, wanted to pursue his own career, Victor would always wish him success in his undertakings.

Other companies were very keen to hire his employees, who became diligent and efficient after training under him. However, after seeking employment elsewhere, these employees would come to realize that other companies cannot give them the fringe benefits they enjoyed in Victor's company. As a result, most of these employees would come back to work for him again while those who did not would repay him by asking Victor to become their distributor.

Consequently, the number of products he represented gradually increased, Vans Shoes is one of these.

When he first started his business, it seemed as if he had put himself into a twist and turn journey with its invisible whirlpools, floating and drowning in the business field, as he struggled all alone! He compared doing business to riding a bicycle. At first, it is not easy nor ideal. But after continuous practice of pedalling and riding, riding a bicycle would soon become smooth.

Victor succeeded in making some money. Gradually, he paid off his

香圃與慈濟的因緣除了母親好善樂施的影響，也因為他認識華商會的慈濟人唐榮謀（Julian Tong），兩人相識三十幾年，有鮮為人知的一段趣事！

王香圃的太祖父有一間關公廟，夏天放學時沒地方去，母親希望他去廟裏打掃，因此常聽到關公義薄雲天的正義故事，所以他覺得一個人做事就是要講義氣。

三十幾年前，年輕氣盛的王香圃曾經跟唐榮謀的弟弟打架，就為了那滿腔的正義感。老師常說他好管閒事，為朋友打抱不平去打架，不吃眼前虧。因事他去找唐榮謀理論，這樣相識的兩人，卻變成生意上的好夥伴。

他曾經目睹唐榮謀為孩子發愁，形容枯槁、心事重重，直到加入慈濟後，面容一百八十度轉變的過程；他發現慈濟的善良理念影響了許多人，包括母親和他自己。他做生意講究「誠正信實」，他認為證嚴法師說的這四個字是做人的基石。

王香圃的外孫是慈青，好友唐榮謀是慈濟人，母親是虔誠佛教徒，慈濟在萊特島救災的大貢獻眾所皆知。受助的菲律賓人開始感恩華人，而王香圃終於找到了一個安心捐助的港口。他的一家公司，生產十個小時的商品，就分享其中兩小時的利潤給附近的學校。「這種分享是需要培養的，當你開始去分享時，心靈的喜悅就來了。」

華人在菲律賓抬頭是近三十年的事，很多地方都有華商會，馬尼拉更有華商總會。海燕風災發生時，慈濟以工代賑，華商會一起募款幫助菲律賓人，當時王香圃捐了一百萬披索，但他覺得自己做得還不夠。知道慈濟需要用錢，他總是開心地捐，

debts and could afford to let his parents enjoy a better life in their old age and also let his own children pursue good education.

Once, he gave some money to his mother. Later, he discovered that his mother had never used the money for herself. Instead, she used it to help others. When he asked his mother why she did this, she answered that it made her heart feel very happy to do so! After this incident, Victor would often give her money so that she could do charity. He hopes that through this, his mother would always be happy.

With courtesy, without hate and discrimination against the poor, Victor Siasat treated his employees as if they are his own siblings. Now, his employees reciprocate his kindness, just like when there is love in the heart, you would understand the sensation of the other pair of eyes. He had drilled himself with such a steady pace, he speaks in a low and steady tone, yet his voice is lively and unrestrained like a flying bird.

Going through many difficulties himself while young, Victor Siasat would immediately respond to someone who is in need, otherwise he will feel uneasy. At times he would come up with some fund raising activities, but her mother would remind him: "If you do not know where your money goes after donation, you lose the meaning of giving an aid."

His mother enjoyed watching DAAI TV and was deeply influenced by Master Cheng Yen's teachings. Victor's affinity with Tzu Chi, apart from his mother's influence in doing charitable deeds, also came about because of his acquaintance with Julian Tong, a Tzu Chi volunteer from the Chinese Chamber of Commerce. They had known each other for more than thirty years, and they have an interesting story which people rarely know about!

Thirty years ago, the young and idealistic Victor had once fought with Julian's younger brother because of his stance of fair justice. Victor's teacher often said that he always liked to interfere with other people's business, to fight

因為他相信所捐出的錢，一分一毫都會用在刀口上。

他會主動問唐榮謀慈濟需要用款嗎？當時奧莫克大愛村的孩子們需要教育助學金，他就捐了一百五十萬披索！

人在買賣江湖中打轉，一路走來歷經滄桑，他的想法是：「我們這輩子能賺的錢都是天註定的，有時候一件生意非常盡力爭取，卻求不得，很多生意他根本未想過要爭取，可是它們卻都自己找上門！」

王香圃深深感受著天知道他努力了那麼久，才終於走到這裏。歲月彷彿讓他擁有飛鳥和魚的能力，淘起順流隨緣的心態，盡本分但結果不強求，前腳走後腳就放，這樣自然能以寬廣而知足的角度去看待世界。

最近一件溫暖的事蹟，是他捐贈了七千多雙 Vans 鞋子，給奧莫克大愛村的鄉親老少，他謙虛地說：「那批鞋是橡膠底，有時效性，所以分享給奧莫克大愛村的居民。」

Vans 是名牌鞋，七千多雙賣出去可是一筆龐大收入啊！王香圃卻還是搖著頭，重複直說自己做得還不夠。

發送當天，很多居民沒上班都來排隊領鞋，因為這鞋子的價格超出他們一日收入的好幾倍，甚至是好幾個月的薪資。村民說：「它很珍貴，我無法買得起。」因為數量多，本土志工討論後，決定也嘉惠給隔壁幾個里以及他們的幹事、市政府員工、警察、醫護人員或未成年犯罪機構，以廣結善緣。

發鞋子之前，志工會先介紹慈濟精神理念，再帶他們參觀環保站，說明做環保的重要。如此，分享的就不僅是物資，還有愛的種子。來自未成年犯罪機構的十一歲男孩佛朗西斯，曾

for justice for the sake of his friends. Over some matter, he went to see Julian for an argument, but they ended up as good business partners instead.

He once saw how distressed Julian was with his children. He looked haggard, with loads of worries in his mind that weighed him down. When he became a Tzu Chi volunteer, his appearance drastically changed.

He discovered how Tzu Chi's wholesome concept had influenced many people, including his mother and himself. He emphasizes on "Sincerity, Integrity, Faith, Steadfastness" in managing his business. He believes that these four words, which Master Cheng Yen teaches, are the cornerstones of human etiquette.

Victor's grandson is a Tzu Ching. His friend Julian is a Tzu Chi volunteer. His mother is a devout Buddhist, and Tzu Chi's great contribution to the disaster relief in Leyte is well known to the public.

The Filipinos who benefited from the disaster relief began to appreciate the Chinese, and Victor has finally found a harbour where he can donate with peace of mind. In one of his companies, which produced ten hours of merchandise, he would share two hours of profit to the nearby schools. "This act of giving needs to be cultivated. When you start to give, splendid joy emerges from the heart."

When Typhoon Haiyan struck, Tzu Chi adopted a "Cash- for-Work" Clean up Program. The Chinese Chamber of Commerce joined in raising funds for the Filipino typhoon survivors. At that time, Victor donated a million pesos. Yet, he felt that he had not done enough.

Knowing that Tzu Chi needed money to carry out its charity works, Victor is always happy to donate, confident that each donation to Tzu Chi will be used for the right cause. One time, the children in Ormoc Great Love Village needed educational grants, and so he donated more through Brother

經從鄰居家偷錢去打電玩，他的父親去世了，母親得扶養他們四個兄弟姊妹。王香圃的善舉感動了孩子，他學習到：「要保持一顆純潔的心，付出不期望回報，也想努力完成學業，未來成為對社會有貢獻的好人。」

七千多雙鞋子，溫暖的不只是鄉親老少的腳，還有他們的心，而王香圃的每一念都像是花圃盛放了春花。他今日的成就，歸功於母親對他的教導，一念一畝福田，至今依舊埋首樂於耕耘。雖然他沒有加入慈濟，但他的心早屬於慈濟！

王香圃把倉儲七千多雙 Vans 名牌鞋，贈予奧莫克大愛村及附近鄉民，大人小孩拿到新鞋都興奮不已。
Victor Siasat donated more than seven thousand pairs of Vans Shoes to the residents of Ormoc Great Love Village. The villagers, young and old alike, were so excited upon receiving the new pair of shoes.

Julian.

Victor said: "The money we earn in this lifetime is predestined. Sometimes we tried so hard to fight for businesses which eventually ended in vain. However, there are many business enterprises that we never even thought to fight for but came knocking at our door!"

Victor believes that the Heavens have witnessed how long he had worked hard to achieve the success he is now enjoying. Time seemed to give him the capabilities of the bird and the fish, which obediently follow their predestined affinity. Doing one's best without demanding for the result, after moving one foot forward, leave the hind foot behind – in this way, one would naturally look at the world with a broad and contented perspective.

Recently, there was a heart-warming incident when he donated more than 7,000 pairs of Vans Shoes to the village folks, both young and old. He said humbly: "That batch of shoes is made of rubber soles. There is a validity period, so we gave them to the residents of Ormoc Great Love Village."

Vans Shoes is an expensive brand in the Philippines. These seven thousand pairs of shoes could have earned him a huge amount of money! Yet Victor shook his head and repeated that he was not doing enough.

Those seven thousand pairs of shoes warmed not only the feet of the village folks but also their hearts. Each of Victor's thoughtfulness is just like the 'Million Bells' spring flower blooming gloriously in the flowerbed.

His achievements today are attributed to his mother's gracious guidance. A seed of good deed blossomed into a field of blessings which he continues to cultivate and nurture. Although he has not become a Tzu Chi volunteer, his heart has long been devoted to Tzu Chi!

(Translated by Si Hoo Ooi)

善良和風陣陣吹

Breeze of Hope in Ormoc Valley

慈濟志工與大愛村民，口誦「南無本師釋迦牟尼佛⋯⋯」跪拜時把額頭俯貼地面，三步一跪祈禱天下無災難。

Tzu Chi volunteers and villagers performed the three steps and one bow pilgrimage while chanting the name of the Buddha.

從臺灣飛往馬尼拉艾奎諾國際機場，出關後，炎熱的夏陽讓我們每走一步就汗流浹背。二十四歲的李慈光，車子停得老遠，走近我們時，淋漓的汗淌過他的臉頰，他擦也不擦，應該是習慣了這種氣候帶來的不適。

我們在餐館用午齋，送菜速度很慢，李慈光說這是菲律賓人的民族性。李慈光是李偉嵩的小兒子，奧莫克大愛村興建期間，都是他陪著李偉嵩看前看後。

身材圓滾滾的李慈光，不羈的外表下有一顆細膩的心，攝影極富禪意。他喜歡穿一件多功能的草綠色背心，背心上有許多小口袋，所有寶貝都擺在口袋裏，要什麼，手就順勢一取，像個帥氣的牛仔。

從國內機場再到獨魯萬的丹尼爾羅穆亞爾德斯機場，一出

Upon arrival at the Manila International Airport from Taiwan, our backs are drenched with sweat from the scorching summer sun.

As 24-year-old Light Lotus Lettuce Lato Li walks towards us from his parked car, sweat was pouring down his forehead, yet he makes no move to wipe it. He must be accustomed to the discomforting heat brought by the local climate.

Light Lotus Lettuce Lato Li is the youngest son of Alfredo Li. Both were present throughout the construction period of Ormoc Great Love Village, witnessing and supporting the process.

According to his parents, Light's name holds a special meaning. He was named "Light" because his birth brought happiness to the family. "Lotus," meanwhile, symbolizes their belief in Buddhism and "Lettuce" because the family are vegetarians. Lato and Li are the family name of their parents.

機場，那棵大葉欖仁樹熟悉地站在老地方。向晚的天空，漫天灰紫色的霞光下，一顆好似即將燃盡的火球，掩在大葉欖仁後面，自葉身的隙縫透出黃澄澄的光亮，向世人宣示它曾經如何在白天照亮人間。

從獨魯萬到奧莫克市必須繞過兩小時山路，坐在黃昏的車裏，忽醒忽睡。車子繞過山腰，左彎右拐貼著山壁急駛，菲利士（Felix Cascara）眼神專注地開車，歷經長途跋涉的我們疲累得直打瞌睡，直到車行平地不再顛簸才逐漸清醒。

這麼多年過去，潘信成曾陪伴帕洛人民一起蓋大愛屋，駐紮此地八個月；而我曾在海燕風災發生後，參加第三梯次義診，我們都深刻體會過萊特島的痛。此刻再回到萊特島，已非昔日殘破印象，繁華又再度回來，街上霓虹閃爍，頹圮已不復見。

我們住在離宿霧港口很近的奧莫克市二十七小區，各國救援組織早不見蹤影，只有慈濟仍陪伴獨魯萬及奧莫克大愛村。居民們在災難後一無所有，雖有救援組織提供房子，但是孩子的教育不能停，心靈寄託的教堂也需要復原，種種需求的考量，慈濟決定留下。

藍天白雲的身影持續在萊特島穿梭付出，慈濟為聖嬰教堂重建，並趕在二〇一四年平安夜前，讓大主教約翰（John Du）為廣大人民舉行莊嚴的彌撒儀式。與會者重新找回心中的依靠，更重要的是把人與人之間的互助模式帶入這個城市，見證宗教的和諧。

當時李偉嵩代表慈濟出席彌撒儀式，並接受大主教的感謝狀。萊特島民數度於絕望中重燃希望，他們深刻了解到崩毀的

Beneath his carefree appearance, the stout Light Lotus Lettuce Lato Li has a caring heart, and his photography skills are enriched with Zen thoughts.

He loves to wear a multi-function grass-green vest. The vest has many small pockets, where he keeps his treasures. Whenever he needs them, he can pull them out swiftly, similar to a stylish cowboy.

We flew from Manila Domestic Airport to the Daniel Z. Romualdez Airport in Tacloban City. As we step out of the airport, the Indian almond tree remains standing in its usual place.

The evening sky is streaked with the colors of violet and gray, and the imminently burned out sun gradually falls behind the Indian almond tree. Streaks of golden light leak through the cracks of the leaves, as if declaring how it had brightened the world earlier in the day.

From Tacloban City, it takes two hours of driving to reach Ormoc. Sitting in the car upon dusk, we are half-asleep and half-awake.

Felix Cascara, the driver, was intensely focused in driving us through the winding road, around the mountains. Having gone through a long journey, our exhausted selves doze off with our backs still upright. We only begin waking up when the rugged roads have become smooth.

In 2014, months after Typhoon Haiyan struck, Apollo Pan took part in the construction of the Tzu Chi Palo Great Love Village for about eight months. I participated in the 2017 Medical, Surgical and Dental Mission in Tacloban City where our medical team treated no less than 6,000 patients. Back then, we noticed that the province of Leyte had recovered from the devastation and that the economy was even booming.

We stayed in a place close to the port area facing Cebu City. No other disaster relief organizations remain in sight, only Tzu Chi continues to

世界能藉著拼湊重新得以完整，因為愛和信賴是那堅實的漿糊。

　　陪伴奧莫克大愛村屆滿五年的今日，李偉嵩有太多感觸在心頭。二〇一九年四月二十八日，奧莫克大愛村舉行朝山與慈濟中小學動土典禮，這樣一件大事，帶給大愛村民很多希望。

　　動土前，慈濟辦公室後面的大操場上堆起了一個圓形沙堆，正中間立著一支從中小學預定地上取得的廢棄水管，筆直高聳，上面掛著一個由奧莫克本土志工環保回收的木條，紅色告示板上面寫著「慈濟奧莫克市中小學動土典禮，二〇一九年四月二十八日吉時，GROUND BREAKING CEREMONY」等字樣，頂端是慈濟會徽，往下拉出傘狀紅色布條圍住圓型土堆，充滿喜氣。

　　主持臺長桌以湛藍色的布覆蓋，四周布置鮮花，採自村子周圍河邊遍生大自然的給予，有藍色鳶尾花、各顏色的百日菊，插在卡南加（Kananga）大愛村砍來的香蕉樹身上，很是美麗。

　　主持臺和預定地之間，兩個用竹子拼湊的看板，上面懸掛橫布條「WE LOVE 上人」，另一個用廢棄的 PP 板做的大型看板寫著「I LOVE TZU CHI」；黃土地上一排大石頭漆上海水藍，顯得湛亮耀眼；寶特瓶剪出一朵朵花和葉子，漆上不同顏色，高低參差插在泥地上，儼然是一個美麗花園。整個動土典禮的布置都是本土志工發想打造，就地取材或以回收物再製而成！

　　李偉嵩就是這大愛村的大家長，村民是他的家人，他們善良純真的各種發想，好比孩子在白紙上作畫，充滿童趣又不失真誠，那麼用心，把環保落實在生活及各種活動裏。

　　我們沿著中小學預定地走著，尋找地點安置相機，從高處往下拍攝這個將點燃夢想的地方。

accompany Tacloban City and the Great Love Village in Ormoc City.

The villagers lost everything after the disaster. Even though other organizations offered shelter, there are still other pressing concerns that are left unsolved. Children's education must not stop, and churches must be rebuilt. With this in mind, Tzu Chi decided to stay.

The Tzu Chi volunteers continued to devote their efforts to the people of Leyte. Tzu Chi helped rebuilt Sto. Niño Church of Tacloban City. The construction was finished in time for the Christmas Eve of 2014, allowing the archbishop John Du, to host a grand mass to celebrate the holy eucharist. Parishioners were able to reassemble their spiritual refuge, and most of all, the works of Tzu Chi allowed everyone to witness the harmony among different religions.

April 28, 2019 is a significant day for Tzu Chi. It is the 82nd birthday of Master Cheng Yen. It is also the 53rd founding anniversary of the Buddhist Compassion Relief Tzu Chi Foundation. Thus, it was chosen as the date to hold the ground breaking ceremony for the construction of Ormoc Tzu Chi Elementary and High School building.

Prior to the day of the ceremony, the village was a beehive of activities. Men took up the heavy work while women prepared the decorations. The youths took care of the programs. The lyre and drum band gave their all to declare their happiness. The residents of the three other Tzu Chi villages in Kananga came to help out too.

They put up a big signboard with the words, "I Love Tzu Chi." Written in an arch at the entrance of the site are the words, "We Love You, Shangren." This was their way of expressing their gratitude to Master Cheng Yen, who believes that education is the way out of poverty.

All the materials used for the event such as bamboo, banana trunks,

一隻大黃牛悠閒地在草原裏吃草，看我們來到附近也毫不介意。牠習慣了溫和的人群，不受侵擾，仰頭看我們一眼，又低下頭自顧自地吃草。離大黃牛大約五十公尺有一面廢棄水泥牆，潘信成矯捷地跳上牆，把相機架在牆上，打算以縮時錄影全程記錄朝山與動土典禮。

　　沙堆周圍黃土上，有朝山的地標，是用收集來的瓶蓋釘在地上；辦公室桌上，有小朋友手拿的旗子，是以廢紙彩繪而成。辦公室乾淨的衛生間，由過去來自宿霧的工程師以簡易屋改造而成，本土志工自己挖化糞池，用水泥砌了洗手臺。

　　天黑了，村內一盞盞亮起的 LED 燈，共三百支，是林烏醋集團執行長莊志得發心捐贈，讓大愛村入夜之後變得十分安全，尤其是老人家。

　　福緣匯聚，人生的面面風景，有時像繞著迂迴的路，會回到最初。

　　山風習習吹來的同時，大愛村民陸陸續續聚集，不論男女老少都穿著白色上衣，表示他們的誠意和清淨之心。

　　大家有默契地六人一排，隊伍整齊，有些才三、四歲大的孩童也穿著白上衣，夾雜在大人身邊，年紀大、行動遲緩的老人也不落人後，黃土石子路上的隊伍綿延到幾乎看不見盡頭。

　　瘦瘦高高的蔡昇航手持引磬走在隊伍之前，宏亮著聲音，用流利的菲律賓語再次解說朝山儀軌，接著開始口誦：「南無本師釋迦牟尼佛……」跪拜時把額頭俯貼地面，三步一跪祈禱天下無災難。

　　信奉天主教的大愛村民愈聚愈多，連卡南加三處小大愛村

flowers and leaves were gathered from around the village and from the recycling center. Plastic bottles are cut into the shape of flowers and leaves, painted with diverse colors, and placed on the grassland at different levels. A beautiful garden is created. Volunteers came up with this idea, wanting to only use easily accessible and recyclable items!

Alfredo Li is like a father to the Great Love Village and the villagers are his family. Like children's expressional drawing on paper, everyone's kind and innocent thoughts are filled with childlike joy and sincerity. Their thoughtfulness puts environmental protection into real-life events and application.

As we walk along the area where the school will soon rise looking for a place to set up our camera, we take a birds-eye view of the place where the hopes of many will be soon ignited.

A cattle is languidly eating grass, but it is not bothered by our presence in the slightest. It is accustomed to the calming personalities of the locals and is undisturbed. It raises its head to glance at us, then lowers it again to continue enjoying the grass.

Fifty meters away from the cattle lies an old concrete wall. We position a camera on top of the wall to film a time-lapse of the entire ceremony.

When night falls in the village, a total of three hundred LED lights would lit up, one by one. These lights are donated by Mr. Charlie L. Ching of the "Lim O Chu (Diana) Foundation". This allows the villagers, especially the elderly and the women, to feel safe after dark.

In the early morning of April 28, 2019, the villagers began to gather. Each of them wore white shirts, representing their sincerity and purity of hearts. They had only one thought in their mind: to beseech the All Mighty to grant Master Cheng Yen good health and longevity.

的村民也都來朝山，跟著蔡昇航三步一跪拜。他們虔誠地跪下來，把頭抵在有許多沙石的地上，依著佛教儀式，雙手放掌在頭部兩側，他們的長褲與雙手都沾了沙塵，但他們一點也不以為意，滿眼都是感恩之情。

奧莫克大愛村的第四度朝山，一路虔誠禮敬，李偉嵩、顏長偉、蔡青山、蔡萬擂等菲律賓資深慈濟人領在最前。去年穿著綠衣的維希也換上白衣，身邊多了一頭母牛「艾菲達（Alfreda）」，艾菲達身上背了兩串香蕉，憨憨的一雙大眼睛，乖巧地挨在維希身邊，讓人看了打從心底憐惜。

跪拜時，只聽見維希對著艾菲達一直說：「Luhod…Luhod…Luhod…」意思是「跪下…跪下…跪下…」可能圍觀的人太多，艾菲達受到干擾不肯聽話。最後蔡昇航過去跟著維希一起跪下來，艾菲達也就跪下來，並把頭抵在黃土上，姿勢很虔誠，兩隻大眼睛朝下望著。

維希欣慰地撫摸艾菲達的頭，跟著艾菲達一起站起來，那一幕讓大家的心一陣沸騰，掌聲不斷響起，難以相信牛兒也懂得感恩、跪拜！

主持臺前擺放了熱騰騰的壽桃、村民做的糕點、維希的兩串香蕉、波羅蜜，朝山這一天同時是證嚴法師的壽誕，村民感恩法師的大愛，紛紛來此隔洋祝壽。蔡青兒和慈青里莎（Rhiesa Roxas）共同主持慈濟中小學動土典禮。

蔡青兒是蔡萬擂和郭麗華的女兒，哥哥蔡昇航、姊姊蔡奇珊和研發多項獲得世界專利的蔡昇倫，全家奉獻大愛在慈濟。

里莎個頭很小，卻已經是高中生，她在學校經常主持節目，

Everyone neatly and synchronously lined up in rows of six. Some children are only three to four years of age, and wearing their white tops, they wobbled beside the adults. The physically-challenged elderly did not lag behind. The shuffling line seemed to stretch infinitely along the golden dirt road.

Michael Siao led the front of the line with his sonorous voice. He explained the meaning behind the three steps and one bow pilgrimage. After taking three steps, everyone would kneel and bow down with their foreheads touching the ground. This cultivates their sincerity and humility.

It was not an easy pilgrimage for the road was paved with pebbles and sand, but the villagers were not bothered by the dirt in their hands and in their knees. Instead, their eyes are filled with gratitude. There were even villagers who brought with them jackfruits, papaya, flowers, a bunch of bananas and vegetables as gifts of love for Master Cheng Yen. It was a very touching scene.

One incident worth mentioning is the participation of the carabao named Alfreda to the pilgrimage.

Two years ago, Alfreda was sold by her owner. Tzu Chi Ormoc team bought the carabao, fearing that it will be slaughtered once it gets sold to the wrong hands. A resident named Vergelio offered to look after Alfreda.

Over time, the carabao and Vergelio developed a special bond. Vergelio taught the carabao to kneel, to bow down and he named her, Alfreda.

During the pilgrimage, Alfreda carried two bunches of bananas on her back and obediently kept beside Vergelio. Upon kneeling, Vergelio whispered to Alfreda, "luhod…luhod…luhod", which means to "kneel…kneel… kneel…"

Perhaps, distracted by the numerous people around. Alfreda refused

臺風穩健，蔡青兒是她的偶像。里莎因為愛動物而想素食，她在大愛村與慈青們一起家訪、做環保，當老師是她的志向。

夏日正在舞動，我拿著攝影腳架跟隨來自臺灣的人文真善美志工張義川滿場跑，捕捉感人鏡頭。

忽然一個個美麗的音符，從背後慢慢超越我，又慢慢落在我背後。那音聲來自菲律賓名歌手吉諾（Gino Padilla），傳達歌詞中成為能給人溫暖與力量的人。

在那一刻，全場的目光充滿了鼓舞，而演唱者在備受矚目中閃耀著光輝，不僅是他絕美的音聲，更因為曲子的內涵如此動人⋯⋯

「Thank you for giving me such a warm embrace
感謝你 給了我 溫暖的擁抱

Staying by my side when I feel sad
讓我擺渡過 生命低潮

Now my heart's full of love I won't bend in the wind
一顆心 裝滿愛 風再大 不飄搖

Lend my shoulder for people to cry on
學會把肩膀 借別人依靠

Sincerely I give you an understanding smile
用真心 給了你 了解的微笑

Staying by your side to end your worries
陪著你解開 心事困擾

Just when you raise your head and your tears flow no more
看著你 抬起頭 淚停了 那一秒

Oh how it moves my heart
感動在胸口圍繞

to obey. Later, as Michael joined Vergelio in kneeling, Alfreda kneeled down too. With a sincere posture, she rested her head on the ground with both eyes glancing downwards.

Vergelio proudly patted Alfreda's head and together, they stood back up. This scene touched the hearts of the villagers and suddenly, everyone was clapping. How incredible! Even carabaos understand how to be grateful and to pay respect! Thus Master Cheng Yen reiterates that animals have feelings and souls too. They deserve our respect and protection.

After the pilgrimage, the ground breaking ceremony started. Maureen Siao and Ormoc youth Rhieza Roxas hosted the ceremony.

Maureen is the youngest daughter of Tzu Chi volunteers Manuel and Teresita Siao. Along with her siblings, Michael, Michelle and Marshall, the entire Siao family are dedicated Tzu Chi volunteers.

Meanwhile, Rhieza is still in high school. She looks up to Maureen when it comes to hosting. Rhieza dreams of becoming a teacher someday.

It was a hot summer day. I was assisting the volunteer videographer I-Chuan Chang from Taiwan, holding my camera and tripod to capture touching moments. Suddenly, I was surrounded by gentle music notes. They come from the well-known Filipino singer Gino Padilla. At that moment, everyone was mesmerized by the singer's voice and the song's meaning.

"Thank you for giving me such a warm embrace
Staying by my side when I feel sad
Now my heart's full of love I won't bend in the wind
Lend my shoulder for people to cry on
Sincerely I give you an understanding smile
Staying by your side to end your worries
Just when you raise your head and your tears flow no more

I know there's love in this world that's worth waiting for

我相信人間有愛 值得去期待

Shielded hearts will open up eventually
長久封閉的心 終究會打開

Wounds will heal when we forgive; Doubts will vanish when we care
體諒會化解傷害 關懷會化解疑猜

Trust is the most moving love
最動人的愛 是信賴」

雖然中文版我已聽過無數次，然而從吉諾歌聲中傳達而來的感覺，特別療癒。

奧莫克這個菲律賓萊特島海邊的城市，烈陽與海潮熱溼人們衫袖，但不要忘記陽光與海水的教養，大愛村正捧在這陽光海水的掌心上。

吉諾首次演唱英文版的慈濟歌曲是二〇〇九年凱莎娜颱風（Ketsana）釀災時，在馬利僅那市（Marikina）受慈濟人唐榮謀邀請，藉由溫暖音聲療慰人心。

入行三十多年的他，過去在五光十色的舞臺上唱跳情歌，只歡愉了某一小撮人淺表的感覺，而今他以單純的莊嚴清謳微吟，曲中的大愛、理解與慈悲，如輕步的雲霧散播到民眾的心田，傳達慰藉與分享。他驚訝地發現，經由慈濟歌選，自己的聲音達到助人的巨大力量，帶給人們鼓舞與希望。

吉諾是一位虔誠的基督徒，但他意識到大愛的付出，沒有宗教的區別。他深深被慈濟歌曲中幫助、理解、寬慰與尊重的大愛所震撼，當災民受到大愛感動而淚下時，他的內心也同時接收到滿滿的回饋。

Oh how it moves my heart
I know there's love in this world that's worth waiting for
Shielded hearts will open up eventually
Wounds will heal when we forgive
Doubts will vanish when we care
Trust is the most moving love"

The first time that Gino sang a Tzu Chi song was during the Typhoon Ketsana (known as Ondoy in Philippines) disaster relief in 2009. Invited by Tzu Chi volunteer Julian Tong, Gino sang in Marikina City and calmed the people's hearts with his soothing voice.

Being in the music industry for more than thirty years, he has transformed his flashy style in the past, which was enjoyed by the audience on a superficial level, to his current performances filled with love and compassion. He discovered that through Tzu Chi songs, his voice bears the immense power of sending hope and joy to his listeners.

Gino is a devoted Christian; however, he realizes that there is no distinction in religion when spreading great love to others.

Gino knows that Tzu Chi has been benevolently active in the Philippines for over twenty years, helping those who suffer and are in need. He is following the footsteps of Tzu Chi. There are many Chinese descendants and Ormoc Great Love Villagers who share the same thoughts with Gino: they want to be able to tell a good story to their grandchildren in the future.

The groundbreaking ceremony begun on a very festive mood. The Philippine flag, Buddhist flag and Tzu Chi flag led the youth band and the village children into the school ground.

The children were marching with joyful hearts and eyes glowing with hope. The parents were beaming with gratitude knowing that a school built by

吉諾知道慈濟在菲律賓行善濟貧、為病苦救助深耕二十餘年，他跟著慈濟的腳步走了起來，菲律賓的許多華商與奧莫克大愛村民都跟吉諾有許多共同感受，他們想說一個好故事給未來的子孫聽。

　　動土典禮開始了，奧莫克大愛村五十公頃土地捐贈者、前奧莫克市長艾德華夫婦、李偉嵩家族、蔡萬擂家族、奧莫克教育部規畫幹事等人，圍著土堆，人手一支鏟子挖了沙堆，期盼慈濟中小學快快平地起。

　　慈濟中小學動土，為大愛村平添無限希望。在慈濟獎助學金下求學的慈青人手揮著旗子，另一手拉著大愛村孩童，成行列歡欣齊走，和順的風吹著慈濟旗與菲律賓國旗，飄蕩著希望，隊伍裏稚齡孩子們展露笑臉……

　　艾德華感性致詞：「非常感謝慈濟在海燕風災後，不間斷對奧莫克付出，至今依然陪伴著我們。」

　　李偉嵩的二哥李偉峯則說：「我們捐這個學校是為了紀念父母過世三十三周年……」他眼眶一度泛紅而語噎，硬是止住了又接著說：「對大愛村的孩子們，將來的生活會進步會更好。」

　　奧莫克教育部規畫幹事瑞安（Ryan Bughao）接受採訪時說：「大愛村有一千多戶居民，孩子們上學要走一段非常遠的路，如今這裏即將興學，對這些孩子們是很重要的。」

　　海燕風災後，善循環一路匯眾愛，建村又興學，五年來肯定有許多波折艱困在其中。然而最後畫面聚焦在奧莫克大愛村，彷彿能看到未來這兒的子子孫孫，他們在感恩、尊重、愛的風氣裏薰陶長大，善良的和風陣陣吹……

Tzu Chi means better quality of education.

Edward Codilla was emotional as he delivered his speech. "We give our biggest thanks to the Tzu Chi volunteers, who never cease to extend a helping hand to the villagers."

Bienvenido Li said "Our family is donating the high school building to honor our parents because we love them so much…"

With red eyes and a slight sob, he continued, "…for the children of the Great Love Village, to give them a better future and a better life."

During the interview of Mr. Ryan Bughao, the representative of the Department of Education, he said, "The Ormoc Great Love Village has more than one thousand families, and before, the children must walk long distances to reach their school. The opening of this school embodies invaluable importance for these children."

"The schools are envisioned to benefit not only the children of Tzu Chi Great Love Village. It will also accept students from the neighboring barangays. One can dream that someday, a president of our country will come from our village."

After the Typhoon Haiyan, the cycle of kindness continually accumulated love from many people along the way. From rebuilding a village to establishing a new school, innumerable challenges and hardships were encountered in the past five years.

Nevertheless, the focus is now in the Ormoc Great Love Village. One can envision the future generations growing in an environment of gratitude, respect, and love, as the breeze of hope continues to blow….

(Translated by Erin Lin)

左上／菲律賓名歌手吉諾經常出現在慈濟愛灑活動中，為愛高歌鼓舞人心的演出，讓他此生再也無憾。

(top left photo) Filipino singer Gino Padilla frequently attends Tzu Chi's activities. People are inspired by his performances because he sings from the heart.

左下／奧莫克大愛村慈濟中小學動土典禮前，慈青一手牽著村裏孩童，一手舉著慈濟會旗或菲律賓國旗，歡喜入場。

(bottom left photo) During the groundbreaking ceremony, the Tzu Ching guided the village children to the school ground.

上圖／慈濟旗幟飄揚在菲律賓藍天白雲裏，奧莫克大愛村孩子們圍成一圈表演手語歌，盼教育帶來希望。

(top photo) The Tzu Chi flag flutters against the blue sky and white clouds. The Great Love Village children form a circle to perform a sign language song. They expect that education will bring hope here.

義診嘉惠貧病
華燈初上
The Lights Turned on at Sunset

小男孩獻花給諾伊（右一）、羅蘭多（後排右三）、菲米雅（中間拿花者），向這些為病苦者奉獻時間的醫師們致敬。
A little boy gave flowers to Dr. Noel (right), Dr. Rolando (3rd from right in the back row) and Dr. Femia（middle）to thank them for dedicating their time and skill to serve less-privileged patients.

臨近中秋，往年常有颱風威脅，今年特別寧靜，也不炎熱，清爽而不黏膩的空氣，異常舒服。

二〇一九年秋分的花蓮靜思堂，我以學員身分參加國際人醫年會，和三位英國、一位荷蘭、一位新加坡的醫師，以及臺灣藥師林幸惠同組。

首日午齋，就發現李偉嵩正巧坐在臨桌，他說諾伊醫師（Noel Maico）就在他後面那桌。

我拉長眼睛望，看見熟悉的圓臉、髮色蒼蒼的諾伊，他也瞧見我了，便開心地笑。

有著慈眉善目的諾伊醫師，人雖沈默，心卻很溫暖，頭腦冷靜、決斷果敢。奧莫克大愛村建成滿五年，諾伊醫師便已三度參加慈濟國際人醫年會。

Every year as the Moon Festival draws near, a typhoon would threaten the festivities. But this year is particularly calm. The weather is not too hot, with an exceptionally relaxing fresh and non-humid atmosphere. In the autumn of 2019, I was one of the participants of the TIMA Annual Convention in Jing Si Hall. I was in the same group as three other participants from England, a participant from Holland, a Singaporean medical doctor as well as the Taiwanese pharmacist Shine Lin.

On the first day, during lunch, I noticed Alfredo Li sitting at the table next to ours. He told me that Dr. Noel Maico was at the table behind him. I looked over to the other table and saw the familiar round face and grey hair of Dr. Noel. He also saw me and smiled. Amiable looking Dr. Noel Maico is a quiet person. Yet he has a warm heart, a cool mind, and is both resolute and daring. When the construction of the Tzu Chi Ormoc Great Love Village was completed after five years, Dr. Noel came to attend the Tzu Chi International Medical Association, or TIMA, Annual Convention for the third time.

菲律賓每年都有許多醫師與會，從早期的呂秀泉醫師、史美勝醫師等人，到近年奧莫克大愛村的駐診醫師也來參加。二〇一八年，諾伊醫師、羅蘭多醫師（Rolando Tomaro）與其夫人菲米雅醫師（Femia Tomaro）同來；這次，諾伊醫師又帶領七位醫師來觀摩，感受國際人醫的智慧慈悲善行。

　　史美勝醫師在二〇〇九年凱莎娜颱風席捲菲律賓時，自己的家也遭受嚴重侵襲，但他仍依約前來臺灣，並講授三十分鐘課程。

　　雖然心繫家園，但慈濟人醫會經年馳援菲律賓義診，他點滴感恩在心頭，覺得答應的事一定要做到，講完課隔天才又回菲律賓。

　　史美勝的眼科義診團隊，早已自馬尼拉的眼科中心跨及菲律賓各島嶼，近日還遠至寮國。

　　在大隊未抵寮國前，他便與臺灣的葉添浩醫師先歷經重重關卡去勘災，了解當地眼科設備，並掌握將面臨的各種挑戰，當日即開始手術義診，嘉惠人民。

　　種種奔波與久站，都需要體力、經驗和無盡的耐心，如果沒有足夠的慈悲善根，每走一步都將吃緊受縛，因為心會抗拒自己的身體。

　　但史美勝從未引以為苦：「上人給我這麼大一個機會，讓我能在菲律賓施展所長，幫助窮人，我心中只有感激！」

　　寮國，荒涼草原中立著屋舍、童話顏色般的建物與憨厚人群的國度。義診前，史美勝又先去教導當地醫師操作當地醫院預先購置的先進儀器，直到熟練為止，有效率而不知疲累是一

Every year, many doctors from the Philippines would attend the convention. In the early years, these would include Dr. Siu Chuan Leh and Dr. Antonio Say, among others. Today, new resident physicians of the Ormoc Great Love Village would also come to participate. In 2018, Dr. Noel joined along with Dr. Rolando Tomaro and his wife, Dr. Femia. This time, Dr. Noel led a group of seven doctors to observe and experience the compassion, wisdom and kindness of TIMA.

When Typhoon Ketsana struck the Philippines in 2009, Dr. Antonio Say's house was also seriously devastated. Despite this, he went to Taiwan as scheduled and delivered a 30-minute lecture. At the back of his mind, he was worried for his homeland. As TIMA has been assisting the Philippines with its medical outreaches over the past years, Dr. Say was deeply grateful and he felt that he must carry out what he had promised to do. After delivering his lecture, he returned to the Philippines the next day.

Dr. Say's ophthalmology team has already served in many places across the Philippines, from the eye clinic in Manila to various islands. Recently, they even crossed oceans to participate in a medical outreach in Laos. Before the team arrived in Laos, Dr. Say and Dr. Tian Hao Yeh, who is from Taiwan, had already encountered many challenges – from assessing the disaster to understanding the local ophthalmic facilities and preparing for possible problems that may come up. On their arrival in Laos, they immediately started performing surgeries.

All these activities, including the need to stand for a long period of time to perform the surgeries, takes physical strength, experience and immeasurable patience. Without sufficient compassion and kind intentions, every step one would take would be hard-pressed and one will eventually get stranded because the heart will resist one's body's stress. Nevertheless, Dr. Say never thought of this as painstaking: "Since Master Cheng Yen has given me such a great opportunity to use my capabilities to help the poor in the Philippines, my heart is deeply grateful!"

種使命感，只要看到病人的微笑，就煙消雲散……

年底將近，好似開鍋的熱騰在隱隱約約煮沸中，不似秋日，什麼都淡淡的。

二〇一九年，奧莫克大愛村延續前一年的內外科義診，並由慈青隊伍深入偏鄉，主動尋找白內障、兔唇、疝氣、甲狀腺腫的病患，加以登載統計，預計十月二十五至二十七日三天，讓更多人重獲健康。

這些善舉是窮人一生不敢期望的，如果不是李偉嵩與志工們共同發願，如果沒有醫師們的悲心，他們將一輩子受病魔折騰而沒有明天。

我常覺遇見生命中美好意外，有時是蒼天自有安排，人生走著走著，有時會有一段旋律浮上心頭，和那張一同哼唱的面容，當我們覺得獨自，其實並非如此。

奧莫克大愛村人醫會的成員中，羅蘭多醫師是外科，諾伊醫師及菲米雅醫師是內科。目前諾伊固定每月第二與第四個星期六在大愛村義診。

諾伊的故鄉在奧莫克，當年他的家也遭受風災，目睹李偉嵩帶領志工和民眾重建家園，汗水淋漓啞著嗓子安撫大家情緒、安排義診。當時諾伊服務於市政廳衛生單位，李偉嵩邀請他加入國際人醫會，他沒有一絲猶豫，因為他的悲心早已被啟發！

他很明白慈濟是佛教團體，他們是天主教，但慈濟從來不談宗教，只談感恩、尊重、愛。

慈濟以地球為一個大家庭，在這個地球上居住的人都是慈濟的親人，大愛精神發揮到極致，這令諾伊打從心底尊敬，願

In Laos, houses stand on desolate grassland, with fancy coloured buildings like the ones you see in fairytales. The people are honest and simple. Prior to the medical outreach, Dr. Say taught local doctors how to operate the hospital's newly bought ophthalmic machines until they are familiar and proficient. Efficiency and setting aside oneself shows deep commitment. The smiles from the patients are enough to melt all their exhaustion away.

The hecticness as the year draws to a close is like a pot hazily boiling hot. Unlike autumn, everything seems so dull.

In 2019, Tzu Chi Ormoc Great Love Village held a medical, dental and surgical outreach like it did the previous year. Tzu Chings went deep into the rural villages to look out for patients with cataracts, cleft lip, hernia and goiter, among others. Many patients were treated throughout the three-day outreach, which ran from the 25th to the 27th of October. Such kindness was beyond any that these patients dared to expect. If not for the collective aspirations of the volunteers, led by Alfredo Li, and the compassionate hearts of the medical doctors, they would have continued to be tormented by their illnesses.

I often feel that every wonderful encounter in my life is arranged by the Heavens. As we journey through life, in times when we feel all alone, a melody would spring forth from our hearts together with an image of someone humming along. Among the TIMA members in Ormoc Great Love Village are a surgeon, Dr. Rolando Tomaro and two general practitioners, Dr. Noel Maico and Dr. Femia Tomaro. Presently, Dr. Noel visits the village every second and fourth Saturday of each month to hold a free clinic for the villagers.

Ormoc is Dr. Noel's hometown. His family is among the survivors of Typhoon Haiyan. In the aftermath of the tragedy, Dr. Noel witnessed how Alfredo Li led other volunteers and the residents in rebuilding their community. Drenched in sweat and with voice hoarse from lack of sleep, Alfredo still managed to comfort the typhoon survivors and arrange the medical outreaches.

意把心中的無相化為具象，真正去實踐而不是空口說愛。

之後，諾伊離開市政廳，展翅放空，他想自在做慈濟事，平淡才能永遠。

他意識到，當我們足夠美好的時候，會希望自己成為更好的人，尤其是看到跟自己一樣具備付出能力的人，比我們付出更多、更得法時，你會被深深激勵，被全然感染。

千里之路始於初步，合抱之樹發於毫芒，證嚴法師常講：「財富要有愛心才有用，意即用在有愛心、用在對的地方，它才發揮了真正的價值與意義。」這也就是為何有那麼多菲律賓的實業家願意把堆在銀行的錢拿出來做大用。

諾伊與羅蘭多、菲米雅目睹自己的同胞曾經如何痛苦絕望，絕大部分得不到良好的教育，因為抽菸、喝酒、賭博的惡習，使得整個社會彌漫汙濁而看不見希望，諾伊過去只有「愛莫能助」的感慨！

如今，有這麼一個慈濟團體來，既不是菲律賓人，宗教信仰也和他們不同，甚至語言都有隔閡，卻把萊特島從廢墟中理出一條無盡的希望……啊！不再是夢！而是以齊心協力打造好的舟子，帶領奧莫克大愛村的孩子們，找到學習與航向恩賜生命價值的方向。

在飄搖與沈澱之間，諾伊等人需要讓舊事釋然，而新事尚待消化，展開自己鑲黃而充滿價值的人生另一章節。

諾伊在奧莫克大愛村每月的兩次義診，與身為護理師的夫人一起貢獻寶貴時間，他們開創了固定駐診大愛村的先例，好似融入大家庭的一員。

At that time, Dr. Noel was working at the City Hall's Health Department. When Alfredo invited him to join TIMA, he immediately agreed. He knows that Tzu Chi is a Buddhist organization while Dr. Noel and the typhoon survivors are Catholics. But Tzu Chi never discussed religion, only gratitude, respect and mutual love. In Tzu Chi, everyone is our family.

For this reason, Dr. Noel regards Tzu Chi highly. He is willing to put the lessons into action instead of just talk about love. After that, Dr. Noel left his job at the city hall so that he could spread his wings and carry out Tzu Chi's work with ease of mind. He realized that when we feel good about doing good, we tend to want to become an even better person. When we see people whose dedication to give their time and skills is stronger than ours, we tend to feel inspired.

The journey of a thousand miles begins with the first step; the huge tree grows from a tiny seed. Master Cheng Yen often said: "Wealth must be abound with loving kindness to become useful, which means that only when wealth is used with loving kindness, can it accomplish its true value and purpose." This is also why so many Filipino entrepreneurs are willing to take out their money from the bank to accomplish great feat.

Dr. Noel, Dr. Rolando and Dr. Femia have witnessed how their fellowmen suffered due to their illnesses and poverty. Majority of them do not have an opportunity to receive a good education because they indulge in the ill habits of smoking, alcoholism and gambling, which resulted to the society becoming permeated with impurities. They could not even envisage any hope. In the past, as much as he wanted to help, Dr. Noel could only sigh and feel so helpless.

And then Tzu Chi came into their lives. Many of its volunteers are not even Filipinos. They have different religious beliefs and spoke different languages. Yet they have triggered hope to spring from the ruins of Leyte… Alas, this is no longer a dream! This is a good boat that was built from

雖然市政府安排醫師來大愛村看診，但服務對象只限於孕婦，絕大多數的老人與孩童無人關心，諾伊學習慈濟人的寬容，守護著弱勢族群與村民的健康。

　　他真心希望去治療那些貧病之人，使他們重拾尊嚴，並因此改變他們某些根深蒂固的觀念。

　　一次義診時，諾伊看到一位村民因血壓高無法接受手術，為了那也許是她人生唯一的治療機會，諾伊給她吃了降血壓藥，等待近一小時後血壓恢復正常，才將她送至手術室。他知道這有些冒險，但是病患如果不接受治療，將會失明。

　　諾伊並非十分富有，但他願意義診。因為一次國際人醫年會時，一位馬來西亞醫師分享他的感受給諾伊：「我不嚮往高薪，願意免費提供服務，動機只為了減輕病人的痛苦，因為當他們身體健康時，我心靈上的快樂勝過千金萬兩。」

　　諾伊更加堅定，穿越並捕捉生命已然到站的真理，就是此時此刻此念。但人的意志是流動的，偶爾他也無法完全掌握住那光和影的挪移。

　　病患蕾德兒（Ledel Lubon）動過甲狀腺手術後，諾伊一直在治療她。

　　蕾德兒不懂術後必須不輟地服用甲狀腺素，因此變得極度慵懶，不整理家務、不上班工作、意志消沈，家裏一切都要體弱多病的母親操勞，包括照顧蕾德兒的小孩。這使得她的母親愁容滿面，充滿無力感，總是無助地以淚洗面，眼神呆滯，不知未來要飄向何處？

　　直到有一天，我把這病解釋給蕾德兒聽，她才明白自己的

everyone's efforts and aimed at leading the children in Ormoc Great Love Village to find a course of learning so that they can sail towards a life direction filled with value.

Amidst uncertainties and settling down, Dr. Noel and the others ventured out to another chapter in life that is full of value. Dr. Noel and his wife, who is a nurse, have committed to conduct free clinics twice a month at the Ormoc Great Love Village. By doing so, they have set an example for medical professionals and even ordinary residents in Ormoc. On their part, it seems as if the couple has joined a big family in Tzu Chi.

Although the city government arranges for their doctors to conduct free clinics at the Great Love Village, their services are limited to pregnant women. The elderly villagers and the children were not taken care of. Dr. Noel emulated Tzu Chi volunteers' boundless love in safeguarding the health of the villagers. He truly hopes to provide medical care to the impoverished patients so that they could regain their dignity and change their negative deep-rooted mindsets.

Once, during a medical outreach, Dr. Noel met a patient who was told that she could not undergo surgery because of her high blood pressure. Knowing that the medical outreach could be the patient's only chance to receive treatment, Dr. Noel prescribed a medication to manage her blood pressure. They waited for nearly an hour until the patient's blood pressure returned to normal. Afterwards the patient was brought to the operating room where she underwent a successful surgery. Dr. Noel knew that what he did was risky, and yet if he did not do it, that patient would not have had the chance to be treated. That patient would have become blind.

Dr. Noel is not a wealthy doctor. Still, he is very much willing to dedicate his time and skills in doing medical outreaches. An incident during a TIMA Convention which he had participated in has stayed in his heart and mind. A Malaysian physician told Dr. Noel: "I don't yearn for a high salary. I

錯，然後回到諾伊那兒就診，持續服藥，病情才漸有起色，家庭恢復生氣與希望。

美麗的喬娜琳（Jonalyn L. Rubia）因種種波折，陷入躁鬱雙極性的深淵，諾伊為她治療一年多始終無效。許是命運的安排，我瞧見在極度憂傷邊緣徘徊的喬娜琳，經李偉嵩同意，透過藝術治療，結合音樂、詩歌和繪圖的種種波長，將喬娜琳心底絲絲縷縷的悲傷情緒抽離，淚水宣洩出來後，得以平靜並騰出一片寬廣。

李偉嵩對諾伊說：「昨天我跟一位馬尼拉的華商說，當你躁鬱得睡不著時，尚未吃鎮靜劑之前，應該先來個藝術治療。」

諾伊則回答：「是的，我曾看日本 NHK 節目，提到音樂、藝術的結合確實能醫治心理疾病遠勝於服藥。我也相信透過繪圖能抒發心中的某些情緒，而得以舒坦。我就很想在自己診所做音樂療法！」

諾伊認為，有些人的高血壓並非起因於體內的高脂肪，而是壓力使然。若能有個寬闊的房間，讓他們置身其中接受音樂治療，使他們靜心，或許能不藥而癒。

人間的愛閃閃，不在相見，只在心中有念。

二〇一七年啟德風災，刮來大量風雨，使奧莫克大愛村遭受嚴重水災。

唐榮謀在一次勘查中，發現了小男孩克勞斯（Claus Bleine Casadar）和小女孩芮宣堇（Reyshenzy Andojar）都有兔唇，列了名冊報給慈濟，尋求醫療協助。

外科醫師羅蘭多知道後，在李偉嵩陪同下，拜訪了芮宣堇

just want to provide medical services to ease the suffering of patients. When they are healthy, the spiritual happiness I feel surpasses all the money in the world." Hearing this, Dr. Noel grew even more determined to grasp the truth about life, which is all the more present at the very moment and at this very thought in giving of oneself for others. However, as humans, our willpower often fluctuates. Occasionally, one cannot totally be firm on certain things.

After a patient, Ledel Lubon, had thyroid surgery, Dr. Noel continued to provide her with medical treatment. Ledel did not know that she has to take Thyroid hormone regularly. As a result, she became extremely lazy in doing the household chores. She refused to go to work and fell into a depression. Her aging and sickly mother took charge of the household chores as well as taking care of Ledel's children. The situation had made Ledel's mother gloomy, exhausted and helpless. Her face was stained with tears and her eyes seemed lifeless. She was filled with anxiety for what the future holds until one day, Dr Noel explained to Ledel her symptoms. That was when Ledel realized her suffering was her own doing. She went to see Dr. Noel for treatment again. With regular medication, her health gradually improved and the family regained their vigour and hope.

After going through consecutive traumatic experiences, the beautiful Jonalyn L. Rubia suffered from bipolar disorder. Dr. Noel treated her for more than a year. But it seemed that she was not making any progress. Perhaps it was fate that I met Jonalyn while she was on the verge of extreme distress. With consent from Alfredo Li, I performed art therapy on Jonalyn. Art therapy combines music, poetry and drawing. After one session, Jonalyn was able to express her pent up emotions and cry all her tears. The strings of sorrow and grief that entangled her for so long were finally coming undone. She grew calm and gradually opened herself up.

Alfredo told Dr. Noel: "Yesterday, I told a Chinese entrepreneur in Manila that if he suffers from bipolar disorder and could not sleep, he should try art therapy before taking sedatives." Dr. Noel replied: "Yes, I have watched

的父母，表示願意免費幫芮宣萱動手術。他知道兔唇手術費是一筆龐大數字，奧莫克大愛村的災民無法負擔，只有透過免費醫治，才有機會看見芮宣萱美麗的未來。

芮宣萱的母親早已為女兒的面容惆悵了好幾年，意料之外，在水災的苦惱中，卻因禍得福，她不知該如何訴說心中對羅蘭多與慈濟的感恩，只一味因高興與感激，不停流下歡喜而悸動的眼淚。

順利動完手術的芮宣萱，露出微笑，好像知道這是她生命的轉捩點。

至於克勞斯，父母在他還小的時候，見他能說話、能吃、能長大，不覺得兔唇有什麼大問題；可是當克勞斯進入小學，同學開始嘲笑他的兔唇，他自己反而希望能動手術。羅蘭多也幫克勞斯動兔唇手術，非常成功。

羅蘭多心裏的歡喜無可言喻，有如天啟，幕將掀起時，你永遠不會知道將面對什麼景色。而今，他一如盞盞孤燈，在一個熟悉又似陌生的地方，為兩個新生命醞釀下一季美麗的元素。

現在的克勞斯已經是個快樂孩子，他在學校品德功課都很好。當我們前去關懷時，克勞斯一聽音樂，就開始跳起舞來，孩子展現了律動的可愛，純真的歡迎讓我們動容，也感染了他童稚的簡約心情。

羅蘭多醫師有著重感情的濃眉，略方的臉總含蓄地微笑，還有一雙散發溫暖與誠懇的眼睛。他從小在貧困的家庭長大，父母親是辛勤的甘蔗田工人，兒時也隨父母在田裏工作過，他能體會勞動者的心情。

the Japanese NHK program. It mentioned how the combination of music and art can really cure mental illnesses far better than any drug. I also believe that drawing helps a person express his emotions better and bring him comfort and ease of mind. I really want to do music therapy in my clinic!"

Dr. Noel also believes that hypertension is not a result of high fat in the body but of stress. If you have a spacious room, treat them with music therapy. Let them calm their minds. Perhaps they could be healed without medications. Love in this world twinkles like stars. It goes beyond seeing each other, but lies in keeping each other in one's thought.

The Tropical Storm Kai-Tak in 2017, brought lots of wind and rain, flooding Ormoc Great Love Village. During a survey, Julian Tong discovered that a little boy named Claus Bleine Casadar and a little girl named Reyshenzy Andojar have cleft lip. Julian submitted their names to Alfredo so that they can be helped with their medical needs.

When Dr. Rolando Tomaro, a surgeon, heard this, he joined Alfredo in visiting Reyshenzy's parents. He told them that he is willing to perform the operation on their daughter, free of charge. He knew that the cost of a cleft lip surgery is expensive and Haiyan survivors could not afford it. Only through a free medical treatment can they see a beautiful future for their daughter.

For several years, Reyshenzy's mother grieved because of her daughter's condition. But after their homes were flooded, blessings seemed to pour down on their family. Her gratitude towards Dr. Rolando and Tzu Chi was beyond words. Tears of happiness flowed freely down her cheeks. After the surgery, Reyshenzy broke into a hearty smile. She seemed to understand that this is the turning point of her life.

Claus Bleine grew up like a normal kid. He can do what every other kid normally does such as eating, playing and walking, among others. As such, it did not occur to his parents that he could suffer a great deal because of his cleft

他試著想，若不幫這兩位稚齡孩子動手術，能想像他們未來得承受許多異樣眼光，那種心裏的傷口，是藏在「無所謂」背後的極大無奈，與拿不出龐大一筆錢來為孩子解決痛苦根源的絕望！

　　他的夫人菲米雅醫師，有雙明快的大眼，清秀的面容中帶著無瑕的笑容，她敏銳地察覺先生的心思，熾熱心腸促使她無條件站在羅蘭多的角度來應和。

　　羅蘭多對菲米雅的感情揉合了愛與被了解，他知道菲米雅愛發言，也了解她的發言都是正確、有建設性的。

　　他們是互補的一對夫妻，羅蘭多十分感謝上天讓他擁有了解他、愛他的菲米雅。「因為沈靜，所以聽見花的墜跌。」用這句話來形容他們夫妻的靈犀，太恰當了。

　　菲米雅身為女人，又為羅蘭多誕下一對兒女，怎會不理解有個兔唇孩子的焦心？那種心理創傷不只孩子會，父母更甚。所以，她和羅蘭多要阻止這種傷害的造成。她明白羅蘭多修復了克勞斯與芮宣萱的兔唇，也會同時修復他們父母的心。

　　行醫的路上，夫妻倆已擁有優渥的生活，但他們未曾忘記走過的苦。

　　那種兒時的記憶總會一輩子藏在我們小小的心靈裏，雖然它被更大的幸福包圍著，但在某些時候，總會偷偷在幸福的門邊跟著別人流淚。

　　當他們看著慈濟人一言一行、良善與慈悲的教導，又去了臺灣參加國際人醫年會，他們更加理解，原來那麼多國家有那麼多醫師，不論貧富差距，都做著同樣的善行。這時，他們內

lip. It was only when Claus Bleine started attending classes in grade school and his classmates would make fun of him that they realized he needed to have surgery. Dr. Rolando also fixed Claus Bleine's cleft lip.

Words can hardly express the joy in Rolando's heart. Just like the dusk, as the curtain of darkness was about to be unveiled, you would never know what scenery you would face. Now, he is like the lonesome lamp in a familiar yet strange place, nurturing the beautiful elements of the next season for two new lives. Claus Bleine has become a bubblier child. His character and academics are all excellent. When we went to visit him, he danced for us. He welcomed us warmly, which was very touching.

Dr Rolando has thick eyebrows, which makes him look perpetually serious. But his slightly squared face always smiles implicitly, with warm and sincere eyes. He grew up in a poor family. His parents worked in the sugarcane plantation. In his childhood, he would also follow his parents to work in the field. Thus he understands the harsh life of a laborer, making it easy for him to empathize with the less-privileged.

If he had not helped those two children to undergo surgery, Dr. Rolando could only imagine the suffering they would have to endure from people who do not understand their condition. Such kind of wound will scar their hearts and make them feel helpless. As for the parents, they will despair for not being able to give the money that their children need to undergo a surgery.

Dr. Rolando's wife, Dr. Femia, has a pair of sharp and bright eyes. Her elegant face always wears a flawless smile. She is sharp in perceiving her husband's thoughts. Her empathy allows her to stand in his husband's shoes. Dr. Rolando's love for Dr. Femia comes with a broad understanding. He knows that Dr. Femia likes talking. He also believes that her speech is proper and constructive. This is why Dr. Femia is officially appointed as the spokesperson of the Tomaro family. Dr Rolando and Dr Femia are a loving couple who complement each other. Dr. Rolando thinks he is quite lucky to

心的光亮徹底被點燃！

他們在奧莫克大愛村為孩童做傳統割包皮手術，在四小時內開了一百五十刀，除了兔唇、割包皮，他們希望還能有更多付出。

因為發現付出的喜悅，是會重回自己心上的。他們滿足也祝福奧莫克大愛村的居民，守護他們的健康。

羅蘭多與菲米雅的一對兒女，都在看著父母為奧莫克大愛村所做的每一件善事，李偉嵩曾說：「我的許多華商朋友聚會時，都會提到自己的父母，因為父母的身教，所以今日他們也學習父母付出奉獻。」

菲米雅參與國際人醫年會回來後，很愛閱讀證嚴法師的著作，她對法師的智慧與處世文字，除了喜愛與佩服之外，也樂於分享給朋友。

諾伊與羅蘭多夫婦都覺得自己與法師有一種無形的牽引，但他們無從說明那是什麼，也許是因為有一個共同的、美好世界的願望，不僅僅是我們生活的地方，而是整個地球。他們心中問著：「長牆，華燈初上，你的去處是何方？」

有成就的人，都具備了一些特質，他們有智有德，也都經歷過艱辛歲月的洗鍊，善良教導我們要有同理心，便捨不得別人苦了。面對新時代所需要的深度學習，知識的累積已不再足夠，我們需要親自去體驗、動手做，與團隊合作而激盪出大愛的火花。

奧莫克大愛村的諾伊與羅蘭多、菲米雅，他們期望自己是那點燃火炬的人。

have such an understanding and loving wife. "In complete serenity, one can hear the stumbling of flowers." It is most appropriate to use this phrase to describe the consonance of this pair.

Dr. Femia gave birth to a son and daughter. How could she not understand the anxiety of a parent for having a child with cleft lip? That kind of psychological trauma affects the child, but it is even more heartbreaking for a parent. Hence, she and her husband would try to prevent such harm from arising. She realized that when Dr. Rolando fixed the cleft lips of Claus Bleine and Reyshenzy, he also healed their parents' hearts. Along the path of their medical practice, this couple enjoys a luxurious lifestyle. And yet they have never forgotten the hardships they have experienced.

Those childhood memories will remain in our little hearts throughout our lifetime. Although it is now surrounded by blessings and happiness, at certain times, we would still secretly shed tears with others.

They observed that Tzu Chi volunteers' every word and action communicates kindness and compassion. When they went to Taiwan to attend the TIMA Annual Convention, they understood better. Indeed, there are so many volunteer doctors from different countries. Regardless of the gap between the rich and the poor, they were all doing the same good deeds. The light in the couple's hearts has been lit up! When they returned home after the convention, they performed traditional circumcision surgeries for 150 children in Ormoc Great Love Village within only four hours.

Apart from cleft lips and circumcision, they hope to have more opportunities to put their love into action, because they found that the joy of giving comes back to them. Helping others gives them a sense of satisfaction and they wish to safeguard the health of the Ormoc Great Love villagers.

Dr. Rolando and Dr. Femia's son and daughter have been observing every good deed that their parents have dedicated in Ormoc Great Love

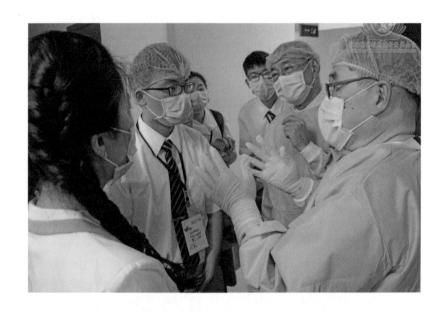

Village. Alfredo Li once said: "Many of my Chinese business friends would mention about their parents during social gatherings because of their teachings. Today, they are also learning to follow their parents' example in contributing to society."

When Dr. Femia came home after the TIMA Annual Convention, she came to love reading books authored by Master Cheng Yen. She admires the Master's wisdom and her way of dealing with the world's problems, and Dr. Femia likes to share all these with her friends. Dr. Noel, along with Dr. Rolando and his wife, feel that they have a deep affinity with Master Cheng Yen, but they could not explain how or why this could have happened. Perhaps it is because they have a common vision of a wonderful world, by creating blessings not only for ourselves, but for the entire world.

Those who have become successful in life have certain unique qualities. They gained wisdom and virtue after going through years of hardships.

Compassion teaches us to have an empathetic heart so that we feel hurt when others suffer. In facing the need for a more in-depth learning in this new era, the accumulation of knowledge is no longer sufficient. We must go and experience things personally, use our hands to do things and work together to awaken the spark of great love. Dr. Noel, Dr. Rolando and Dr. Femia from the Ormoc Great Love Village aspire to be the ones who will lit that torch.

(Translated by Si Hoo Ooi)

左上／手術室內，史美勝醫師指導志工如何引導病患進入手術流程。
(top left) In the surgery room, Dr. Antonio Say instructs the volunteers on how to guide the patients through the surgery process.

左下／手術室外，民眾耐心等候接受免費手術。
(bottom left) Outside the surgery room, patients wait for their turn to undergo surgery.

環保護大地

綠芽綽約一碧千里

Beautiful Greenery for Thousands of Miles

二〇一七年，奧莫克市長理查（Richard Gomez）與菲律賓分會執行長楊國英簽署市議會議案，由慈濟在該市一百一十里推動環保分類。
In 2017, Ormoc City mayor Richard Gomez and Tzu Chi Philippines CEO Henry Yunez signed the City Council memorandum that permits Tzu Chi to promote recycling across all 110 barangays of Ormoc City.

頹圮與廢棄代替了曾經優雅的西班牙建築，雖然已將狼藉清除運走，房子已無法使用，但人總是有感情的，依戀陪伴自己走過長遠歲月的一切，即便裏面已空無一物。

前些日子，我在大愛村那五十公頃的寸寸土地散步時，聞到淡而隱密的花香，像是沾了露水草莖的氣味，總是特別感動。彷彿飄散而來的風，仍然擁抱著、靜靜地、耐心地安撫著村民曾經驚懼的心。

大愛村要動工時，菲律賓慈濟人請示證嚴法師。法師秉持回歸大自然原貌、疼惜地球的想法說：「使用鋼筋水泥要挖山開礦，必須破壞大自然，鋼筋過了一段時間可能生鏽腐蝕，重新被拿掉，破壞山林等於是傷害人類自己，就用竹子代替鋼筋來建造簡易屋吧！」

What were once elegant Spanish-inspired houses have been replaced with collapsing and uninhabitable structures. Although the mess left by the typhoon have been cleaned up, the survivors will always carry in their hearts the sadness it brought. The place that they thought would shelter them for a long, long time was almost wiped out in just a snap of a finger. A few days back, when I took a walk on the 50-hectare land that has been transformed into a village, the breeze smelled of grasses covered with morning dew. I was very touched. It was as if the wind was embracing every resident, patiently and quietly calming their once frightened hearts.

When the construction of the Great Love Village was about to start, Alfredo asked Master Cheng Yen for advice. The Master reminded him to preserve the earth's natural resources. She said: "To use reinforced concrete, mountains have to be excavated and mined, destroying nature. After a while, the steel bars will corrode and then it needs to be removed. Destroying nature is also harming mankind. Let us make use of bamboos in building the houses

從整地到簡易屋組裝完成需要幾個月時間。當時附近甘蔗園的農工與村民大都失業，正為生活煩惱。李偉嵩、李伯芳、蔡昇航等人，開始發起「一披索一支竹子」的「以工代賑」方案，聚集大家一起做「福竹磚」。

於是，男女老少都歡喜地動起來，上千支竹子取自大地的恩賜，竹子砍了，還會再長，而且速度很快。眾人驚訝於法師的智慧，沒想過竹子竟可以這樣使用，不僅深深佩服，也對疼惜大自然的信念，有了初步的概念。

另外，又帶動住在臨時收容所的災民，也一起來做福竹磚，災民想到將有安身之地，紛紛歡喜付出。

這些村民、災民從開始建簡易屋，便與慈濟志工們齊心協力一起忙活，很多人都住進了大愛村，比如班傑明（Benjamin）、泛尼托（Juanito）、艾維斯（Ives）、大衛（David）等，他們已成為資深本土志工，也是大愛村的中流砥柱。

患難中一起奮鬥的種種經歷，有如平淡與絢麗交錯的點滴對映。

慈濟在全世界許多地方援建大愛屋，以環保概念所研發的福竹磚，是就地取材、不破壞大自然的綠色製造和環保落實，證嚴法師因而榮獲第三十九屆克羅埃西亞國際環保金牌獎與發明獎。

這些房子的屋齡已進入第六年，幾次的風災、水災，淹水超過屋頂，看起來卻依然新采如昨，彷彿還記得新落成時人們的歡呼、喜迎。

回想風災後緊急發放毛毯時，慈濟志工發現遍地寶特瓶，

instead of steel."

From the preparations to its completion, the construction of the Great Love houses will take several months. At that time, most of the nearby farmers and residents who labored in the sugarcane field were jobless. Taking that into consideration, Alfredo, together with fellow volunteers Ferdinand Dy and Michael Siao started a campaign that encourages everyone to cut bamboos into sticks. Tzu Chi will pay one (1) peso for each bamboo stick. With the "One Peso a piece of Bamboo" slogan, this "Cash-for-Work" program gathered both the elderly and the young ones to work together for the so-called "bamboo bricks".

Although thousands of bamboos would need to be cut down for the program, these plants have a fast growth rate. People were impressed with the wisdom of Master Cheng Yen. Never have they thought of using bamboos in such way. Because of this, environment protection left an impact on everyone. This campaign was also introduced to the disaster survivors who lived in temporary shelters. They were also encouraged to help in making bamboo bricks. The thought of having a place to call home soon inspired them to participate.

Villagers and disaster survivors have been working alongside Tzu Chi volunteers since the construction of houses started. Many of them have already moved into the Great Love Village. To name a few are Benjamin Mingao, Juanito Suco, Ives Famador and David Lumacang. They have all become senior local volunteers, as well as mainstays in the village. Through the good and the bad times, the experiences they shared only brought them closer to one another.

Tzu Chi has built a number of Great Love houses in many places around the world. The bamboo bricks were developed with Tzu Chi's environmental protection advocacy in mind, which promotes the use of locally-sourced materials without compromising nature. This eco-friendly innovation won

那是慈濟研發的淨水器未裝置前，民眾購買瓶裝水留下的垃圾。於是，清走廢棄物又多了遍地寶特瓶。

李偉嵩隨機示教，一手拿著寶特瓶，一手捧著毛毯說：「你們知道這個毛毯是用寶特瓶做出來的嗎？」

災民驚訝得面面相覷，寶特瓶竟能織成如此柔軟又保暖的毛毯？

大家真是開了眼界，於是開始拾起滿地的寶特瓶。從那之後，回收寶特瓶變成全民環保運動。

時光漫漫，好日子才過不久，災難又降臨，好像腐朽的事物總有微細的線條留下，久久便要滲入一些苦濁！

二〇一七年六月，奧莫克市與鄰近城鎮受到強震災變，村民無家可歸，慈濟在卡南加的希羅杜甘（Hiloctogan）援建簡易屋五十間、里薩（Rizal）七十二間、聖嬰（Santo Niño）一百二十間。

另外，奧莫克重災區達瑙湖里（Lake Danao）的災民，已住在破爛不堪的帳棚長達一年半了。慈濟想援建簡易屋的願望已久，但總有些事不得不臣服，直到奧莫克市政府終於買了一塊地，才由當地居民自己整地，奧莫克大愛村的志工協助興建了一百多間。

有時心願宛如守候已久的夜鷺，在靜默中蟄伏，於枯枝上守候，以一種無為而有所為的生命態度，來去之間自在隨緣。

奧莫克大愛村以綠色環保建造的簡易屋，多達五個村莊，一切努力變成巨大的環保楷模。

五個村的村民之間，也因為這層關係，有更深的情誼牽連

Master Cheng Yen the 39th Croatian International Environmental Gold Medal and Invention Award. It has been six years since the construction of houses were completed. Despite the numerous typhoons and roof-high floods that the village has experienced since then, the houses still look new, standing tall and sturdy, welcoming the residents.

Recalling a relief distribution of blankets after the typhoon Haiyan disaster, Alfredo Li saw a lot of plastic bottles scattered everywhere. Before the Tzu Chi-developed water purifier was installed in the area, people have to buy bottled drinking water. Even though tons of garbage have been disposed, plastic bottles still littered the streets. While holding a bottle in his one hand and a blanket in the other, Alfredo then asked the crowd: "Do you know that these blankets are made from plastic bottles like this?" People looked at each other, surprised. How could the plastic bottles turn into a soft and warm blanket? It was really unbelievable!

Alfredo Li explained that a technology in Tzu Chi Taiwan converts plastic bottles in fibers which are then made into blankets. Hearing this, the people began to pick up every bottle they saw on the streets. Eventually, this environmental protection activity has become a public environmental protection movement.

Good days never last long enough before another calamity strikes. It seems like every bad experience will leave a mark and the pain will be felt from time to time. In July 2017, Ormoc City and other nearby towns were struck by a strong earthquake, leaving numerous residents homeless. Tzu Chi extended help by building fifty (50) houses in Barangay Hiloctogan, Kananga. Seventy two (72) houses were built in Barangay Rizal and one hundred twenty (120) were put up in Barangay Sto Niño.

Lake Danao is also one of the hardest hit barangays in Ormoc City. Residents have stayed in dilapidated tents for a year and a half. Since after the earthquake, Tzu Chi had plans to build houses for these quake survivors. But

著。有如來自同一株大樹的身軀，分出了五條大小迥異的枝幹，卻都遍生了茂密的綠葉。

二〇一九年二月在奧莫克市，首次舉辦大型華人春節活動，奧莫克市的大賣場 SM Mall 邀請志工去介紹慈濟。

這突如其來的邀約，是因為奧莫克市已開始體認到環保的重要性。

奧莫克本土志工泛尼托主管環保團隊，他以堅定而驕傲的話語介紹證嚴法師後，再向廣大的民眾闡述來自寶特瓶回收所製造的產品。

「我們收集寶特瓶、塑膠製品、廢紙、鐵罐……其中，寶特瓶能經由抽紗製成毛毯、衣服等，而能微波用的塑膠可以製造福慧床，有些資源回收的物品也可以當二手物再賣出。不光如此，最重要的是環保能還給地球清潔的環境，我們需要拯救地球母親。」

在慈濟，賣出回收資源所得又充作基金，回饋在慈善、教育、醫療等志業上。

一位同學瑪恬分享：「我們曾經去臺灣，學習如何管理自己的時間。今日大多數年輕人不懂時間的寶貴與價值，如果我們能把握時間去做一些善行、善待別人，我們的國家將會充滿無限希望！」

曾聽過，栽植樹木需要十年，培養人才需要百年。所以古賢管子說：「十年之計，莫如樹木；終身之計，莫如樹人。」培育人才是長久之計，時間之於年輕人更是多麼珍貴的事，而悲心的培養得落實在生活。

there were a lot of things to consider. Until finally, Ormoc City government bought a parcel of land and let the residents handle it by themselves. Over a hundred houses were built with the help of volunteers from Ormoc Great Love Village.

At times, vows are like night herons staying dormant, waiting in dead branches. It is life's philosophy in doing something without being attached, being carefree in whatever outcome. There are already five barangays of Ormoc that have adopted the practice of using environmentally-friendly materials to build their houses. Constructing the Great Love Village has also left a great impact on environmental protection. Residents of these villages have formed a good relationship with each other and treat each other like families. They are like the five tree branches that came from a single huge trunk. Each branch varies in size, but each has grown dense with green leaves.

In February 2019, a large-scale Chinese New Year festival was held in Ormoc. The SM shopping mall invited volunteers to introduce Tzu Chi to the people. This unexpected invitation came because Ormoc residents have started to realize the importance of the Tzu Chi volunteers' efforts in pushing for environmental protection.

Ormoc local volunteer Juanito Suco is in-charge of the recycling team. He felt proud as he was introducing Master Cheng Yen to the people. He also explained how PET bottles can be turned into different new products. "We collect PET bottles, plastic products, waste paper and cans, among others. PET bottles can be processed into yarn and eventually made into blankets and shirts. On the other hand, plastic products that are microwave safe can be turned into Tzu Chi collapsible beds. Moreover, other recyclables can also be sold as second hand items. Recycling can keep our environment clean. We need to save Mother Earth," he said.

In Tzu Chi, all funds generated from its recycling program are reverted back to charity, education and medical care.

泛尼托與瑪恬的分享，提醒大家「化無用為大用」與「分秒不空過」的概念，都讓民眾有新的體認、心的悸動。

奧莫克大愛村有市區二人組瑪里露（Marilou Arciso）與蘿拉（Lorna Capucao），她們在奧莫克市區四處撿拾寶特瓶做環保，一方面也維持市容清潔。

她們深知環保是珍愛地球、維護生態健康的善行，因此做得十分歡喜。有時推著三輪的小回收車穿梭在巷弄裏，那身影被夕陽拉得長長的，似乎象徵著環保之路永相隨。

奧莫克大愛村在環保的努力與付出，終於獲得二〇一九年六月菲律賓的獨立節邀約。

遊行活動那一日，大愛村本土志工和慈青樂隊得以參與，受到市民認同與支持。

市長和政府官員向慈濟團隊揮手，市長感動地說：「感恩慈濟環保志工這幾年在城市裏的付出，更感恩證嚴法師對海燕災民的救助從不間斷。」

獨立節活動結束後，志工們快速回收寶特瓶及清掃市容，幕幕點滴，為市民樹立難忘並值得學習的典範。

這一切也昭示著，奧莫克市民看到的慈濟，不只是救災、蓋大愛村、環保救地球，還有培育菲律賓的青年，走向更美好的人生路途。

每年十一月一日是菲律賓的清明節，菲律賓民眾跟臺灣人一樣，都會去掃墓，但多人集中的地方易產生垃圾，奧莫克的墓園亦是如此。

本土志工和慈青在這一天來臨之前，他們用大圓框套上袋

One of the students, Marithel Valiente, shared her experience: "We have been to Taiwan and learned time management there. Many young people nowadays do not realize how precious time is. If we can spare time to do charities and help those who are in need, our country will have a bright future." An ancient Chinese philosopher, Guanzi, once said: "A tree will only need ten years to achieve its full growth, but it will take a lifetime to cultivate one's skills." Cultivation takes time. That is why every second is precious especially for the young ones, and nurturing compassion for all should be reflected in our daily life.

Juanito and Marithel's talks reminded everyone to "turn things perceived as useless into great use" and "to waste no second." The audience were not only impressed but also learned something valuable. Marilou Arciso and Lorna Capucao, both volunteers of Ormoc Great Love Village, have been going around the city to collect PET bottles and other recyclables, thus keeping the surroundings clean. They understand that recycling is one way of cherishing the earth's resources and they are very happy to be of service. Sometimes they can be seen pushing a recycling tricycle in different villages.

All their efforts and the hard work they put in doing recycling paid off when they received an invitation to participate in the June 2019 Philippine Independence Day celebration. During the parade, Filipino volunteers from the Great Love Village and the Tzu Ching musical band were recognized. They also received the support of their fellow Ormoc residents. Ormoc's city mayor, along with other city officials was seen waving to the Tzu Chi team. The mayor was emotional as he said: "We are thankful to Tzu Chi Foundation for all their contributions to our city. We are also grateful to Master Cheng Yen for her continuous support to Haiyan survivors." After the activities, the volunteers quickly collected plastic bottles and helped clean the area. Their actions have set an example and a valuable lesson for the people. Moreover, Tzu Chi has been part of Ormoc not just in the first phase of the disaster relief, the construction of the Great Love Village and the advocacy for environmental protection, but also in the development of the Filipino youth towards a better

子，又製作慈濟快報、環保資料、靜思語，分組並進去收垃圾，並分享資訊、靜思語給民眾。

他們已經在清明節發心這麼做第二次了，得到市政府、警察、神父和社會人士的讚賞與認可。

菲律賓人都深刻理解，慈濟帶動村民與年輕人把城市變乾淨了，而本土志工與慈青已經把環保愛地球深深刻印在心上。

習慣的養成，非一朝一夕可改變。

愛默生（Ralph Waldo Emerson）有一句名言：「習慣不是最好的僕人，便是最壞的主人。」這句話適切地表達了習慣的影響力。

環保，並非只是外在環境維持那麼狹隘，它更需往內心求善良、節約、感恩、尊重與愛的理念，這是心靈環保。

比如所謂的三好——口說好話、心想好意、身行好事。奧莫克大愛村不論在浴佛節或歲末祝福活動，都會教導孩子們為父母洗腳，透過行動來感受孝順的重要。

一個對的、正向的、善良的依歸與學習，都是心靈的環保。

時時提醒自己保持一顆潔淨的心，能善待他人，也愛惜自己，珍愛萬物、尊重眾生、體恤各種人情緒的衝突，經常保持單純的信念，平淡靜定於每個當下，是現代人最亟需學習的心靈環保。

菲律賓人最需要實踐的還有身體環保，就是三不——不抽菸、不喝酒、不賭博。

有一次採訪前奧莫克市長夫人薇歐莉時，她很開心地告訴我，奧莫克大愛村近百分之八十的人已戒此惡習。

life path.

November 1 is the observance of the All Saint's Day in the Philippines. Like the Taiwanese, Filipinos go to the cemetery to visit their loved ones who have passed away. But wherever there is a gathering of people, garbage easily piles up. The same goes with Ormoc cemetery during this holiday. A day before November 1, Filipino volunteers and Tzu Chings busily prepared garbage bags and grouped themselves into teams. They also prepared Tzu Chi's publication and environmental protection materials as well as Jing Si Aphorisms to share with the public. This was the second year that they will do recycling activity and raise awareness on environmental protection in the cemetery. The initiative is supported and recognized by the city government, police, priest and the community.

Filipinos have realized that it was Tzu Chi who motivated everyone to keep the city clean. Environmental protection and loving Mother Earth will always be in the hearts of Filipino volunteers as well as of Tzu Chings. Habits are not developed overnight. There is a famous saying by Ralph Waldo Emerson: "Habits are either the best servants or the worst masters." This best explains how influential they are. In doing recycling, one should not just think about preserving the beauty of environment. It is even more important to seek inner goodness, conservation, gratitude, respect and love.

Let us take the example of the Three Goodness: Speak good words, think good thoughts, do good deeds. Whether it is the celebration of the Buddha Day or Year End Blessings, Ormoc Great Love villagers would teach the children to show their love and respect towards their parents by washing their feet. In order to protect our spiritual environment, we must have a positive and a right way of learning. Remind oneself to maintain a pure mind. Be kind to others and also love thyself, cherish resources, respect all living beings, be sensitive with people's emotional conflicts. Keep your thoughts simple. Most of all, be calm and quiet in dealing with everyone. All these are what people nowadays should learn to nurture their spiritual environment. The most

這是走向希望未來很重要的一大步！因為萊特島人賺錢不易，所得若無法供應孩子們就學，而是揮霍在抽菸、賭博、喝酒上，那等於是不歸路，意味著孩子將步向自己後塵，永遠無法翻身。

黑暗到光明的過程並非只有兩樣景，黑暗爬過千山萬水，而光明又橫越萬水千山而來。改變，需要具備那股暗伏的堅定力量。

落在草地上的葉子，一葉鮮黃疊過一葉烙黃，優美地躺在大地寬廣的懷裏，閃著光，發出淡淡的泥土氣味。我們總裹著一層厚厚的泥土，而望不見地球母親的傷口。

茹素這件事，除了是心靈的環保也是身體的環保，更是整個地球的環保。

如今在奧莫克大愛村茹素的人愈來愈多，比如泛尼托一家人、慈青莎德拉娜、羅伯特、艾莉莎……

許多本土志工因著各種因緣理解了什麼是「愛」，理解到還有更高層次的愛是珍惜地球，不殺生，發自一念慈悲心進而願意茹素。

為了響應一月十一日「世界蔬醒日」，奧莫克大愛村展開活動。

泛尼托事先帶領本土志工們向村民說明蔬醒日的意義，邀請他們最少茹素一日，答應參加的家庭就在門外貼上參與信條，上面寫著「I support 1.11 Ethical Eeating Day（111 世界蔬醒日）」。

有一位村民聽完志工的說明後，十分感動，她說要自己貼

important thing that Filipinos need to practice is to care for and protect their body by applying the Three No's namely, No smoking, No Drinking and No gambling.

When I had a chance to interview the former first lady of Ormoc, Engr. Violeta Codilla, she was delighted to tell me that almost 80% of the Great Love Village residents have been practicing the three No's. This is already a big step moving toward a better future. It is not easy for Leyte folks to earn a living. And yet, instead of saving the money to support the education of their children, they would use it to sustain their ill vices. They are leading their children to follow in their wrong practices, therefore making it difficult to free themselves from the cycle of poverty. Transforming someone or something requires determination. It cannot be done overnight.

Vegetarianism is not only beneficial for our spirit and physical bodies but also for the environment. More and more Ormoc residents are shifting to a vegetarian lifestyle. An example would be the families of Juanito Suco, Tzu Chings Sandrane Pepito and Robert Ejada as well as Alyssa Candela. Because of various affinities, many Filipino volunteers have understood the meaning of "compassion." They also realized that a higher level of compassion means cherishing the earth, not killing all living beings and committing to a vegetarian lifestyle.

As part of the observance of the Earth Ethical Eating Day on January 11, a series of activities has started in the Great Love Village. Filipino volunteers, headed by Juanito Suco, explained the significance of the event to the villagers. At the same time, he invited them become a vegetarian at least for a day. Those who will participate will post a note with the words, "I support 1.11 Earth Ethical Eating Day" on their doors. A resident was very touched after learning the importance of being a vegetarian that she eagerly posted the note herself.

At the end of the event, 119 families or a total of 417 residents surprisingly committed to be vegetarians. Filipino volunteers then

在牆上。

蔬醒日當天，願意吃素的家庭有一百一十九戶，總共四百一十七人，出乎預料的多。

本土志工將煮好的鹹綠豆湯，送至參與茹素的村民家，那是一種關懷，也是一種鼓勵與肯定。

其中，耶美琳達（Emmelinda Mysterio）發願要親手做素食菜餚參加蔬醒日。

李偉嵩去了她家看她煮菜，耶美琳達說到做到，煮了兩道菜——炒南瓜和地瓜葉，地瓜葉還是她自家種的，第三道菜是志工帶給她的鹹綠豆湯，她的家人們都笑開懷。

每個月第三個星期日，大愛村志工們發放臺灣愛心米給弱勢家庭、年老力衰或有病纏身無法工作的村人，讓他們能安心度日。

瑪里露和凱薩琳（Catherine Daligdig）意志堅定，不管路有多泥濘，還是扛著大米往前走，也有慈青來幫忙。阿曼達（Amanda Gabas）奶奶收到大米非常感動，就砍她種的甘蔗回饋給志工。

菲律賓與臺灣一樣，是以米飯為主食的國家，他們的飯量尤其大，收到大米的弱勢家庭向志工們表達感恩之情。李偉嵩說：「布施者持著慈悲的心，滋潤著受惠者的心靈。這種愛的交會就是慈悲的學習。」

「量周沙界，心包太虛故，知意根清淨，是以圓滿一千二百功德。」慈濟人秉持證嚴法師所說，不畏辛苦，投入一切不計較，以誠意付出。

prepared "munggo (mung beans)" soup and brought them to the families who participated. What they did was an act of care, encouragement and affirmation. One of the residents, Emmelinda Mysterio, committed to prepare only vegetarian dishes on observance of the Earth Ethical Eating Day. Alfredo went to visit her to see how she will cook the vegetarian dishes. Emmelinda prepared two dishes – fried pumpkin and sweet potato leaves. The sweet potato leaves were harvested from their own backyard. The third dish is the "munggo" soup which was prepared by the Tzu Chi volunteers. Her family was so delighted when they tasted the dishes.

Every third Sunday of the month, Filipino volunteers would distribute Taiwan rice to indigent families, the elderly, or those with serious illnesses or are jobless for them to move on their lives with peace of mind. Volunteers Marilou Arciso and Catherine Daliglig were determined to carry the sack of rice no matter how filthy the road is. Tzu Chings came to help as well. Amanda Gabas was so touched when she received the rice sack. She then went to her backyard and cut some sugarcane as gifts to the volunteers.

Both the Philippines and Taiwan are similar in having rice as their staple food. Rice beneficiaries especially the indigent families expressed their deep gratitude to the volunteers. Alfredo Li said: "The donor has a compassionate heart which encourages the spirit of the beneficiary. The mutual exchange of love between these people is a life's lesson on compassion."

"Because our mind is broad to accommodate the vast universe, our mind would be pure, thereby, it perfects a thousand and two hundred merits." Adhering to Master Cheng Yen's teaching, Tzu Chi volunteers give their best sincerely without complaints.

Filipinos who are good in singing and dancing, find it easy to hum a song, but a struggle to solicit donation. Only through heart-breaking life experiences do they speak out, like petals of flowers opening slowly. A resident named Rollie Capuyan would knock at every door, encouraging people to

善於歌舞的菲律賓人，清唱容易，募款難。只有痛徹心扉的人生體悟，方能將心底話娓娓說出，如花一般緩緩地層層地綻放。

村民如利（Rollie Capuyan）會挨家挨戶做環保。他利用被丟棄的電鍋和其他回收物，組成烤鍋。一個烤鍋可以賣給村人兩百披索，年紀雖大，也獨居，但他不僅環保資源回收，還自創、自力更生，他不向命運低頭。

梅（May Entero）也走出村子，向其他小區的公共市場及商店等募款，至今已經在她的故鄉普羅克‧塔隆（Purok Talong）有了許多捐助者。

她有一本勸募的列冊，日復一日依著自己規畫的路程去勸募並做環保：「有禮貌地打招呼，說明慈濟在島上做了哪些慈善，介紹竹筒歲月，不要求捐多，只需盡力便可，最重要的是這些捐款可以幫助更多的同胞。」

她總會想起極度災苦時，慈濟馳援熱食、大米、毛毯、生活物資與慰問金，並舉辦義診。她的募款將會去救更多人，這些想法支持她勇於勸募，梅說：「證嚴法師說過募款主要是啟開人的一念善心，我很受感動。」

她誠懇的身形與真心的言語，總是深深打動著結識的人們。

有心做，就不難。深入了解善良的意涵，人的面容就自然產生柔和的光彩，人與人之間信賴的建立，都是一個「愛」字，而這個字即便不說出口，對方也能從所展現的誠懇與慈悲感受得到。

二〇一九年三月，奧莫克大愛村本土志工在奧莫克市的羅

become donors. At the same time, he would promote Tzu Chi's recycling program. He can turn discarded electric cooker into a barbecue stove, which can be sold for two hundred pesos. He lives all by himself even at his old age. He is not only protecting the environment but is also making use of available resources, turning them into useful items.

May Entero goes to the public market and various shops to collect donations from her regular donors. So far, she has already gathered a lot of donors from her hometown in Purok Talong. She keeps a donation record book, which helps her track the donations she receives. Her daily routine is to collect donations and then do recycling. She said: "I would greet the donors politely, and explain to them the good deeds that Tzu Chi has done. I would also introduce to them the concept of the bamboo bank. I do not ask them for a big amount of donation. Instead, I encourage them to share whatever they can. The important thing is that the donations can help our fellow Filipinos."May would always reminisce how Tzu Chi had responded to their needs in their most difficult time: from preparing hot meals to the distribution of rice, blankets, basic needs and cash assistance. Tzu Chi also organized a medical mission to cater to those in need of medical attention. She knows that everyone's collective donations can help more people. May added: " I was very touched when Master Cheng Yen said the purpose of collecting donations is to open someone's heart and mind". This has been her motivation to continue inviting more donors. Her sincerity leaves an impression especially to those people she has just met. If you have the determination to do what is right, nothing is impossible. When a person fully comprehends the true meaning of kindness, it is reflected in his attitude. Love is the only thing that can build trust between people.

In March 2019, local volunteers went to Robinsons mall to raise funds for three African countries that were devastated by a widespread flooding. These volunteers have experienced firsthand the struggles of a disaster victim. Only them can understand the suffering in those difficult times. The country that was the worst affected by the flooding was Mozambique, which is even

賓森廣場（Robinson Mall），為非洲三小國的水患募心募款。他們曾經飽受類似的苦難，怎不感同身受那分心疼？

尤其受災最嚴重的莫三比克，是比當初萊特島還要窮困的國家，想到他們一無所有的窘境與困頓，便燃起志工們滿腔的熱血；愛如泉湧，連小孩子也舉著「Send Love To Africa（援愛到非洲）」的牌子。

許多民眾一見本土志工和慈青九十度鞠躬接受捐獻，莫不憶起當年自己也是這樣被疼惜、被尊重、被陪伴著煎熬過那步履維艱的日子，便都伸出愛的手，紛紛捐助。

稚齡的孩子看在眼裏，都是教育。雖然他們小小心靈尚不知苦，但是看見父母兄長與民眾互動的和美景象，也一一學習著九十度鞠躬。

有一次，李偉嵩散步到靠近海邊的公園，看見達尼羅（Danilo Jumao-as）和潔西卡（Laine Dejesica）夫妻在賣花生，賣的量很少，他心想這樣怎麼維持生活呢？

夫妻倆說，他們用的三輪車是借來的，賣了花生後必須給那人抽傭金。

李偉嵩非常不捨，於是買了一部車焊接改裝成三輪車，送給他們。這麼一來，他們除了公園還能去別的地方，有慶典都會去賣，開始有了歡喜的生活。

最寶貴的是，夫妻倆如今一邊賣花生，也一邊撿拾寶特瓶給奧莫克大愛村，他們覺得這是回饋慈濟唯一的方式。

原本心高氣傲的菲律賓人不願做的環保回收與勸募，如今竟如綠芽綽約，一碧千里……

more impoverished than Leyte province. With the disaster victims' situation at the top of their minds, the volunteers became even braver in soliciting donations to help. Even the children are holding a signage which says, "Send Love to Africa".

When people saw that the volunteers and Tzu Chings would bow at 90 degrees while accepting donations, they were reminded of how Tzu Chi had treated them with respect, showered them with kindness, and accompanied in their most difficult days. Then, they would reach out their hands, this time to help others.In the eyes of the young children, these are all valuable lessons in life. At their age, they may not understand what suffering is yet, but as they see their parents or elder brother or sister interact lovingly with the people, they follow their example and bow at 90 degrees as well.

One day when Alfredo Li was walking along the park at the seaside, he saw Danilo Jumao-as and Laine Dejesica selling peanuts along the street. However, he noticed that they were not selling much. He thought, "How could this couple sustain their daily needs?" The couple told him that they would borrow a tricycle to sell the peanuts to other areas. By day's end, they will give a percentage of their income to the tricycle owner. Out of pity for the couple, Alfredo bought them an improvised tricycle. With this, the couple could sell peanuts not just inside the park but in other places as well. They can also sell peanuts whenever there is a festival or celebration. The most rewarding thing is to see this couple pick up every plastic bottle they see on the streets while selling peanuts. For them, this is a simple way of giving back the assistance that they have received from Tzu Chi.

Those who were initially hesitant to help out, especially in recycling and fund raising efforts, are now like fresh sprouts popping out in numbers from the ground, transforming the landscapes into beautiful greenery for thousands of miles.

(Translated by Celia Chang)

左上／假日，慈青領著村裏的孩子們，人手一個大塑膠袋準備做環保，這是每個星期固定的愛地球教育。

(top left) Bringing along garbage bags, the Tzu Ching guide the village kids in preparation for their recycling Activity. This is an education on environment protection conducted weekly.

右上／奧莫克大愛村民致力於環保推動，獲得二○一九年六月菲律賓政府舉辦的獨立節活動邀約，受到市民認同與支持。

(top right) With all the hard work and efforts that Great Love Village volunteers have put in, they were invited to participate in the Philippine Independence Day celebration last June 2019, during which they have received recognition and support from the whole city.

左下／瑪里露和凱薩琳不管路多泥濘，還是扛著大米往前走。阿曼達奶奶收到大米後，回贈自己種的甘蔗。

(bottom left) Volunteers Marilou Arciso and Catherine Daliglig were determined to carry the sack of rice no matter how filthy the road is. Amanda Gabas was so touched when she received the rice. She went to her backyard and cut some sugarcane as gifts to the volunteers.

教育人文與家訪

每一個笑容都值得紀念

Save Each Smile in My Mind

二〇一八年底，在眾人愛心資助下，奧莫克慈青終於有機會到臺灣參
加靜思生活營，拿到護照，開心不已。

By the end of 2018, the Ormoc Tzu Ching finally had the opportunity
to attend the Still Thoughts Life Camp in Taiwan. They were so happy
when they received their passports.

淅瀝瀝下雨了，路面潮溼，絲絲雨絮如織。我坐在簡易教
室的桌旁，風吹著雨絲，卻沒有涼爽的感覺，反倒是黏糊
糊的；衣服被空氣的溼潤貼著皮膚，渾身燠熱，但放眼望著雨
滴綢繆過窗外的原野，一分恬靜的美麗襲上心頭。

　　我正坐在這世界某一個角落，四周綠野、好友相隨，有屋
擋雨，有鳥飛過，可愛而矯捷地站在樹叢裏，樹下一隻牛慢條
斯理吃著草，牠們好像認識很久了，聽著自然滴答滴答的敲響，
奏著音樂。

　　我看施嘉怡用滑鼠在電腦上謹慎地製圖，坐在斜對面的阿
莫斯與隔鄰的羅伯特一直忙著電腦轉檔或擷取訊息。

　　志工們陸陸續續來了，一張張白色小椅子整齊地排滿屋，
大家安靜地坐下來，這是常態的默契；背後的一個白色布簾開

It was raining and the road was wet. I sat beside one of the tables inside the temporary classroom. The wind was blowing in some rain showers. It didn't feel cool, but rather humid, and my clothes felt sticky, making me uncomfortable. But as I look out of the window and gaze at the grass field, I felt a sudden sense of peaceful beauty. I sit here sheltered against the rain with good friends around me, while we're surrounded by the grass land. I listened to the melody of nature. The birds flew by, settling under the tree, where a carabao was slowly chewing grasses. It seems like they knew each other already for a long time.

I saw Ericson Go Giap working intently in front of the computer. Sitting next to him were Amos Matugas and Robert Ejada. Both were busy transferring and downloading information from the computer as well. Volunteers, Tzu Ching and others were coming in continuously and sat down quietly on the small white chairs. A familiar music filled the room, then "Life Wisdom" started to play on the white screen. This is their daily routine.

始了熟悉的《人間菩提》音樂聲響起，每週一到週五下午三點是所有村民、志工、慈青聽證嚴法師說話的固定時間，有空的人都可以來。

他們莊嚴地坐直，兩手交疊放掌，聚精會神。「啟智教養院的人雖然智能障礙，但他們的心是那麼單純，很可愛啊！」影片中，法師看著他們比手語後，就拿了兩籃餅乾和竹筒歲月吊飾送他們，他們各個歡喜感謝。

一位環保老菩薩九十四歲了，依然健朗，臉上很多皺紋，可是看起來卻是那麼慈祥，做環保十八年，還愈做愈健康。從前未做環保時，老菩薩晚上睡不著覺，做了環保後，不服藥也睡得好香甜。

「愛」有如一把鑰匙，啟開人人的心扉，展現自信與微笑。

看著這些翻譯成英文的影音檔，本土志工紛紛上臺分享心得。法師的言語在每天下午雨露均霑，在每個人的心田種下良善的啟發，結出滿滿慈悲的稻穗。

法師非常重視教育，因為教育不光是讓人長智識、學一技之長，教育還讓孩子了解孝順的重要，對有生命或無生命的事物都能善加愛惜。

心境轉變，人的言行舉止也會隨之改變，當你懂得體恤，說話便不再尖銳；當生活中失去珍愛，也能善解失去只是因緣不具足。

多年前看到一則真實故事，情節至今深印在我的腦海未曾褪色。

一百多年前的某個午後，英國一個鄉村田野裏，一位貧困

Every Monday to Friday at three o'clock in the afternoon, they would gather together to listen to the sharing of Master Cheng Yen.

Everyone sits upright, paying close attention to the video. "Although the kids from Qizhi Education and Nursing Institute are mentally incapacitated, they have a pure and sincere heart." In the video, Master Cheng Yen is seen giving away boxes of biscuits and bamboo banks to the kids after the latter's sign language presentation. The kids are very happy and thankful.

A 94 year old elderly volunteer has been involved in recycling activities for the past 18 years. Before she started volunteering at recycling centers, she had difficulty in sleeping. But the more she got involved in recycling activities, the healthier she became. Although wrinkles are already evident on her face, she still looks kind and compassionate.

"Love" is like a key to everyone's heart. It can make someone smile and can give someone confidence. Filipino volunteers were all excited to share their insights after watching the English translated videos. The teachings of Master Cheng Yen is like raindrops pouring over, nourishing the innate goodness of everyone. Master Cheng Yen values education. She believes that education is not just gaining knowledge and skill but also teaching the importance of filial piety and to appreciate and cherish all living and non-living things. Once our mental state has changed, our behaviour will follow. You will only learn empathy once you become cautious when you speak. Moreover, you will eventually understand that losing someone or something was only due to a cause and effect relationship.

There was a true story I've read few years back, and it seems the storyline was already stored in my memory. More than hundred years ago in England, there was a poor farmer who was busy working in the field. Suddenly, he heard a voice that was calling for help. It was a young man who accidentally fell into the water. The farmer did not think twice and immediately jumped into the water to save him. Later on, the farmer found out that this young man came

的農民正在勞作。忽然，他聽到遠處傳來呼救的聲音，原來，一名少年不幸落水了。農民不假思索，奮不顧身地跳入水中救人，孩子得救了。後來知道這獲救的孩子是貴族公子。

幾天後，老貴族親自帶著禮物登門感謝，農民拒絕了這分厚禮。他想，當時救人只是出於自己的良心，不能因為對方出身高貴就貪戀別人的財物。

但故事到這兒尚未結束。老貴族因敬佩農民的善良與高尚品德，感念他的恩澤，決定資助農民的兒子到倫敦去接受高等教育。農民接受了這分饋贈，因為讓孩子受到良好的教育是他多年來的夢想。

農民的兒子終於有了走入世界殿堂、改變自己命運的機會，老貴族很開心為自己的恩人完成夢想。

多年後，農民的兒子從倫敦聖瑪麗醫學院畢業了，他品學兼優，後來被英國皇家授勳封爵，並獲得一九四五年的諾貝爾醫學獎。他就是亞歷山大 · 弗萊明，青黴素的發明者。

被救的那位貴族公子也長大了，在第二次世界大戰期間患上了嚴重的肺炎，但幸運的是依靠青黴素，他很快痊癒。他竟是後來的英國首相邱吉爾。

農民與貴族，都在別人需要幫助時伸出援手，卻為自己的後代甚至國家播下了善種。人的一生，往往會發生很多不可思議的事情，有時候，我們幫助別人或感恩別人，冥冥之中似有輪迴。

善良與愛就如同花朵與果實，他們自然地傳遞生命的動力，也感染著每一個人的美善人生。「愛出者愛返，福往者福來」，

from a noble family.

A few days later, the young man's father went to see the farmer in order to thank him for saving his son's life. He brought gifts for the farmer. However, the farmer refused to accept it. For him, saving the man was the right thing to do in that situation. He should not accept anything in return just because the man he had saved turned out to be a member of a noble family.

The young man's father was impressed by the kindness and morality of the farmer. He offered to support the farmer's son so he can study in London. The farmer accepted this because he had always wanted his children to have a better education. It was a good opportunity for the farmer's son to see the world and gain more knowledge and experiences.

A few years later, the farmer's son finally graduated from St Mary's Hospital and Medical School in London. Because of his excellent academic performance, he was honoured by the Royal British and won the 1945 Nobel Prize in Medicine. He is Alexander Fleming, who discovered Penicillin. The young man who was saved by the farmer had grown up as well. He was diagnosed with pneumonia during World War II. It was the penicillin that helped him recover. This young man is Sir Winston Churchill, who became the Prime Minister of United Kingdom.

The farmer and the noble father had offered a helping hand to each other in times of need, thus cultivating goodness for the next generation and even for their country. In life, there are always unexpected things that could happen. Sometimes when we help or express gratitude to someone, there seems to be a law of nature that works wonders..

Kindness and love are like flowers and fruit. They are passing on the natural beauty of life and influencing each and every one as well. "One who shares love and blessings will receive the same in return". Education is the medium to generate kindness and love.

教育，便是傳播良善與愛。

埃德溫（Edwin Codilla）是在達瑙湖附近開披薩店的老闆，當初興建其他四座大愛村時，慈濟志工總會招待本土志工去吃披薩。久了，埃德溫自覺亦曾受慈濟恩惠，又有這層交會，更加深他對慈濟的了解與感佩，便來奧莫克大愛村為孩子們免費上英文課。

奧莫克大愛村的孩子們，在蔡昇航、彭本語、施嘉怡三人小組的教育下，各個乖巧、知禮數、有人文。

是年教師節，孩子們前一天便開始在簡易教室裏布置，他們要為英文老師帶來驚喜，表示感恩與敬意。彩帶、彩球、一張大大的海報上面用五顏六色的彩紙剪了「HAPPY TEACHER'S DAY」教師節快樂。

教師節當日，埃德溫一進教室，發現溫暖而充滿綺麗的布置，孩子們更一一獻上自己從大愛村五十公頃土地上摘來的花，用彩帶綑綁出一個個美麗花束，九十度鞠躬送到埃德溫手裏、懷裏。他情不自禁地淚溼了眼眶！

想想人生當中，再如何努力、再好的運氣也無法賺到全世界，但就這滿懷花束和九十度的鞠躬，深深撼動了埃德溫內心纖細的情感。他將永生難忘，擁有比財富可貴上千萬倍的愛與感動。

世上亙古不變的，除了雲月伴隨古樸的老樹，還有我們心中閃亮的愛。

孩子們的教育金來源，極大部分來自菲律賓華裔商人的捐助。顏長偉捐助獎助學金之外，知道孩子上課要走三公里去很

Edwin Codilla is the owner of a pizza store in Lake Danao. When the other phases of Great Love Village were still under construction, Alfredo Li would often invite volunteers to have pizza in his store. As time passed, he came to learn and understand more about the foundation. Edwin became very grateful to Tzu Chi. Later on, he decided to go to Ormoc Great Love Village and teach English to the kids for free.

Under the supervision of Michael Siao, Rey Penalosa and Ericson Go Giap, the kids at Ormoc Great Love Village become very obedient, talented and polite. A day before the Teacher's Day, students gathered inside their classroom to decorate. They wanted to surprise their English teacher with a simple gift that will demonstrate their respect and gratitude towards him. The students used ribbon and balloons and made a colorful poster that reads "HAPPY TEACHER'S DAY".

On the day of the celebration, Edwin was filled with warmth when he entered the classroom and saw the colourful decorations. One by one, the students bowed 90 degrees as they give their personally hand-picked flower bouquet to their teacher. Edwin could not help it. His eyes filled with tears. In reality, no matter how hard you work or how lucky you are, you cannot have everything. But the flowers and the students' respect have deeply touched Edwin's heart. This unforgettable experience will surely surpass the monetary wealth a hundred and thousand times.

In this changing world, aside from the ageing trees, the only thing that would not change is the love in our hearts. The source of educational fund mainly came from the donation of Chinese businessmen in the Philippines. Eric Ngan did not just donate scholarship but also a big white truck to fetch students going in and out of the schools. This was after he learned that many of these students walk three kilometres every day in order to reach their school and the same distance going back home.

Alberto Beltran volunteered to drive for the students every day. With

遠的地方，回家又是三公里，從天亮走到昏暗，很是不捨，於是捐了一部純白的大卡車，用來接送孩子們上學。

村民亞伯特（Alberto Beltran）自願每天載孩子上下學。從此，孩子們不勞父母操心，加上有林烏醋集團捐贈的 LED 燈矗立在黑暗的角落，奧莫克大愛村就像一個孩子們不失航的終點站。

李偉嵩常常得意地形容這大卡車，不但載孩子上下學、志工們外出活動、環保資源回收、大節日時接送四個大愛村的村民……簡直是萬用的萬能車！

教育是一輩子的事，還有很多華商也樂於捐助，慈濟牽引的善良和風，滾滾不絕捲襲所有人熱騰騰的心，如鑽石般堅硬而晶澈！

孩子們申請助學的背後，都是一篇篇感人的故事。而申請助學並非無償上學，他們利用假日做環保或是家訪，幫獨居或行動不便的老人清掃家園，從勞動中體會賺錢不易，用辛勤、陪伴來抵償助學金，也啟發善念、愛和悲心。

家訪時，關懷老人健康並做紀錄，在做中感受人我之不可分，同理心地將老人家當成自己的親人，學會體恤、孝順。這些無不是實踐著證嚴法師的教導——「苦人所苦」。

透過實踐理解到老一輩的人沒機會念書，無賺錢能力，老年生活是如此黯淡，年輕人就會更奮發向上。

比如他們去家訪艾德華多爺爺（Eduardo C. Oracion），一位七十歲的單身漢，他的父親是中國人，母親還是少女時在工廠上班，遇見他的父親，然後有了他。

this, the parents won't be worried about their transportation anymore. Moreover, the owner of Lim O Chu (Diana) Foundation donated the LED lamp posts, which light and guide the students on their way back to Ormoc Great Love Village. Alfredo Li is proud of this big white truck because it serves not just as a school bus for the students, but also as a service vehicle for volunteers whenever there are activities such as recycling. It is also used for other events at the Great Love Village. This truck is really multi-functional.

Victor Siasat would always ask Julian Tong if Tzu Chi needs donation. Without hesitation, Julian would say, "Yes, we do." Education is a long term assistance and many Chinese businessmen were willing to donate. Because of Tzu Chi's initiative, a lot of people are willing to be part of this circle of love.

There were many touching stories behind each scholarship application. Scholars are also not getting the assistance for free. On school holidays, they join recycling activities or home visitations to aid recipients. They helped those living alone or disabled elderly to clean their houses. From volunteering, the students come to realize that earning money is not easy. Moreover, volunteerism teaches them to become more compassionate and kind.

During home visits, students are not only caring for the elderly but are also taking down notes for record-keeping. From there, they learn how to treat these elderly as their family, how to be understanding, compassionate and respectful. All of these are from the teaching of Master Cheng Yen "To experience other people's sufferings as if they were your own".

These activities also motivate the scholars to study well as it gives them an understanding of the consequences of not finishing one's education. If they miss this wonderful opportunity, they will also miss the chance to earn a living. There is an elderly named Eduardo C. Oracion who lives by himself. He is 70 years old. His father is Chinese while his mother was a factory worker when they met each other. Eduardo's father wanted to take him to China when he was only seven months old. However, China was a very conservative

在他七個月大時，父親歸國想帶走他讓他在中國受教育，但是當時的中國還很封閉，他的母親認為自己不會被夫家接受，就抱著他逃走了！

之後他的母親另組家庭，又生了三個孩子，他被孤立了。情感上，他像是一臺小小的電扇在窗簾底下旋轉，吹得窗簾微微掀起，又闔上，只發出很小很小的聲響。非婚生子的祕密，一直壓在他心頭上。

生命裏每一趟旅程每一幕，都是一個慎重而孤獨的約定。

艾德華多的家在海燕風災時被摧毀，繼父與母親往生，他與同母異父的弟妹遷居的房子又因政府擴大道路被拆除。幾經輾轉，艾德華多住進奧莫克大愛村，弟妹們搬到馬尼拉，他開始了獨居生活。

他為左鄰右舍維護環境，鄰人見他年老又獨居，有時會給他一些小費，或買他種的花妝點門面。有時人家問他，對生活還有雄心嗎？他都說自己老了，能三餐溫飽足矣！

艾德華多七十年的歲月，應該有過夢，但那些夢彷彿已經變成厚厚的沈積岩，仔細再聽，是否還有流水的音聲？或者流淚的嗚咽？

他的內心一定還有與母親相依時的記憶。如今，他立在樹叢間，只想傾聽微風中綠葉搖晃的細瑣，歷經長久的風雨，他仍擁有自己完整的一顆心，不容易。

現在他懷抱感恩，把自己的前塵往事像剪髮一般梳理。他要回報慈青孩子們定時去探望他，幫他打掃家裏及帶來歡愉，他珍惜在奧莫克大愛村的點點滴滴，每日都聽得見樹葉花草對

country at that time and his mother was anxious that she may not be easily accepted by his family. So she decided to run away, taking Eduardo with her. After that, his mother had started another family and gave birth to three more children. Eduardo then became lonely and isolated. The allegations being hurled at his mother for giving birth without getting married have caused him so much pressure.

Every chapter in Eduardo's life only seemed to grow more serious and lonely by then. Eduardo's house was destroyed when Typhoon Haiyan hit. He also lost his mother and step-father. He then lived with his step brothers and sisters. However, they were relocated once again because of the local government's road widening project. Eventually, Eduardo moved to the Ormoc Great Love Village alone while his siblings transferred to Manila. They have been living separately since then. Eduardo would help keep the neighborhood neat and clean. Knowing that he is living alone, his neighbors would offer him small token or buy some of the flowers he planted. Sometimes they asked him if he still have the eagerness to move on. He simply replied that he is old and having three meals a day is already good enough for him.

Eduardo have dreams. But these dreams seemed to be met with a lot of hindrance. He remembers the days when his mother was with him. Now, he is all alone, standing in the bushes, listening quietly to the sound of the gentle wind. It is not easy for him to move on after all that he had been through. Yet he is very grateful to the Tzu Chings who visit him regularly and help him with the household chores. These Tzu Chings have brought him so much happiness. Eduardo treasures all the memories he had in the Ormoc Great Love Village. In fact, you would hear him talking to the flowers and trees everyday.

Another beneficiary is Anacorita Cuyos. After she broke her right arm, Tzu Chings were very active in visiting this elderly. As Anacorita cannot do the cooking anymore, Tzu Chings would bring with them hot meals during their visits. This simple gesture warms not only Anacorita and her husband's

他說話的聲音。

　　還有安娜考瑞特（Anacorita Cuyos）右手骨折後，孩子們更加勤快來看他們兩老，因右手無法煮食，孩子們非常貼心地每晚送飯菜來，溫暖他們的不只是胃，還有心窩。

　　說來如此細瑣的事，為何總是閃亮亮的，教人一再拼圖而不厭其煩？

　　奧莫克大愛村即將邁入第六年的此刻，當年擔任慈濟菲律賓分會執行長的李偉嵩，對萊特島特別有一分情感，他雖然是宿霧人，但他在萊特島生活過一段時間，算是他的第二個故鄉。海燕風災發生時，起先他幾乎忘了米沙鄢方言要怎麼說，但長期陪伴後的今天，一回生二回熟，早已朗朗上口。

　　善良與微笑一樣，是有感染力的。

　　二〇一七年，奧莫克大愛村又遭水災，透過以工代賑鼓勵居民復建家園。李偉嵩告訴我：「耶誕節那天，我好懺悔！」問他為什麼？

　　原來，在奧莫克大愛村裏，他巧遇年僅九歲的小女孩卡爾琳（Angel Carlene Pantig），當時，她穿著單薄的衣裳對他說：「Sir Alfredo（李偉嵩），Merry Christmas.」

　　李偉嵩說：「在菲律賓，如果陌生人或是孩子對你說『Merry Christmas』，就是要錢的意思。」那時他以為小女孩想跟他要錢，加上他正忙著處理水災的事，兩相權衡，他沒理卡爾琳。但後來志工跑來跟他說：「卡爾琳是要捐五十元給慈濟救災，不是要錢。」

　　孩子心念單純，卻被自己平白誤會了，他懺悔不已，趕忙

stomachs but also their hearts.

The Ormoc Great Love Village has been sheltering Typhoon Haiyan survivors for almost six years already. Alfredo Li was then the CEO of Tzu Chi Philippines office. Although he grew up in Cebu, he always has a special place in his heart for Leyte. Many years ago, he stayed in Leyte for a time and he had considered it as his second hometown. When Typhoon Haiyan struck the province and brought him back to this place again, he found that he had almost forgotten how to communicate in Bisaya, the local dialect. But after continuous interaction with the locals, his tongue got used to the dialect and now he can fluently speak it again.

It goes the same with kindness and a smile. It can easily influence others. In 2017, Ormoc Great Love Village faced a flood disaster. It was through the launching of the cash-for-relief program that the residents were encouraged to clean up their homes. Alfredo Li tells me that he felt very guilty that Christmas Day. I asked him why. He said he met a 9-year old girl named Angel Carlene Pantig in Ormoc Great Love Village. She was just wearing simple clothes while greeting him "Sir Alfredo, Merry Christmas".

"In the Philippines, when someone greets you a Merry Christmas, it means that person, especially among kids, is asking for a gift money," Alfredo recalls. He thought the little girl was asking for a cash gift and had ignored her since he was busy coordinating for the disaster relief. A volunteer later told him that Carlene would like to donate 50 pesos to Tzu Chi. She was not asking for money at all!

A child's mind is naive and pure. Alfredo felt guilty for misinterpreting the intention of the child. He then immediately went with other volunteers to visit Carlene. Her Grandmother told them, "Sometimes I would ask her for money from her savings but she often refuses to give me." Carlene would go around the village singing Christmas carols to earn money, which she wants to donate to help others, just like what Tzu Chi volunteers are doing.

跟志工到卡爾琳家裏拜訪。卡爾琳的祖母說：「平常連我要跟她拿錢都很難的。」這五十元，是小女孩到處唱耶誕歌曲報佳音賺來的，目的是想學志工們救災助人。

卡爾琳學習李偉嵩的良善，就像孩子學習大人的言行舉止，那是影響孩子一輩子的教養。

李偉嵩自小接受父母身教的洗禮，父親常教誨他成功時勿忘「造橋鋪路」，他來不及讓父母親看見他對社會做出奉獻，如今卡爾琳的五十元讓他想起那情景，他不想再有後悔，便與家族商量，希望在大愛村興建學校，落實教育。

大愛村的孩子們每天走三公里路去上課，既勞遠又危險，李偉嵩希望能在大愛村興建中小學，實踐證嚴法師「安身、安生、安心」的願，提供一個便利又優良的學習環境。

奧莫克大愛村因海燕風災而矗立，靠近奧莫克大愛村的兩所小學，學生捐出他們存了許久的竹筒，願為建校基金盡心力。

蔡昇航陪伴本土志工們與會，孩子們抱著存滿愛心的竹筒，等待倒進大甕裏。這些孩子們來自奧莫克中央學校，海燕風災後皆曾接受慈濟幫助，存竹筒如今已變成他們生活的日常。

奧莫克中央學校老師說：「現在孩子們來上學，第一件事就是把零錢投進竹筒，每一枚硬幣都是一個心願，他們祈禱奧莫克中小學能儘快美夢成真。」

利洛安中央學校的孩子，也積極響應。老師說：「作為學校的老師，鼓勵學生養成儲蓄的習慣，是我們的責任，雖然孩子存進竹筒的金額不多，但長期累積下來是大愛心。」

這兩所學校多數來自奧莫克大愛村家境清苦的學生，志工

For Carlene, Alfredo Li is her role model. She wanted to adopt his kindness just like how a child is learning every word and action of the adults. Alfredo Li was raised by his parents with good teachings and morals. His father would always remind him to give back to others when he becomes successful. However, his parents were not able to witness all of his contributions to society anymore. Now, Alfredo was reminded again of his parents because of Carlene's donation. He doesn't want to have regrets again. He decided to discuss with his family the plan about building a school in the Great Love Village to give everyone a better education.

The children from the Great Love Village will need to walk three kilometres to reach the school. Alfredo Li hopes to build an elementary and high school inside the village in order to provide the students with good quality and more accessible learning environment. This is also included in Master Cheng Yen's action plan for the said housing community which is "to provide permanent housing, job programs and temporary shelter."

Because of Typhoon Haiyan, the Ormoc Great Love village was built. Students from nearby schools donated the contents of their bamboo banks. Each of them would like to be part of the construction of the new school. With the assistance of Michael Siao and Filipino volunteers, students lined up one by one, holding their bamboo banks then poured their coin donations into a big jar. These students were from Ormoc City Central School. They were once a beneficiary of Tzu Chi, now this is their way of giving back and helping others. Teachers of Ormoc City Central School shared, "Every day as the students came to school, the first thing they would do was to drop a coin into the bamboo bank and say a prayer. They prayed that their dream of having an elementary and high school will soon come true."

The students of Lilo-An Central Elementary School are also supporting this project. Teachers said, "As teachers of the school, it is our responsibility to encourage our students to practice saving their money. Although it is not a large amount, it gathers everyone's compassion."

們用愛灌溉他們的心靈，希望有天善的種子也能萌芽。

其中奧莫克中央學校校長羅伯特說：「很感恩慈濟為我們的孩子送來文具，還教導孩子們環保、手語，他們捐出的竹筒只是小小的回饋。」

孩子們的點滴愛心，串流成河而為建校盡心力，也將照亮自己的未來。

慈濟中小學預定面積八點七公頃，教育部官員來大愛村查看土地，很滿意又感動，又看了學校的建築圖，說：「慈濟捐贈的學校莊嚴又美麗，未來將成為萊特島的地標。」

羅伯特先生（Robert Jardin）是奧莫克最大一所小學的校長，他看了也極為感動，說：「我們學校有兩千五百名學生，我會勸他們每兩天捐一塊錢，來幫慈濟蓋學校。」

二〇一九年六月，證嚴法師行腳到臺北，我在新店靜思書軒有緣得見施恭旗一面，他穿著簡單的一身白，眼神篤定而誠懇，尚未來得及交談，一行人便匆匆上樓去見法師了。

事後李偉嵩告訴我，法師在會談中也指示要為孩子們興學，施恭旗知道後捐出一億菲幣作為建設基金，搶著要蓋慈濟小學。

在菲律賓分會，現任執行長楊國英、前執行長蔡萬擂、李偉嵩，都屬當地的實業家族，這些社會菁英在找到信仰與價值後，全力為當地社會奉獻，無悔無求。

李偉嵩說施恭旗也是實業家菁英：「菁英的眼睛都是雪亮的，他們會觀察你們是否真心為苦難人做事？」

李偉嵩與施恭旗相識於海燕風災過後舉辦的茶會裏。

「志工準備餐點，邀約各方人士來分享。用餐前，播放以

Most of the students of these two schools are from poor families of Ormoc Great Love Village. With the love and companionship given by volunteers, they hope that their effort would prosper someday. Robert Jardin, principal of Ormoc City Central School said, "We are very grateful to Tzu Chi Foundation for donating school supplies to our students. They even teach the students environmental protection and sign language. The money from bamboo banks was just a small contribution from us." Every drop of kindness can accumulate into Great Love, just like the raindrops that can form a river. The eagerness of students to help in the construction of the school somehow reflects the brightness of their future.

Tzu Chi Elementary and High School will have an area of 8.7 hectares. Officers from the Department of Education were very touched and satisfied after conducting an inspection at the Great Love Village. While looking at the construction plan, they said "the school donated by Tzu Chi is very beautiful and solemn; this will become a landmark of Leyte province." After learning about the plan, Principal Jardin of Ormoc's largest elementary school was so touched and said, "Our school has 2,500 students, and I will encourage them to donate one peso every other day to help Tzu Chi build the school."

When Master Cheng Yen travelled to Taipei in June 2019, I was fortunate to meet Carlos Chan at the Jing Si bookstore in Xindian. He was wearing a simple white outfit and he looks so down to earth. He was in a hurry to meet with Master Cheng Yen that I did not get a chance to talk to him. Later, Alfredo Li would tell me that Master Cheng Yen has also advised that Tzu Chi needs to build schools for the children. Carlos Chan immediately committed to donate one million pesos for the construction fund. In the Tzu Chi Philippines office, the current CEO Henry Yunez, former CEO Manuel Siao and Alfredo Li are all local entrepreneurs. But after discovering the value of their lives, they have dedicated themselves to contributing to the society without asking for anything in return.

Carlos Chan is also a local entrepreneur. Alfredo Li said, "Privileged

工代賑相關影片。我注意到，他很認真在看影片。之後我起來講話，把在獨魯萬勘災，一直到廢墟打掃乾淨才離開，過程詳細講了一遍，感動了他。」

　　然後他問我：「可以找個安靜地方談一下嗎？」

　　施恭旗說他想見證嚴法師，於是透過安排飛來花蓮，連同太太、孩子、孫子、兒媳跟女兒都一起來。與證嚴法師一席談話後，他問我：「一間簡易屋多少錢？」我說大概十萬。施恭旗說：「我負責一千間。」

　　他觀察這位知名實業家：「當晚一行人回到飯店，施恭旗居然要助理與女婿合睡一間房，女兒跟媳婦睡一間。搭飛機不買商務艙，他們坐經濟艙！」

　　李偉嵩感動於一個實業家敦厚的內心，傳承良善家風的精神、節儉不豪奢的態度，可是對社會的奉獻卻那麼慷慨、那麼低調。

　　目光即是鏡頭，華麗的蛻變，最美的依舊是平淡。

　　或許山嵐消失了，山會失去氤氳靈氣，若是天色太亮了，天地萬物將不再靜默，若是我們的身邊沒有誰，我們亦歡喜屬於自己。但是如今奧莫克大愛村的村民們，均殷殷相互守望。

　　再回頭望望凹陷的過去，慈濟教育帶給村民們輕輕哼起歌，用滿腔的熱愛繼續前進，以右手掌貼著自己的左胸口，像是繞了一條迂迴的遠路，回到最初，通往更潔淨而明亮的地方，坐在那純良的土地上，永恆的畫面裏，他們記得生命中陪伴的，每一個笑容都值得紀念……

people have sharp eyes. They would observe if you are really extending help to the needy." Alfredo Li and Carlos Chan met during a tea gathering after the disaster brought by Typhoon Haiyan. "Volunteers have prepared snacks and invited different people to share their insights. Videos regarding cash for work programs were also played. I noticed Carlos was paying attention to the videos. After that, I shared our relief efforts in Tacloban City. I also mentioned that we did not leave the city until we have cleaned up the place." Carlos then approached me and said "Can we go to a quiet place where we can talk?"

Carlos Chan said he wanted to see Master Cheng Yen. Through the arrangement of Tzu Chi office, he flew to Hualien in Taiwan together with his family. After the meeting with Master Cheng Yen, Carlos asked me how much does one prefab house costs? About a hundred thousand pesos I said. Carlos said, "I will take care of one thousand units." Alfredo Li was observing this businessman. "When we got back to the hotel, Carlos Chan instructed his assistant to share the same room with his son-in-law, while his daughter and daughter-in-law shared the other room. Their plane tickets were in economy class instead of business class." He was truly touched by Carlos Chan. He is a businessman who knows how to stay down to earth despite his popularity and success. He is generous and contributes to society while keeping a low profile. Simplicity would always be the best.

When the mist dissipates, the mountains lose its ethereal beauty. If the sky is too bright, all things are not silent. If we don't have other people around us, we belong only to ourselves. But for now, the people of Ormoc Great Love Village are eagerly watching over and helping one another. Looking back, Tzu Chi has taught the villagers to hum their song, to move forward with passion, as if taking a U-turn from afar, and returning to where they've started, which is headed towards a cleaner and brighter destination. Sitting in that fine piece of land, capturing a moment of eternity, they remember every acquaintance in life, and every smile is worth remembering.

(Translated by Danny Tam)

右上／實業家施恭旗（左六）認捐奧莫克大愛村一千間簡易屋，以及一輛高儲水量消防車以及慈濟奧莫克小學。

(top right) Entrepreneur Carlos Chan (6th from left) donated a thousand unit of prefabricated houses to Ormoc Great Love Village, a fire truck with huge water storage capacity, and the Tzu Chi Ormoc Elementary School.

左上／在靜思生活營中，施嘉怡教導孩子們如何簡單地做出一道美味三明治。

(top left) During the Jing Si Life Camp, Ericson Go Giap is teaching the children how to make a delicious sandwich in an easy way.

左下／平價披薩店老闆埃德溫充滿智慧和愛心，他撥空在奧莫克大愛村教孩童學習英文。

(bottom left) Edwin Codilla, the pizza store owner, is full of wisdom and love. He would spent time to teach English to the kids at Ormoc Great Love Village.

浴佛典禮
陽光與海水的教養
Brought up in Sunlight and Ocean

奧莫克大愛村舉辦二〇一九年浴佛典禮，人人點亮心燈，懺悔己過，祈禱天下無災難，迎向更美好的未來。

The 2019 Buddha Bathing Ceremony was held at the Great Love Village. Everyone lights up their heart lanterns and repents for their faults, praying that there be no more disaster in the world and looking forward to a glorious future.

炎夏漫無目的，即便我們坐在車裏，沿著樹蔭下彎彎曲曲小路，透過林間葉隙，依舊晒得我雙眼睜不開，所幸閉目沈思起來。

二〇一九年五月十二日，萊特島舉辦大愛村建村以來第四度浴佛節，早上在獨魯萬，下午於奧莫克，逐年增多的浴佛人數，是人們對慈濟信賴的表徵，與宗教完全無關，是「愛的陪伴」那溫暖與倚靠。

萊特島居民隨著歲月流逝，當年慘痛傷痕逐年退去，他們所信仰的宗教心靈依歸已得以修復，遠自臺灣越過千山萬水而來的慈濟教導，讓所有分裂的家庭和睦、讓不孝順的孩子如倦鳥歸巢回到父母身邊、讓孩子從看不見未來而至今敢於作夢……

浴佛節前一日，我們到了辦公室，聽見施嘉怡正教導幾位

Even inside our van, travelling through the winding alleys under the shade of the trees, the summer heat pierces through the gaps between the leaves of the trees making it hard to open one's eyes. With my eyes close, it brings me some thoughts....

On the 12th of May, 2019, the Buddha Day Ceremony was held at Leyte. This was the fourth Buddha Day Ceremony held here since the village was built. In the morning it was held in Tacloban City, and later in the afternoon in Ormoc. The yearly increase in the number of people attending the Buddha Day Ceremony implied that more and more people are developing good faith in Tzu Chi. It has nothing to do with religion but with the warmth and steadfast "loving and caring support."

One day before the Buddha Day event, we came to the office and heard Ericson Go Giap teach the Chinese language to several children in the Great Love Village. He patiently taught them Romanized pinyin, slowly, word per

大愛村孩子學中文，耐心地一個拼音一個字慢慢教。

這裏是菲律賓的一個島，曾經發生慘痛災情的地方，在距離臺灣那麼遙遠的村子，這些孩子們竟然熱愛學習中文？不僅如此，他們的手語也比得非常入心，平日待人接物、參與發放或是家訪，都是九十度鞠躬，身形和美而莊重。

窗外飄著細雨，不知明日浴佛會怎樣？

我經過河堤，想摘點薄荷草或是羅勒，發現河的兩岸開滿了白芒，漫漫綿延，順著風的韻律如浪蕩漾。

坡上的狗尾草，細毛凝露有如睫毛上的淚；幾隻白鷺鷥佇立涼涼水中，歪著頭在風中啄整羽翼，世界如此細密又如此溫良安靜。

途經艾德華多爺爺的花園，忍不住關照了一眼牛角瓜淡淡的紫花。

因為兩株靠得近，成簇的紫花便相互支撐著彼此，我莞爾一笑，想起奧莫克大愛村的教育三人小組裏，彭本語與施嘉怡兩位職工的處境。

老師出身的施嘉怡，因為腦瘤需依靠枴杖走路，而有護理背景的彭本語與他同租一屋，就近照顧。無論外出或在辦公室廚房用齋，彭本語都會幫施嘉怡帶一份，親如兄弟的情感，支持彼此行走人間。

他們自馬利僅那市跟著蔡昇航移師到奧莫克，來這裏培育慈青，三人都是慈青大學長。施嘉怡自慈青時代就喜歡設計，奧莫克大愛村這兒的海報、浴佛用衣服圖騰、教導孩子中文的教具，都是由他設計。

word. Here in one of the thousands of islands of the Philippines, a place which had once faced a tragic disaster, a village, so far away from Taiwan, have these children who are so keen to learn Chinese! Not only that, they are also very well-versed in the sign language performance. On normal days, when they interact with people, participating in the relief distribution or home visitation, they bowed at 90 degrees, their physique were so graceful and solemn.

It was drizzling outside, so I wondered how it would be like tomorrow during the Buddha Day Ceremony. As I pass through the river dike, and thought of picking some mint or basil, I noticed that both sides of the dikes are full of silvergrass stretching far across the plains. These silvergrass bend along the rhythms of the wind like dancing waves. The dogtail grasses along the slopes have fine mists like the tears in eyelashes. Standing tall in babbling water, several egret tilt their heads to peck on their wings. The world is just so delicate, gentle and peaceful.

Passing through Grandpa Edward's garden, I couldn't help but to take a look at the light purple flowers of Calotropis gigantea. As two plants were close together, the clusters of purple flowers are mutually supportive of each other. I smiled and recalled the three-member education team of Ormoc Great Love Village and the situation of the two employees, Rey Peñalosa and Ericson Go Giap.

Ericson is a teacher by profession. He once suffered from brain tumor and is now relying on crutches to walk after his surgery. Meanwhile, Rey with his nursing background, stayed closed to Ericson to take care of him. They rented a house together. Whether they eat out or have their meals in the office kitchen, Rey would always get a share for Ericson. They are as close as siblings, mutual supporting each other in walking their paths in this world. They followed Michael Siao as he moved from the city of Marikina to Ormoc. They came here to nurture the Tzu Chings as all three were once Tzu Chings.

Since his years as a Tzu Ching, Ericson has liked designing. Today, the

有時，我探頭看簡易教室，彭本語正親身示範著《慈悲三昧水懺》的手語，他逐句比著手勢，微笑掛在嘴邊；蔡昇航就跟孩子們坐在椅子上，等著彭本語教一個段落，他再起身繼續講解下一段經文。

　　蔡昇航用羅馬拼音、英文、中文這樣合著，教大愛村的孩子們學習水懺經文。

　　蔡昇航大半時間都待在奧莫克大愛村，有時三人小組移師保和島。他志為慈濟終身志工，每個月回馬尼拉家裏的時間少之又少，常與另一半黃亮亮分隔兩地。

　　某日，蔡昇航用手機不知跟誰說話，我們正要用早齋，突然聽見他清亮的聲音說：「阮是恁尪啦（閩南語，我是你的丈夫啦）！」

　　一旁的我們面面相覷狐疑地望向他，是否兩人太久沒聯絡，黃亮亮到底是故意還是真認不出蔡昇航的聲音？也許是我們的表情太有趣，蔡昇航突然笑不可仰！

　　蔡萬擂與郭麗華夫婦真不容易，四個孩子全都奉獻給慈濟，李偉嵩家族也是。他們就是菲律賓在慈濟的兩棵大樹。

　　施嘉怡連續設計了四年浴佛節衣服及各種海報，他設計好，蔡昇航決定顏色和款式。李偉嵩說，自己只是出一隻手，指一個方向！

　　比如二〇一九年的浴佛，志工們要演出《慈悲三昧水懺》中的「夢歷六道」，施嘉怡就設計了一個「懺」字。蔡昇航決定用淡灰底黑字來呈現，圓形標記放在衣服胸前左上角，看起來簡潔又有意義。

posters of Ormoc Great Love Village, the logos in the Buddha Day ceremony uniforms, the teaching materials used to educate the children in Chinese, were all designed by him. At times, when I peeked in to have a look at the prefabricated classroom, I could see Rey personally demonstrating the sign language of the sutra adaptation of "*The Compassionate Samadhi Water Repentance*". He taught the sign language phrase by phrase, with a smile hanging on his lips. Michael sat with the children on the chairs, waiting for Rey to demonstrate a part of the sign language. After that, he would stand up to continue explaining the next sutra passage. Michael used Romanized Pinyin, English and Chinese simultaneously, to teach the children of Great Love Village the Water Repentance sutra passage. Michael spends most of his time in Ormoc Great Love Village. At times, this Education Team would move to Bohol Island. Michael is a committed Tzu Chi volunteer. His monthly trips back to his home in Manila is getting scarcer and he is often separated from his wife, Carolina Uy-Siao.

One day, as we were about to have our breakfast, Michael was using his mobile phone but the person on the other line probably did not recognize him. Suddenly we heard his clear voice saying: "I am your husband!". As we were just beside him, we looked at him with astonishment. Is it because both of them have lost contact with each other for a long time? Is it that Carolina purposely or truly cannot recognize Michael's voice? Our fascinated expression led Michael to suddenly burst out laughing beyond control. It is not easy for this couple, Manuel and Teresita Siao. All their four children are dedicated to Tzu Chi. It is also the same for Alfredo Li's family. They are the two big trees of Tzu Chi in the Philippines.

Ericson had, for four years consecutively, designed the uniform and various posters for the Buddha Day Ceremony. After he designed, Michael would decide on the colours and style. Alfredo said, "I only use my hand to point out the direction!" For instance, during the Buddha Day Ceremony in 2019, the volunteers were to perform the "*Dream of Going Through the Six Realms*" which is derived from the "*The Compassionate Samadhi Water*

有著溫柔嗓音的施嘉怡，平日沈默，縮小自己，樂於配合。出生是早產兒的他，父母住在香港，回菲律賓探望外公、外婆，當時在母親肚子裏才七個月大，就急著來人間報到。

　　由於早產必須留院觀察，當時菲律賓在經濟、醫療各方面的資源又優於香港，就這樣他留在外公、外婆身邊長大。

　　施嘉怡幸運地活下來，並且在學成績優良。他個性比較內向，每天只有往返學校與家裏，不跟同學出去玩，在菲律賓念到十四年級就完成高中學業，直接考大學。但在施嘉怡要上大學時，外公因糖尿病往生了。

　　為了完成大學教育，施嘉怡半工半讀，前兩年他批發衣服來賣，後兩年教電腦，靠著這些收入，他不但能養外婆和自己，也讀到大學畢業，一畢業即留在母校教書。

　　一九九五年，在蔡萬擂的介紹下，施嘉怡認識了慈濟。

　　二○○七年，最親愛的外婆也往生了。「迎著晨曦，尋找溫飽，出發吧！」施嘉怡雖然內向，但他用淡定的生命觀，迎向自己的命運。

　　李偉嵩的小兒子李慈光說：「我要上中二的時候，他原本應該是我的老師，可是很可惜，他到臺灣去了。」施嘉怡很坦然地慢慢說：「我去開腦瘤！」

　　很是震驚的訊息，這個大男孩在那麼年輕的歲月，究竟受過多少精神的折磨？

　　外婆去世的第二年，施嘉怡就罹患腦瘤，但他並不自知，直到蔡萬擂和蔡昇航父子發現他常牙痛，手會顫抖，直覺不對勁，於是安排他於二○○九年前往花蓮慈濟醫院檢查，才發現

Repentance". After Ericson designed the word "repentance". Michael decided to present the words in black with a light grey background. The round-shaped emblem was placed on the upper left hand corner in front of the chest on the shirt. It looked simple yet meaningful.

Ericson has a soft and gentle voice. He mostly remains silent, showing his humility. He is most happy when he is able to help. He was born prematurely. His parents, who were living in Hong Kong, came back to the Philippines to visit his grandfather and grandmother. At that time, he was only seven months in his mother's womb, and he was rushing to come out to this world. After he was born, he had to stay in the hospital for health monitoring. Consequently, he stayed with his grandparents, who raised him. Ericson was lucky to have survived and maintained a good academic record in school. An introvert, his daily routine was to go to school and then go home. He never went out to play with his classmates. In the Philippines, he completed his high school in the 14th grade and was directly admitted to a university. However, when Ericson was about to go to the university, his grandfather succumbed to diabetes. In order to pursue his university education, Ericson followed a work-study program. For the first two years, he bought clothes from a wholesaler and sold them in retail. In the next two years, he taught computer classes and relied on this income to sustain both the living expenses of his grandmother and himself. He eventually completed his study and graduated from the university. After graduation, he immediately became a teacher in his former school.

In 1995, through Manuel Siao's introduction, Ericson came to know about Tzu Chi. In 2007, his dearest grandmother also passed away. "Ushering the first ray of the morning sun, he set off in search of his livelihood!" Although Ericson is introverted, he has an unperturbed sense of life's value and presses on towards his destiny.

Alfredo Li's youngest son, Light Lotus Lettuce Lato Li, recalled: "When I was in second year high school, he was supposed to be my teacher. But it

是腦瘤。

此後輾轉動了四次腦部手術，如今施嘉怡的臉型右邊微腫，影響他的眼睛與說話，但不減他溫文儒雅、俊秀的模樣。

美麗的可能性時時都在發生，施嘉怡身在慈濟，每一次遇見生活的困頓，都會專心地想著，「我只需做好一件事情！」抱著這樣的信念，即便生命隨時因腦瘤而飽受威脅，行動、說話都受限制，但他依然在每一次的任務中發揮自己最大的良能！

奧莫克大愛村的孩子們，眼睛各個雪亮，他們非常尊敬這教育三人組。

每年五月第二個星期日，是佛誕日、母親節、慈濟日三節合一的浴佛大典，即便在多數信仰天主教的奧莫克大愛村，眾人依舊如火如荼練習著手語、鼓樂，場地布置的各種道具都是資源回收再利用做成的。

泛尼托在大愛村裏，不但善於領導，腦筋也很靈光，他深深受環保洗禮，領著本土志工做環保、發放和勸募。

浴佛節或是其他重大節日，他從教育三人組那兒學習到如何場布，所有需要的道具，他腦筋動得飛快，做事又勤勉，是李偉嵩的得力助手。

二〇一六年，奧莫克大愛村在滿是黃土石礫的場地，首次舉辦浴佛。

孩子們演繹《父母恩重難報經》，從日復一日的練習演繹中，孩子們深刻了解到「孝順」的意義和重要性。

而奧莫克大愛村的男兒，個個穿上施嘉怡設計的藍色制服，看起來整潔又剽悍，演繹《行願》——闡述的是唐朝鑑真大和

was a pity that he went to Taiwan." Ericson calmly explained: "I had to go to Taiwan to undergo a surgery for my brain tumor."

It was a shocking thing to hear. How much spiritual torment he had been through at such a young age! Two years after his grandmother's death, Ericson suffered from brain tumor. However, he was unaware of it until both father and son, Manuel and Michael Siao noticed that he often had toothache, his hands trembled and his intuition was not right. They arranged for him to go to Tzu Chi Hualien Hospital in 2009 for a medical check-up and they found out that it was brain tumor. One after another, he underwent four brain surgeries. Now the right side of Ericson's face is slightly swollen, which has affected his eyesight and his speech. Nevertheless, it did not diminish his gentleness and elegant appearance.

Beautiful possibilities happened all the time when Ericson is in Tzu Chi. Every time he encountered difficulties in life, he would focus his mind to think, "I just have to do one thing well!" With such faith, even though his life was always threatened by the brain tumors, even though his mobility and speech were restricted, he still gives his best in every mission.

Every child in Ormoc Great Love Village has sparkling eyes. They regard this three-member education team highly. The second Sunday of May each year is the Buddha Day Ceremony, which commemorates the Three-In-One celebration of Buddha Day, Mother's Day, and Tzu Chi Day. Even though the majority in Ormoc Great Love Village are Catholics by religious faith, everyone still practiced the sign language performance and striking the drums to the rhythm of the music. The various display that decorated the venue were all made from recyclable materials.

In the Great Love Village, Juanito Suco is not only good in leading people but is also very clever. He firmly believes in the importance of environmental protection and leads the local volunteers to carry out recycling work, as well as other volunteer activities like relief distributions and

尚受日人所託，為了傳揚正統佛法，不畏艱難六次東渡日本，不屈不撓、不畏風雨飄搖，那分「願」力與排除萬難「行」在驚濤駭浪上，終至抵達彼岸！

在蔡昇航的解說與彭本語肢體的帶動下，眾人反覆演繹，潛移默化了實踐的意志力，這在生活中是多麼彌足珍貴！

他們演繹時動作矯捷有力，目光炯炯如炬，在黃土石礫上又站又跪，膝蓋磨啊轉啊，燠熱的氣候裏日日揮汗練習，那分毅力是透過什麼念想？能如此堅定不移！

尤其，演出鑑真大和尚與弟子等三位僧人，為了演出此角色，必須剃光了頭。事後接受採訪，他們說：「雖然我們信奉天主教，但是這個演繹是教導我們做好人，並沒有違背我們的信仰。」

馨香一念，猶如一朵夜裏暗香浮動的野薑花，逐漸濃郁地散播了整個奧莫克大愛村。

二〇一七年，我到菲律賓參與義診，義診結束時，我們排排坐在白色小椅子上，村民為我們帶來了一分驚喜。

這年，他們浴佛典禮時的「鐘鼓」，是以資源回收的水桶和鍋子取代。以大愛村土地上砍來的竹子做鼓棒，水桶都敲到凹陷，鍋子也敲破了，不知已經練習過多久，才能凹陷、破成那樣？

看了這獨步全球的鐘鼓演繹，大家莫不為他們那分純樸可愛而開懷地笑，也讚歎村民的點子如此克難，卻又不失環保再利用的新義。

然後，他們還準備了一場跨宗教信仰的《無量義經》演繹。

fundraising drives. From Ericson, Rey and Michael he learned how to decorate a venue. Juanito is very smart as he is hardworking and diligent. He is a competent assistant to Alfredo Li.

In 2016, the Buddha Day Ceremony was held for the first time at Ormoc Great Love Village. At that time, it was a site full of loess and gravel. The children performed the sutra adaptation of *"Profound Gratitude to Parents"*. From the daily rehearsals, the children had come to understand the meaning and importance of "filial piety."

The men of Ormoc Great Love Village wear the blue uniform designed by Ericson. They looked clean, swift and fierce as they performed *"From Vow to Action"* which tells the story of how during the Tang Dynasty, the eminent monk Ven. Jian Zhen set out to Japan to spread the orthodox Buddha-dharma. He made six attempts to go to Japan, unafraid and unyielding to the wavering storm, with such "aspiration" that helped him overcome all difficulties until he finally come ashore! Driven by Michael Siao's commentary and motivated by Rey Peñalosa's body language, everyone took their roles in the performance seriously. This subtly influenced their willpower to practice and realized how precious this is in life! In their performance, their action was vigorous and full of vitality. Their eyes were bright like a torch as they stood and then knelt down on the loess gravel, with their kneecaps grinding and turning. Under the hot climate, they practiced and sweated every day. How could they uphold such perseverance and unwavering determination? In order to play the roles of the three monks, the eminent monk, Reverend Jian Zheng and his disciples, the performers have to shave their heads bald. After the performance, when interviewed, they said: "Although we are Catholic in faith, this performance teaches us to be good people who do not violate our religious faith." A thought of incense fragrance liken to the wild ginger flower emitting its fragrance secretly in darkness, gradually spreads across the Ormoc Great Love Village.

In 2017, I came to the Philippines to participate in the medical outreach. When it was done, we sat together on the small white chairs and the villagers

奧莫克大愛村的居民，別開生面的整齊穿著，展現獨特的演繹，以《無量義經》中〈無量法門〉展開序幕。

他們依舊採用竹子當鼓棒，水桶作鼓，鍋子為鐘，當「靜寂清澄，志玄虛漠，守之不動，億百千劫……」音樂響起時，擊響法鼓，敲下法鑼，一響、二響、三響，聲聲震撼人心，警醒人們要去除無明，時時向善。

最後更是展現村民的熱情奔放，由泛尼托敲著玻璃瓶的巧思，接續〈環保歌〉表演。

輕脆的音符跳躍著，大家隨著音樂又唱又跳，歌聲洪亮，「世界災難頻頻傳，慈濟發揮正能量……」村民舉起「支持慈濟基金會，一起來做環保」的標語，希望能喚起更多人的環保意識。

泛尼托說：「這些材料或許看起來很簡陋，但是對我們來說，所擊出的每個聲響都是非常具有意義的。」展現最虔誠與最真誠的心，在在顯示出他們的純真與用心。

原本已逐漸黯淡的天色，在村民們的表演下，人人的心都整個亮了起來。

最後，我們與他們手牽手圍成一個很大的圓。這分情誼並非忽然發生的，而是從二〇一三年海燕風災後，蔡昇航、彭本語、施嘉怡三人帶動，最後泛尼托等人逐漸挑起大梁，自己獨創風格，完成一場圓滿的浴佛活動。

到了二〇一八年，泛尼托、大衛等本土志工，更自行發想演繹〈地獄之門〉。

什麼樣的人會進地獄？受什麼刑罰？做什麼好事可以當天

brought us a surprise. That year, the materials for the "drums and bells" performance was replaced with recycled buckets and pots. The drumsticks were made of bamboo cut from the Great Love Village. The buckets were knocked until dented. Even the pots were hit until damaged. Just imagine how long have they been practicing to make these dents? After watching this uniquely innovative bell-and-drum performance in the world, surely anyone would be fascinated by its pure simplicity and would laugh beyond control. They also praised the villagers for overcoming their difficulties without forgetting to put environmental protection into practice.

Then, they also performed the Sutra of Infinite Meanings, which transcends religious faith. The residents of Ormoc Great Love Village, really opened up a fresh outlook. Dressed so properly and neatly, they performed their unique take on the Infinite Dharma Paths, which is extracted from the Sutra of Infinite Meanings during the opening ceremony. They still used bamboos as drumsticks, buckets as drums, pots as bells. When the music, "with minds tranquil and clear, vows vast as the universe, they remain unwavering for countless kalpas" echoed, the drums were beaten and the dharma bells were struck simultaneously. One striking sound, two striking sound, three striking sound. Each striking sound jolts the human mind to awaken the people, eliminate their delusions and always strive towards wholesomeness. Finally, they even revealed the enthusiasm of the villagers, with Juanito's ingenuity in striking the glass bottles, followed by the performance of the "*Environmental Protection Song*". The melodious musical notes it creates complement with the song and made everyone sing and dance along with the music.

"World disasters frequently happen; Tzu Chi exerted their positive energy..." The villagers put up the slogan "Support Tzu Chi Foundation, let's come together to carry out recycling work", hoping to raise awareness on environmental protection. Juanito said: "These materials may seem rudimentary, but for us, every sound that it make is very meaningful." With utmost piousness and sincere hearts, it only reveals their pure simplicity and mindfulness.

使？他們自己編劇，志工自己演。

這個演繹，主要勸人要以一顆良善的心念，活在人間。

對於每年的浴佛節，大愛村的村民們似乎對演繹這件事上了癮。

他們總是用資源回收再利用的自創道具，自編平日教育三人組所教的經文，或是以每年證嚴法師特別重視的事件來編導演繹，用純真而樸實的發想引人注目。

二〇一九年演繹《慈悲三昧水懺》的〈夢歷六道〉，則是倡導茹素的重要性。

道具都是泛尼托帶領兒女與所有志工趕製完成。邁入第四年浴佛，李偉嵩早已完全放手讓本土志工自己編劇，只偶爾技癢的時候，看到大家在排演，覺得動作不夠到位，他就會親身示範給他們看，逗得大家笑呵呵！也點醒村人演繹真正的意涵是什麼。

瑪里露飾演愛吃肉的夫人、大衛飾演老爺，為了滿足夫人的口欲，僕人們宰殺豬、羊、牛、魚……冤靈在夜間進入夫人夢中，死前的掙扎與淒厲的叫聲，嚇得夫人夜夜不能眠而痛哭。老爺於是勸夫人茹素，之後便不再做惡夢。

最後，人手拿著由泛尼托手繪的蔬菜或水果，排成人牆開始唱〈呷菜上蓋讚〉：

「大肉大魚 呷尬肥肥

巴肚那圓圓 常常跑醫院

青菜水果 三餐定時

皮膚幼綿綿 手腳也伶俐

Originally, the sky was gradually fading into darkness, but after the performance of the villagers, everyone's heart suddenly brightened up again. Finally, we held hands with them to form a very big circle. This friendship did not happen suddenly but after the Typhoon Haiyan in 2013 and with the motivation from Michael Siao, Rey Peñalosa and Ericson Go Giap, finally, Juanito and the others gradually willingly shoulder the great responsibility as they created their own style to accomplish a successful Buddha Day Ceremony.

In 2018, the local volunteers such as Juanito and David even came up wit their own skit called *"Gates of Hell"*. What kind of people will go to hell? What will be their punishment? What kind of good deeds will turn humans into holy angels? The local volunteers composed their own script, which they performed themselves. This sutra adaptation performance mainly aims to remind people to maintain their wholesome thoughts while they are in the living world.

Every Buddha Day, the villagers of Great Love Village seemed not to get enough of performing. They would always use recyclable materials to make their own props, compose their own theme and script based on the sutra passage that they heard from Michael, Ericson and Rey or on the annual events that Master Cheng Yen laid special emphasis on. They do all these with pure intentions, simply hoping that it will open people's eyes to important truths in life.

In 2019, their performance of the *"Dream of Going Through the Six Realms"* which was extracted from the *"The Compassionate Samadhi Water Repentance"*, is to disseminate the significance of vegetarianism. The props were all prepared by Juanito, along with his children and other volunteers. Entering into the fourth year of the Buddha Day Ceremony, Alfredo Li has already left it completely in the hands of the local volunteers to compose the drama scripts, except on occasions when he sees everyone taking part in the rehearsal but their actions do not seem good enough. He would personally demonstrate how it should be done and it often brings everyone to laughter!

不論初一或十五　不論下雨或好天

呷菜呷菜　上健康

呷菜讓你呷尬百二

不論小孩或大人　不論小姐或先生

呷菜呷菜　上蓋讚

呷菜讓你呷百二」

　　接近黃昏，與會的伊薩卡尼神父上臺演講，之後人醫會醫師也上臺了。曾經接受羅蘭多醫師手術的克勞斯和芮宣董都捧了花束，由他們的父母代筆寫信感謝醫師。孩子的可愛笑容，是醫師們最美的回饋，羅蘭多醫師紅了眼眶。

　　就像慶祝耶誕節那般的歡愉，菲律賓奧莫克大愛村的三節合一慶典，有莊嚴的浴佛儀式，也有溫馨的孝親活動，具體落實在大愛村的每一個家庭。

　　天色整個暗了，在墨色中，蔡昇航用菲律賓語，請大家捧起燈燭，一一點燃，並虔誠地祈禱。克勞斯雖然才上小學，但燭火照亮了他雙眼緊閉虔誠祈禱的模樣，那麼動人。

　　當我們兒時，因為保留了一分美好記憶，所以長大後，偶爾會來探望我們兒時的等待。

　　在生活的最深處，星空好深好美，像是一個善解人意的小孩，懷抱著那善良陪著眾生向前行！

　　夏末的晚風，我細數著在大愛村的每一個日子，腳步輕輕地繞過一棵辣木樹。孩子們向我圍過來，幾天後我即將離開這兒，但孩子們，心不要急，慢慢來，永遠不要忘記，陽光與海水的教養。

He also does this to explain to the villagers the true meaning of performing the sutra adaptation. Marilou Arciso played the role of the wife who loves eating meat. David played the role of the husband. In order to satisfy his wife's appetite, the servants slaughtered pigs, sheep, cows, fish... The grieved spirits visited the wife in her dreams at night. The struggling and mournful screaming before the animals were taken by death frightened the lady, causing her to have sleepless nights, crying bitterly. The husband then advised his wife to practice vegetarianism. After that she no longer had nightmares. At the end of the play, the performers, holding the vegetables and fruits that were hand-painted by Juanito in their hands, lined up to form a human wall and they started to sing together:

"Large meat, large fish, will make you grow fat
With rounded belly, you will always have to go to the hospital
Green leafy vegetables and fruits, with regular three meals
Your skin texture will be fine and soft
Your hands and feet would also move freely
Whether it is the first day or the fifteenth day of the Lunar month
Whether it is rainy or good days
Eating vegetables is always very healthy
By eating vegetables you will live up to the age of 120
Whether children or adults
Either Women or men
The best is to eat vegetables
Eating vegetables you will live up to the age of 120"

As the sun began to set, Father Isagani Petillos, who attended the ceremony, came on stage to express his gratitude. After that, TIMA medical doctors also went on stage. Both Claus Bleine Casadar and Reyshenzy Andojar, who had undergone surgery by Dr. Rolando Tomaro, carried the bouquets, and their parents wrote letters to thank the doctors on their behalf. The children's lovely smile are the most beautiful reward for the doctors, and Dr. Rolando was moved to tears. Just like the splendid joy of Christmas

celebration, the three-in-one celebration in Ormoc Great Love Village in the Philippines had a solemn Buddha Day Ceremony, and also the heart-warming filial piety program, which was concretely implemented in every family in the Great Love Village.

The sky is completely dark. In the darkness, Michael Siao uses the Tagalog dialect to ask everyone to light their candles up one by one, hold it up and pray piously. Although Claus Bleine Casadar is still a grade schooler, he joined in the prayer, the candlelight illuminating his tightly closed eyes.

In our youth, we preserve a delightful memory lane, so after growing up, we would occasionally pay a visit to our childhood anticipations... In the darkest part of life, the starry sky is bright and beautiful, just like a child who is good at understanding others, embracing their kindness to accompany the sentient beings to move forward!

The night breezes in the late summer. I recounted every single day in the Great Love Village as my footsteps gently passed by the Moringa tree. The children came and surrounded me. I am leaving this place a few days later, but children, don't worry. Take your time, you should never forget, the sunlight and the ocean that brought you up.

(Translated by Si Hoo Ooi)

左上／以回收鍋具為鐘、塑膠水桶為鼓，就地取材的桂竹作鼓棒，雖異於一般，但是誠意十足。
(top left) Using kettles as bells, plastic pails as drums and bamboo as drumsticks to perform the same beat with sincerity.

左下／想起母親的養育之恩，珍瑪卡（Jamyca Carlotsa）在浴佛活動中，手拿冰棒，餵母親一口，便潸然淚下。
(bottom left) In the Buddha Day event, Jamyca Carlotsa holds a popsicle to feed her mother. She bursts into tears as she reflects on her mother's sacrifices to raise her.

勤耕土地
都是晚霞的顏色
Dusk Colored It All

羅伯托一公頃半的土地簡直一望無際，隨著季節更替，養土為下年度
農作物做準備，只有遠方的玉米田還欣欣向榮。

Roberto's 1.5 hectares of land seems to stretch on and on. As the
seasons change, the soil is prepared for the next crop, only the corn
fields from the far distance are still flourishing.

河岸滿是晚霞顏色，沿著河廊，我們輕踩步伐往大愛村走。山丘在河岸過去幾百公里處，每當忙完事情在此散步，往往已近黃昏。

　　三房與兩房型的大愛屋之間，平疇綠野尚有部分未加利用，芒草舞著細薄鋒利的長袖，伸手去摸時寸寸都是刀鋒；若是有風輕輕吹起，就變成音樂。麻雀在草長與碎花植物間飛躍，輕快的羽翼，微顫顫地從此處躍向彼處，似難停歇。

　　我們從辦公室出發，最先經過艾德華多爺爺的家。他是一位七十歲的單身漢，看得出他年輕時的帥氣、善良，不輕佻、話也不多、經常微笑著。他的家門口屋頂下，串了一條可以懸掛植物的白色鍊子，一盆綠色九重葛、一盆武竹、一盆黃蝦花……艾德華多爺爺珍愛植物如同親人，軟枝黃蟬盛開了，黃

The riverbank glows with the colors of the sunset. We gently stride along the river coast toward the Ormoc Great Love Village. The mountains are hundreds of kilometers away from the river. Every time we finish work and decide to take a walk, the sun sets as dusk approaches.

Between the three-roomed and two-roomed Ormoc Great Love houses rests an uncultivated piece of land. The dancing miscanthus swings its blades, which are sharp enough that it can cut a hand. Yet when the wind gently blows against it, it creates beautiful melodies. Sparrows soar between grasses and flowers; their wings seem to flap ceaselessly.

We left the office. We passed by the home of Eduardo C. Oracion, a 70-year-old unmarried man. He doesn't talk much but he always wears a kind smile. He is undoubtedly handsome in his youth. A white cable hangs from under his door, allowing plants to hang as decorations. Green bougainvillea, asparagus, lollipop flowers, etc…Eduardo treats plants as if they are family

花蔓藤過屋頂，好似給房子戴了頂黃色皇冠，廊下鵝掌藤與武竹、竹柏，一叢又一叢綠油油圍住他的家。

圍籬外一條小黃土路，旁邊種了一畦畦蔬菜，圍著蔬菜又種了開著紫花的牛角瓜、紅竹、彩葉草、百日菊……我尤其喜歡牛角瓜，這是一種藥用植物，開的花很美，傘狀花、微微的紫色，結了種子後，就像馬利筋或蒲公英一般，飛絮隨風飄逸，而且全年都開花。牛角瓜全株都有乳汁，這些乳汁有毒性，但能治療皮膚病、痢疾、強心，近年還被提出抗癌防癌的功效；它的莖皮纖維亦可造紙。

每次經過這兒，孩子們問起這是什麼花？我都告訴他們用眼睛看，不要摸！我沒問艾德華多爺爺是否懂得牛角瓜的藥用價值，整個大愛村也只有他的花圃看得見這種植物，或者艾德華多爺爺只是愛它四季持續不間斷開著淡紫色美麗花朵呢？

艾德華多爺爺患有高血壓，他知道證嚴法師鼓勵村民善用土地，於是買了苗栽和種子，在自家空地種了許多美麗的花樹與蔬菜。他種了芋頭、白菜、蔥、空心菜、木瓜、絲瓜、南瓜……把環境打理整潔，藉著這些農活維持著身體健康。

一位居民正巧來向艾德華多爺爺買菜，只見爺爺自菜圃拔了幾棵白菜、空心菜和兩條絲瓜放入婦人的提籃，然後收下一點費用。

除了農作，艾德華多爺爺還會理髮，藉著種植和理髮自力更生。七十歲對他而言，彷彿是新生活的開始，而不是結束。

不遠處，聽見孩子們運球上籃的聲音，循著爽朗笑聲的地方望去，兩個籃球框立在空曠的田野間，空地已劃平但尚未鋪

members. As the Allamanda bloom, their yellow flowers climb over the rooftop, presenting the house with a golden crown. A dwarf umbrella tree, asparagus, and Asian bayberry bushes surround his house.

Just beyond the fence, there are a plethora of crops surrounded by purple flowers from Calotropis, Ti plants, Coleus, zinnia, etc...I especially like Calotropis, which are used as herbs for medical purposes. Calotropis flowers are beautiful with their umbrella shape and purple tint. Once the seeds form, they ride the wind and bloom throughout the year, similar to tropical milkweeds and dandelions. The entire Calotropis body contains latex, which is toxic. However, latex is also useful in treating skin diseases, dysentery, and cardiovascular diseases. Recently, it has been suggested that latex may have preventive and curative effects against cancer. In addition, the fibers from the skin of its bark can be used to make paper.

Every time we pass by, the children would ask: "What kind of flower is this?" I remind them to only observe and not touch! I was not able to ask Eduardo if he understood the value of Calotropis as herbs. In the entire village, these species of plants can only be found in his garden. Perhaps Eduardo simply likes those beautiful light purple flowers that bloom all year round?

Eduardo is hypertensive. He knows that Master Cheng Yen encourages villagers to put their back and front yards into good use. Thus he buys seedlings, grows flowers, trees and vegetables in his garden. He plants taro, cabbage, green onions, water spinach, papaya, luffa, pumpkin among others... Through gardening, he is taking care of the environment while taking care of his health.

A villager walks toward Eduardo to buy vegetables. Eduardo picks a few cabbage, water spinach and two luffas from his vegetable garden. He puts it into the lady's basket and then collects the money.

Apart from agriculture, Eduardo also does hairdressing. With these, he is

上水泥。想起慈濟人有很多為大愛村孩子們規畫的藍圖，有動態、有靜態，想法很單純，就是要孩子們從各種學習和嘗試中，找到自己的興趣去發展，開發自我潛能，獲得生活的樂趣與自信。

乘著晚霞餘暉，我們向三房型大愛屋方向走，如果以一個 U 字型來形容奧莫克大愛村的建物，在 U 字開口處是辦公室與道路，U 的左側是三房型大愛屋，右邊是兩房型大愛屋，其他地方是可供開墾種植的平疇綠野。而帕羅（Pablo Celmar）爺爺就住在三房型大愛屋那區。

帕羅爺爺種了許多絲瓜、紫茄，還有一棵棵綠油油的木薯（樹薯），木薯是大愛村居民大宗的澱粉食物來源，將它的塊根蒸熟後壓碎做餅。在我小時候，母親會把樹薯塊根與椰奶渣和在一起磨粉，蔥炒香放一點糖，餅烤好時剪開，將炒了糖的蔥一夾，鹹鹹甜甜香香，很好吃。最簡單的吃法，是將塊根直接切塊悶煮加糖，它的 Q 度很高很美味。

絲瓜收成時，帕羅爺爺常用竹編的容器裝來送給辦公室廚房作為回饋，也賣給鄰居賺少許錢零花。知足，讓他感到踏實而幸福。

繼續沿著河廓走，看到了卡莉朵媽媽（Carlito Yahut）正在採摘絲瓜與辣木葉（Buah Kelor），準備做晚餐。她的辣木長得很高，結了很多長條豆莢狀的種子，故意留了幾條枯乾的種子，打算自己育苗，她也種了香蕉、木薯、白蘿蔔、南瓜。

辣木是奧莫克常見的植物，卻也是很特別的植物，它富含維生素與礦物質、胺基酸，對提升身體免疫力極為有效，大愛

able to support himself. For him, being seventy years old is only the beginning of a new life, not the end.

The sound of children dribbling the basketball and their bright laughter catches our attention. Two basketball nets stand in the middle of a field that is bulldozed flat but has not yet cemented. Looking back, Alfredo Li had contributed in building the blueprint of the Ormoc Great Love Village. For the children, he considered both dynamic and static aspects of activity. His vision is simple: he wants children to learn from different experiences, discover their passions and reach their highest potential.

The sun is setting. We walk toward the Great Love houses with three rooms. The buildings at the Ormoc Great Love Village is shaped like the letter "Y". The bottom vertical portion marks the office and the main road while the upper right portion is the cluster of Great Love houses with three rooms and the upper left portion is the cluster of Great Love houses with two rooms. The remaining land is a flat field that is open to reclamation and cultivation. Pablo Celmar lives in one of the Great Love houses with three rooms.

Pablo plants many luffas, eggplants and cassava plants. Cassava is the main source of carbohydrates for the majority of the villagers. The root can be made into pastry after steaming and compressing. When I was young, my mother grinded cassava roots into powder with coconut milk, fried the mixture with green onions and sugar, sliced the baked cassava pastry, and then fixed the fried and sugary green onions in between. Savory, sweet, and crisp; the pastry was delicious. The simplest preparation method was to dice the cassava into cubes and braise with sugar. Its chewy texture added to the delicious taste.

Once the luffas are ripe, Pablo collects them using baskets made from woven bamboo. He sends some of the luffas to the office kitchen as a token of appreciation. The others, he sells to his neighbors for a little income. He appreciates his steady, simple and fortunate lifestyle.

村民取辣木的葉子入湯，也拿來與麵粉同炸來入飯。

卡莉朵媽媽送我一條已經枯乾的辣木子，堅硬而脆響地敲打著皮膚，好像樂器一般發出沙沙聲，很是有趣。我打開豆莢，裏面的種子比黃豆個頭還大，比無患子小一些，顏色淺褐，外面有絲薄的羽翼，呈現三角形，十分特別。

對心血管有幫助的辣木子，使用要適當，否則會引發嘔吐，這就好比銀杏果（白果），銀杏葉對身體循環有百般好，但白果要入菜需適當，是同一個道理。

從很多的細節，我們總不斷發現植物跟人類一樣，是有脾氣的。

微風慢慢飄蕩，河面與河岸上的植物都是淡金色的，用心去看時，能見到空氣裏浮沈著細細的灰塵，在奧莫克大愛村，感覺時間會變慢。

我們在維希家附近遇見普瑞希索（Precioso Cagalitan），他種的長豆茂密又新鮮，長長的一塊地上滿滿都是，其間又種了蘆筍和南瓜。

李偉嵩與李伯芳剛好散步到這兒，與我們相遇，普瑞希索看到李偉嵩，熱情地摘了好多長豆要送他，李偉嵩趕忙掏出錢來，「不可，不可，你們種菜很辛勞，能善用土地就已經非常感恩你們了！」他多出了一點錢塞給普瑞希索，普瑞希索也開心地收下了。

奧莫克大愛村居民，過去生活懶散，如今他們在大愛村安居樂業，除了居民相互影響帶動，也是因為慈濟志工長期耐心陪伴。陪伴他們度過災後的驚恐與蕭索，陪伴他們一起建立安

As we continue down the river coast, we can see Carlito Yahut harvesting luffas and Moringa leaves to prepare for dinner. Her Moringa plant is very tall and bears many long peapod-shaped seeds. She intentionally leaves a few seeds to grow them into seedlings. She also plants bananas, cassava plants, turnips and pumpkins.

Moringa is very prevalent in Ormoc, yet it is also a very special plant. Rich in vitamins, minerals, and amino acids, this plant is beneficial to the immune system. Great Love villagers put moringa leaves in stews and fry them with flour as a side dish.

Carlito gives me a piece of dry moringa. The hard surface makes a crisp sound as it comes into contact with the skin, as if an instrument creating a rustling sound. I open the peapod to peek inside. The light beige seeds are larger than soybeans but smaller than soapberries. With thin winged structures along the surface, the shape forms an interesting triangle.

Moringa seeds are beneficial for cardiovascular patients, yet it must be taken in moderation. Otherwise, it might induce vomiting. The same principle applies to ginkgo nuts. These nuts are helpful for blood circulation circulation, but must also be eaten in moderation.

By paying attention at the small details, we realize that plants and humans are the same: both have different characters.

The wind blows gently. The plants on the river surface and along the riverbank radiate a mellow golden color. If you concentrate hard enough, you will see the thin sheet of dust in the air. In Ormoc Great Love Village, it feels like time passes by very slowly.

We encounter Precioso Cagalitan around Vergelio Baguion's home. The long peapods that he plants are fresh and abundant. They fill the ground, with asparagus and pumpkins growing in between.

靜舒適綠化的家園，陪伴他們一起感受那破碎的、燦爛的、日常的種種心情。

維希自從辦公室被一把火燒盡，他便一直沒回家住，固守著興建復原中的辦公室、環保站、孩子上課的教室……他想回報證嚴法師對故鄉的大愛，出發心很厚道。厚道，不是示弱，而是因為強大到願意成全。世界終不會辜負那些心裏乾淨，負載美德而努力的人。

維希高大黝黑，待人和氣謙遜，誠正果敢，對事用心又富情義。我說他像《三國演義》裏的關雲長，那麼值得人信靠，只差關雲長是紅皮膚，維希是黑皮膚。

維希不在家，太太對他的任何決定都是百分之百支持，他們住在兩房型大愛屋區，門前土地上的香蕉、木薯、空心菜……便由太太勤快澆灌，幸好時序進入雨季，有了老天來幫忙。

他們在靠近莎德拉娜家那邊，還有一大片香蕉園，是大愛村裏僅次於羅伯托（Roberto Laguna）最能善用土地的居民。

天要完全黑了，維希的太太拿了一串香蕉送給我們，身材高壯結實的傑里（Jery Esperance）醫師一手接了過去，看起來輕鬆，那串香蕉實則不輕，因為有維希澆灌的滿滿的愛。傑里醫師起先與我們慢慢一起走，漸漸地和我們有段距離，想必是意識到手中漸漸沈重的香蕉串吧！

晚霞退去，我喜歡星空，奧莫克大愛村沒有汙染的夜空，群星閃爍。不管別人承不承認、如何解讀，每顆星都是獨一無二的，像星空下的人群，也像這世上每一株每一種植物，都是唯一。

Coincidentally, Alfredo Li and Ferdinand Dy are also taking a walk. When Precioso sees Alfredo, he happily picks a few peas for him. Alfredo immediately takes out his wallet. When Precioso refuses to take the money, Alfredo said: "No, no, you put in so much effort into growing these crops. Knowing that you are using the land efficiently is enough." Alfredo then takes out more money for Precioso and this time, the villager happily accepts it.

Ormoc Great Love villagers once lived an indolent life. Today they live happily and peacefully. The villagers keep each other company. Alfredo and the other Tzu Chi volunteers also spend time with the villagers, helping them to move forward after the disaster, building a comfortable and eco-friendly home for them and empathizing with their daily life encounters.

After Tzu Chi's office inside the Ormoc Great Love Village was burned down, Vergelio Baguion did not come home until the office was rebuilt. He guarded the office, recycling station and classrooms throughout the reconstruction period. This was his way of paying forward Master Cheng Yen's unconditional love. Her starting point is kindness. Kindness is not weak; rather, it is so strong that it inspires willingness to help. The world will not fail those with a pure heart, virtue and perseverance.

Vergelio is a tall man. He is modest and polite. Honest and bold, yet diligent and good-willed. He is like General Guan Yunchang from "The Romance of the Three Kingdoms" because of his trustworthiness; Except General Guan is red-skinned while Vergelio's is brown.

Vergelio is not home at the moment. They live in one of the Great Love houses with two rooms. His wife is supportive of all his decisions. Bananas, cassava plants, water spinach among others grow in their front yard. His wife waters them regularly. Often, Mother Earth would contribute in watering the plants by blessing it with some rainfall.

Near Sandrane Pepito's home, the couple has another banana field. In

隔日午後，我們決定走一趟羅伯托的農田。他的農田既不在三房型大愛屋，亦不在兩房型大愛屋，而在進入大愛村的馬路與河廓之間，一片寬廣的腹地。

　　通往羅伯托一公頃半的土地，盡是乾旱堅硬。可是剛結好的玉米覆在米色包被裏，隱隱透出陽光的色澤，另一側竹架上的長豆，爬高高垂掛在綠葉間。

　　可能是陽光炙烈，菲律賓的長豆比較乾瘦，肉質硬，纖維粗，要細切水煮，老年人才好入口。但奧莫克居民不興如此費工，總是切長段煸乾，他們喜歡細細咀嚼那滋味。

　　高高綠立之中，視線只如隧道窄小，再往前走，豁然開朗，左一片綠彩椒、右一片秋葵，盡頭是一片南瓜，每一片都是豐收狀態，纍纍結實在地上或莖上。

　　山谷曠野，自力更生，豐收的景象靜靜地呈現在陽光下；即使再如何堅硬的土壤，只要用心耕耘，也有辦法讓它發揮滋養農作物的奇蹟。

　　羅伯托戰戰兢兢默默耕作了四年，如今豐收，是他用長期的勞力流汗所掙得！他將手伸向深綠而多汁的秋葵，輕輕一折，脆聲斷成兩半，可見它有多嫩多甜啊！

　　李偉嵩讚歎一聲，請教羅伯托：「這整片農作物，你怎麼澆水？」

　　羅伯托說：「用幫浦自緊臨的河裏打上來啊！」

　　循著羅伯托手指的方向，原來不遠處隱在玉米田邊是一條川流不絕的河水。這條河曾經在一連幾日的滂沱後滿溢釀災，但並非它的錯，它原是滋養大地的血脈，只是源頭的大樹被人

Great Love Village, they come in second to Roberto Laguna for using the empty land efficiently.

The sun is almost completely set. Vergelio's wife offers us some bananas. Dr. Jery Esperance accepts them effortlessly. However, the bananas are heavy; they are filled with Vergelio's love. At first, Dr. Jery walks closely with us, but the distance between us increases over time. Perhaps the bananas are making it hard for him to catch up with our steps.

The sun is completely set. I love the night sky. Ormoc Great Love Village does not have light pollution, so the stars shine brightly. No matter who disagrees, no matter how other people interpret this, every star is unique. Just like every person under the night sky, and every plant in the world. They are all one and only.

The next day, we decided to visit Roberto's farm. His farmland is neither at the three-roomed nor the two-roomed Great Love houses region. His land is vast, sitting between the entrance road of Great Love Village and the riverbank.

Roberto's 1.5-hectare land is dry and tough. The scarcely ripened corn is wrapped inside the cloth bag, subtly reflecting the color of sunlight. On the other side, the green beans grow on the bamboo fence, hanging nicely in between the green leaves.

Perhaps because the sunlight is so bright, the green beans in the Philippines are more shrivelled, tough and thick-fibered. They must be finely cut and boiled in water for the elders. However, Ormoc villagers dislike the amount of work that this preparation entails. Rather, they would often cut the beans into long segments and dry them, then enjoy its flavor and texture.

Walking through these tall plantations, our visions were limited as if were inside a tunnel. But moving forward, the space opens up. To our left is

類砍走，土壤失去大樹根抓地，崩落堵塞了水道，讓河水莫名背負了罪愆。

走近河岸，河水的旅行，從森林墜下平地便溫馴、耐心地在城郊慢慢轉彎，展開又匯聚，偶爾零星的水花跳著舞，打上岸後又回歸安靜流淌，之後默默滲入土壤，歷經長途跋涉，沒有任何埋怨地完成使命。

李偉嵩很佩服羅伯托，問羅伯托一個人怎麼處理這麼龐大的植栽？羅伯托晒得黝黑的微笑特別帥氣！原來他以每天兩百披索的代價，請了大愛村裏六位村民來幫忙，他的妻子則把蔬菜拿到市場賣。

每個月羅伯托都送慈濟廚房很多蔬菜，他的心裏充滿感恩，回饋蔬菜是他表達的方法，每當慈濟有活動時，他都盡心盡力支援。

羅伯托覺得能在大愛村裏生活是多麼珍貴的一件事，能盡情耕耘這麼大片的土地，更是無比幸福。他同時造就六位村民工作的良機，從手心向上變成手心向下的那一刻，感受到證嚴法師寬廣的大愛與智慧、慈悲，如果災難讓他失去所有，那麼是證嚴法師又讓他重新擁有。

一公頃半的農作物，是羅伯托用雙手打拚出來，背後心胸寬大的捐地者則是奧莫克前市長寇迪拉。

在大愛村裏，這些零星分布的農地，像是山谷裏一顆顆巨大的寶石，琢磨自己的成色，默默在山谷的夜裏，靜靜發出豐收的亮光，並且持續不斷還有新的光亮滋生。而所有豐收，都來自一分遙遠大愛的祝福！

a field of green peppers. To our right is a field of okra. Far into the distance, there is a field of pumpkins. Every plot is ready for harvest season.

These wide mountains are full of vigor and strength. The scene of full harvests rests under the sunlight. Even the toughest soil, if cultivated with love, can be utilized to its full potentials, creating agricultural miracles.

Roberto has been farming diligently for four years. His harvest today is the accumulation of all his efforts, which he deserves! He reaches to the juicy okra, gently snaps it in half. So soft and flavorful!

Impressed, Alfredo asks Roberto: "How do you water this entire farmland?" Roberto replies, "I use the pump and get it from the river!"

Following the direction of Roberto's finger, we can see that beside the corn field is a hidden river. This river once overflowed and flooded the village after consecutive days of intense rain. Yet, it was not the river's fault. The river was the nourishing circulation of the earth, but the big tree at the headstream was cut down by humans. Without tree roots to grip, the soil collapsed into the river, blocking the water supply. The river was unfairly blamed for the tragedy.

We approach the riverbank. The water travels down from the forest to the flatland, docile and patient as it waits to turn into the suburban area. It diverges into smaller paths, then converges back again. Water droplets dance sporadically, then splash back into the calm river and finally seeps into the soil. They never complain about the long journey.

Alfredo asks Roberto how he manages to till the vast farmland all by himself. Roberto is tanned and his smile is so handsome! It turns out he hires six Great Love villagers for Php2000 to help him every day. His wife then sells the vegetables in the market.

Every month, Roberto donates a lot of vegetables to the Tzu Chi kitchen. His heart is filled with gratitude, and donating vegetables is his way of expressing it. He also supports every Tzu Chi event.

Roberto is grateful to live in the Great Love Village. He feels extremely fortunate to have the opportunity to cultivate such a big piece of land.

At the same time, he is providing jobs to six villagers, going from receiving aid from others to contributing aid to others. He understands Master Cheng Yen's unconditional love, wisdom and compassion. If typhoon Haiyan had taken everything from him, Master Cheng Yen had led him to starting over and recover everything back.

The 1.5 hectare of crops is the result of Roberto's hard work. As for the land, it was kindly donated by the former city mayor, Edward Codilla.

In Great Love Village, these scattered farm plots seem like huge diamonds in a valley, each possessing their own colors. At night, the harvest glows of abundance, and continue to sprout. All the amazing harvest originates from love and blessing!

(Translated by Jane Lin)

左上／帕羅爺爺絲瓜收成時，常用竹編的容器裝來送給辦公室廚房作為回饋，也賣給鄰居賺少許錢零花。
(top left) When the luffas are ripe, Pablo collects them with baskets made from woven bamboo. He then sends some of it to the office kitchen as a token of appreciation. He also sells some to the neighbors to make some profit.

左下／住在維希家附近的普瑞希索，他種的長豆茂密又新鮮，長長的一塊地上滿滿皆是。
(bottom left) Presioco Cagalitan lives near the house of Vergelio Baguion. He plants fresh, long peapods that fill up the ground.

II. 等待著我們溫柔的梳理
Waiting for Our Gentle Touch

維希 Vergelio Baguion

影響鄰人一起種蔬果

Let's Plant It Forward

朝山這天也是證嚴法師的生日，維希帶艾菲達來為法師祝壽，感恩法師的教導，讓牠保住了性命。

The three steps one bow pilgrimage was held on Master Cheng Yen's birthday, Vergelio brought the carabao Alfreda to thank the Master for her guidance, which spared the carabao's life.

有人告訴慈濟志工李偉嵩（Alfredo Li），有一戶人家需要錢，要賣掉他們的牛。李偉嵩知道這牛被賣出去，定會被宰殺，因此起了一念悲心，把牠買下來。

奧莫克大愛村有很多空地，證嚴法師交代李偉嵩要鼓勵居民去耕種這些土地，因此他想將牛送人養。

因緣際會，維希認養了這頭牛。李偉嵩囑咐他不可殺、不可賣，只可生。維希為了紀念買下牛的善人，便以他的名字為這頭母牛命名為艾菲達（Alfreda）。

維希為何想認養這頭牛呢？因為他希望這頭牛可以幫他耕作，也可以幫幫其他農人的忙。雖然父母留下的田地已經賣給了別人，他也在奧莫克大愛村分配到一個家，可是他仍掛念著有一日能在那塊田地上耕作。

One day, someone came to inform Alfredo Li that there is a family who is in need of money and plans to sell their carabao. The news saddened Li. He knew that the carabao will be slaughtered once it gets sold. Out of compassion for the carabao, he decided to buy the animal to save her life.

There is a vast expanse of vacant land in the Ormoc Great Love Village. Master Cheng Yen asked Li to encourage the villagers to cultivate the land. He thought that this carabao could be a useful gift to the farmers.

In a stroke of fate, Vergelio adopted the carabao. Li reminded him not to kill nor sell this animal but to allow it to reproduce. And in honor of the person who bought it, Vergelio names the carabao Alfreda.

Why does Vergelio wants to adopt the carabao? Because Vergelio believes that the carabao can help him till the land, and even help other farmers as well. Although his parents had sold all their land, and Vergelio was given a house at

他讓艾菲達住在田裏，還在田邊搭建一間小鐵皮屋。他幾乎每天都來看牠，在鐵皮屋裏休憩，雖然燠熱，但他很滿足。

　　小鐵皮屋前有兩棵鄰人種的大芒果樹，他幫忙照顧這兩棵樹，待有收成，鄰人賣了後會給他兩分。若是下大雨，果實被雨打壞，那麼一切的損失都要他承擔。

　　維希基於愛護自然的心情，即使沒有什麼好收入，還是盡心盡力地幫忙。

　　一直到今天，艾菲達還不肯背上犁，維希也無任何收入。所幸，田地雖乾裂嚴重，仍有許多綠草可供牛來食，他不至於有太多損失。

　　自從擁有艾菲達，維希開始教牠如何跪拜。維希說，他希望牛也能跟人一樣有禮貌、知禮數，也希望艾菲達能懂得禮敬諸佛。他深信世間萬物皆有靈性；牛有靈性，更何況是人呢！

　　艾菲達不久前生了一頭小牛，現在又懷了胎。遠遠地，我看見牠用牛角勾起一簇草，原來是有蚊子襲擊牠，牠輕輕地驅趕蚊子，牛孩兒緊緊跟在牠身邊。那一幕讓我想起小時候，爺爺拉著我的小手，跟水牛一起到田裏的情境。

　　世間生命都有靈性，一花一樹一葉、動物或是我們輕踩的土地，都有呼吸。維希珍視一切的靈性，從小在稻田裏摸索著微細的生命，他對待這世上的任何一件事物，總是那麼用心。

　　他的小鐵皮屋外，有一大片放任生長的綠色植物，延伸至夕陽落下與地球交界處，其間似有什麼橫梗著，目光不能及，但花和葉有如鐵打的樹身上的行雲流水，望去永遠是簇新的，望不見有些已枯了。

the Tzu Chi village, he has not given up hope of one day tilling his own land.

Vergelio led the carabao to stay in a farm. He even built the carabao a small metal shelter. He visits his carabao almost every day. It is stifling hot inside the metal shelter but Alfreda stays there without complaint.

In front of the metal shelter are two big mango trees owned by the farm's neighbors. Vergelio helps to take care of the trees in exchange for profit when the mangoes are sold. The only setback would be the rain, which could damage the fruits and then he'll end up getting nothing. But out of Vergelio's love for nature, he still does his best to help even without a decent pay.

The carabao still refuses to pull the plough at this moment. Therefore, Vergelio cannot derive any income from it yet. Fortunately, even though there is a serious drought, there are still plenty of grasses around for Alfreda to feed on. So, nothing much to lose for Vergelio.

Since having Alfreda, Vergelio started teaching the carabao how to prostrate. Vergelio explained that he wants Alfreda to be as polite as a human being. Plus, he expects her to show respect to the Buddha. He believes that all creatures have a spiritual nature. If carabaos have spiritual nature, what more us humans?

Not long ago, Alfreda delivered a baby carabao and is now pregnant with another. From a distance, I saw Alfreda stalking a bunch of grass with her horn. It looked like mosquitoes were annoying her and that she was trying to drive them away. The baby carabao followed Alfreda closely.

That scene reminded me of my childhood; my grandfather used to hold my little hand while we went to the field with our carabao.

Every life on Earth has a spiritual nature. Every flower, every tree, every leaf, every animal and even the land we step on, is breathing.

維希邀請我們去看看他在大愛村的家，我們一起走著走著，來到一戶滿是綠蔭花樹的門前，一條白狗看到維希便立即興奮地奔跳到他身上，熱情地舔他，顯示出主人與白狗之間的感情。動物的愛，是真純不加掩飾的。

家園前面一大片地是公共的，沒人要利用，他種了香蕉、木薯、紫茄、絲瓜、辣椒、空心菜……數也數不完的青菜水果。維希和妻子兩人都那麼勤快，種得好豐美。

問他種這麼多，怎麼吃得完？他說，他喜歡與鄰居分享，若有人要買，他也便宜賣給人。

就在我們聊著天時，鄰人也來了。鄰人說：「他很乖。」我們玩笑地反問：「他很乖，那你呢？」鄰人笑著回答：「我只有睡覺的時候才乖乖。」

鄰人接著說：「他種的香蕉，我都會去摘來吃，他不但不會生氣，還會問我夠不夠？因為看他如此勤快，種那麼多水果蔬菜，我們都被他影響，也跟著種。」

維希心地善良到萬物皆與他有情，他珍愛所有身邊的人事物，懂得感恩，做事殷實。

從他分配到一間大愛屋開始，到認養那頭牛，愛這世上所有生靈，在自家前面空地種水果、蔬菜，勤勞善用每一塊土地，進而影響鄰人來一起種蔬果，護大地。

在酷熱的菲律賓，大多數的人們慵懶度日，今朝有酒今朝醉；但維希卻完全超脫那生性的禁錮，帶動大愛村民來耕種，自給自足。

世界很美，時間有限，無常更近。

Raised on a farm with tiny creatures as playmates, Vergelio has always been so caring to every living being.

Vergelio invited us to visit his home in the Great Love Village. We walked together and found a house bristling with trees and flowers in the front yard. A white dog was so excited to see him that it jumped at Vergelio when we walked up to the house. We can tell how close they were. An animal's love is simple and undisguised.

A big plot of land in front of the house is open to the public, but nobody is interested in making use of it. Vergelio and his wife diligently plant bananas, cassava, eggplant, loofah, pepper, spinach, among countless vegetables and fruits on that land.

We asked him, "How can you eat that many vegetables and fruits?"

He said he loves to share them with his neighbors and to those who are willing to pay, he sells them for a cheap price.

His neighbor came to join us while we were chatting.

The neighbor described Vergelio as a "good guy". We teased the neighbor, "If he is a good guy, what are you?"

The neighbor smiled and replied, "I am a good guy while I sleep."

Vergelio's neighbor continued to tell us, "He never gets mad at me whenever I take the bananas he planted. He only asks if I have enough bananas. We started to plant vegetables and fruits when we saw how hard he works on planting."

Vergelio has a kind and loving heart for all beings. He cherishes and is grateful for whatever he has. He respects Master Cheng Yen and is always

二〇一九年六月中旬，奧莫克大愛村辦公室、環保站、儲藏間，一直延伸到廚房那一大片，因廚房的電線走火釀災，燒掉了。

　　當晚維希與泛尼托、大衛、艾維斯、阿莫斯等村民，都來幫忙搶救，但所剩無幾。

　　失去不必追，幸好儲存大愛村圖文紀錄的硬碟，被蔡昇航帶回馬尼拉，把最重要的歷史保住了。其他的硬體設備，就慢慢再恢復或重新規畫，使之有新面貌。

　　維希從施工那天起，就不回家了，甚至走過家門一步也不入，好比中國舊時代的大禹治水。

　　他白天跟著村人與工作人員整修辦公室的房子，晚間就睡在臨時辦公室，偶爾半夜起來於村裏四處巡邏。他想起兒時偶爾躺在草地上，放晴的夜空綴滿星星，不同顏色的星星，深深淺淺地在漆黑的夜空裏閃爍。

　　如今他在夜裏巡邏，走過草坪，聞著散發的淺淺草香，草地上綴著米色小花，未細看時，還以為那是淚一般的露水。

　　好幾個月過去，幾乎不回家的維希，用寶貴時間換取愛的付出，顧全了持續完成中的建設。他不是為了什麼才決定這麼做，只是想回報證嚴法師曾給他故鄉的愛。

　　與法師在遙遠的時空相隔中，對映如星子，永恆是什麼？一顆心相互永遠珍惜。

　　維希有無數的願要許給法師，他的心隔著海陪著法師向前走，他期待著每一個明天，要一一實現，作為對於法師的種種承諾與祝福⋯⋯

grateful to her.

From the time that he was granted a Great Love house to adopting a carabao, he has learned to love everybody and everything in the world. With his diligence in turning an empty land into a bountiful farm, he has inspired his neighbors to do the same and to care for the Earth.

The hot weather in the Philippines makes many people lethargic, idling their time away. Vergelio, on the other hand, completely transcends such characteristics. He leads the villagers to cultivate and learn to support themselves with their lands.

(Translated by Audrey Cheng)

維希看見慈青們表演水懺手語，也好奇地跟著臺下示範的志工學習。
Vergelio saw Tzu Chings rehearse the sign language on *Water Repentance*. Curious, he joined in and learned from following as the volunteers demonstrate it down the stage.

艾達 Aida Cornito

陪伴於險境的邊緣人

Lonely Person on the Brink

艾達是辦公室最主要的行政人員，對外溝通與大愛村各種訊息發布，掌握有方。

Aida is the Chief Administrative Staff in the office. She is efficient in handling the communications with outsiders and the dissemination of information at the Great Love Village.

在奧莫克市區往宿霧的海邊，大型的百貨公司亮晃晃的燈飾招牌、舞臺上勁歌熱舞的年輕人，與在路邊昏暗裏擺攤的年長衰老，形成強烈的對比。

我們走過一個白色的博物館廣場，水舞池邊凌亂的人群，一棵高大的美洲合歡樹附近，步上一座古老的拱橋，我用手觸摸著它歷史的坑疤，聽說是海底的珊瑚做的。海邊有著很多氣味的風。

我們住的旅店離這兒走路大約需要十五分鐘，艾達的家離旅店有十分鐘，因此每天由奧莫克大愛村回旅店，艾達便與我們同行。

初見艾達，覺得她是個面無表情的人，但是工作認真仔細，後來知道她在政府改朝換代時失去了工作，這在很多國家是常

In downtown Ormoc City, along the sea side facing Cebu, the big department store's bright neon lights and the young people dancing on stage contrast sharply with the aging vendors who stand in the dark side of the road.

We walked past a white museum square. People crowded by the dancing fountain. A tall American hubris tree stands near the old arched bridge. I ran my fingers over the ancient bridge and remembered someone told me that it was made of corals from the bottom of the sea. Various odors were brought in to me by the wind from the seashore.

The hotel we are staying in is a 15-minute walk from the beach. Aida's home is about ten minutes from the hotel; so every day that we go back to the hotel from the Great Love Village, Aida always joined us.

When we first met, Aida had a blank look on her face but she worked

見的事，誠如夕陽之後是黑夜。但不要害怕，我們在世上要能欣賞夕陽的優雅，黑夜的沈默，而光明終究會出現。

失去工作的艾達聽說慈濟正需要人，也知道慈濟是一個很優良的組織，目標是幫助有需要的人。於是二〇一六年七月，她成為奧莫克大愛村辦公室一員，管理大愛村所有受益人的住家，至今已三年有餘。

艾達是少數大學畢業的職工，她原先希望能住在大愛村裏，但因為她與兄姊們四個家庭同住一層公寓裏，算是有居所而不符入住資格，雖然這讓她感到沮喪，但比起無處窩居的人，她覺得自己不該貪求。

不快樂的時候，去做對的事情。艾達非常關注醫療案例，幫助病苦者得以治療，這讓她除了大愛村的行政工作外，更有機會陪伴寂寞於險境的邊緣人，找到心的安寧。

有一回，大愛村為白內障患者義診，她遇到一位五十四歲、雙眼白內障的婦人。

婦人告訴她，當她仍然健康並且目明時，她的孩子們總是命令她完成所有的工作；當她得了白內障，她的孩子們卻要她離開。這讓艾達感到莫名的心酸。

她犧牲自己的健康來撫養孩子，但她的孩子們卻如此輕易地放棄了這個母親；更悲哀的是，她生病後，先生隨即變心和另一個女人在一起。她的情感深深受了傷，長久地為家努力付出，為何生病了換來的是殘酷與無情？

孔子說：「三十而立，四十而不惑，五十而知天命⋯⋯」意思是說，三十歲有所建樹，四十歲不困惑，五十歲理解自然

cautiously and detail-oriented. I learned later that she lost her job during the government transitional period.

This is as common as sunsets and sunrises. It is nothing to be afraid of. We need to appreciate the elegance of the sunset. The light will appear again after the silence of the dark nights.

At the time when she was unemployed, Aida heard that Tzu Chi Foundation was in need of manpower. She had heard many good things about the organization, including its goal of helping people who are in need.

Eventually, in July 2016, Aida became an employee at the office of Ormoc Great Love Village. In the past three years, she has been in charge of managing the houses of the villagers.

Aida was hoping her family can also move in the Great Love Village. However, her application was rejected because her family and siblings are already sharing a house. The news of the disqualification depressed Aida, but only for a while. Eventually, she realized that she was far luckier compared to those people who had nowhere to live. She learned not to ask for more.

Fortunately, she was doing the right thing at the time that she was feeling down. In addition to her routine administrative duties at the village, Aida is also responsible for ensuring that the ailing and suffering villagers, as well as people from outside the village, receive medical treatment and aid. The task gives Aida an opportunity to accompany the lonely people, who are on the edge of danger, and help them find peace of mind.

During a medical outreach for the villagers with eye diseases, Aida met a 54-year-old woman who suffers from cataracts on both eyes.

The woman told Aida that when her eyes were still healthy, her children would always ask her to do the house chores. But after she was diagnosed with

規律……而這婦人卻在五十幾歲，發現她的人生一切都走了樣，完全無法理解過去所有的付出是為什麼？

艾達自己也有孩子有丈夫，自然明白為人母為人妻的心情。婦人因為眼疾，孩子和丈夫都棄她而去，想想她與孩子們、丈夫的那麼多往事啊，就因為病竟然都成為過去了。好感傷！

後來，婦人接受了眼科手術並成功地恢復光明。這是她經過一段漫長的祈禱，盼到了希望！

艾達說：「這位婦人的孩子們得知她恢復了視力，便希望她回家，因為她可以幫忙帶孫子……」

我不可思議地急問艾達，婦人答應了嗎？她說，婦人還是回家幫忙帶孫子去上學。這件事讓艾達印象很深刻。

世間的艱難，常讓人不知道自己靠近誰多一些？不知道自己投入哪個部分多一些？我們總因不想有太多糾結而選擇委屈求全。

艾達常想那婦人為何願意再回到背棄她的孩子與丈夫身邊，甘願帶孫子們去上學？人生充滿細節的緣，無盡的困惑，好像那點點滴滴的明暗背後，都有一股不斷傾盡全力教人順服的力量。

或許心有所愛，永恆就存在；傻傻地做一些勇敢的事，是人的本質……

就快立夏了，奧莫克慈濟中小學的動土儀式即將到來，艾達想到那些回收的寶特瓶，是否可以用創意剪成假花，賦予更多藝術的設計呢？她進入慈濟學會的不僅僅是如何助人、體恤人，還有回收資源再利用來減少開支。

her eye disease, her children do not want her anymore and drive her away. Hearing this, Aida was filled with sorrow for the woman.

The woman had sacrificed a great deal of her health to raise her children. But how easy it was for her children to give up on her! Her husband had also moved out to be with another woman.

Confucius said, "At age 30, one should stand on his own. At age 40, one should not be confused. At age 50, one should know his destiny." It means that in our thirties, we should establish our life. In our forties, we should not be confused, and in our fifties, we should be able to understand the laws of nature.

But this woman, in her fifties, found out that she had lost control of her life. All the hard work that she had put in the past, where are they now?

Aida has her own children and a husband. It was easy for her to put herself in the woman's shoes. Because of her eye disease, the woman had been abandoned by her own children and husband. All those times they have walked together as a family is now in the past. How sad this is!

The woman later on had an eye surgery, which successfully restored her vision. After praying so hard for far too long, it finally became a reality! Aida told me, "When the woman's children learned that she had regained her vision, they wanted her to come home because she can help look after her grandchildren again...."

I asked Aida if the woman had accepted her children's proposal. Aida told me the woman did come home to help take her grandson to school. This incident left a deep impression on Aida.

People would sometimes feel lost in the face of difficult situations, wondering which or who is more important? Which part of our life should we

她曾經來到臺灣，在精舍見到證嚴法師，忽然莫名哭泣起來，自己也不懂為什麼，她無法解釋內心感受。也許是因為證嚴法師對菲律賓做了很多好事，即使不同的宗教信仰，法師的愛卻超越這些太多太多！

　　夜晚，大愛村四周菅芒草隨風吹著窸窣響在耳畔。艾達告訴我，她最想要的是幫助有需要的人，而不求任何回報。

　　悶熱的夏天，不知道為什麼我卻像個笨蛋似的感冒了，感覺自己的鼻塞鼻酸，還有一陣陣的鹹水自眼眶滴下，在墨色的車內，沒有人看見。

艾達帶領村人與志工一起學習手語，雖然信奉天主教，但慈濟手語歌的精神深深打動她的心。

Aida led the villagers in practicing the sign language performance with the volunteers. Although they are Catholics, the spirit of the song deeply touched her heart.

put more time or effort into?

Aida often wondered why the woman would choose to go back to the children and the husband who abandoned her in her time of need, and still manage to care about her grandchildren. The numerous kamic conditions and the endless affliction in our life are consistently teaching us to follow our destiny.

Perhaps eternity exists because we have love in our hearts. It could be human nature to do things recklessly without a thought.

Summer is approaching. The groundbreaking ceremony for the Ormoc Tzu Chi Elementary and Secondary School is getting close. Aida is thinking of those collected plastic bottles. Could they be given new life through art?

After joining Tzu Chi Foundation, Aida has not only learned how to help people compassionately, but also how to recycle resources.

Aida has visited Taiwan and the Jing Si Abode. As soon as she saw Dharma Master Cheng Yen, her tears flowed uncontrollably. She did not understand nor could she explain why. It is perhaps because the Master and her followers have done so many good deeds to the Philippines. The love from the Master and the volunteers' hearts transcends religious beliefs and more.

The LED lights in the Great Love Village began to light up again at night. Aida told me that what she wanted most was to help those in need without asking for anything in return.

It is a hot summer night. I felt like getting a cold with a stuffy nose and salty water coming down from my eyes. Luckily, inside this dark car, no one noticed.

(Translated by Christine Fisk)

泛尼托 Juanito Suco
幸福是彼此關照與支持
Happiness is Caring for Each Other

二〇一八年浴佛節，奧莫克大愛村的本土志工自行編劇演出〈地獄之門〉，道具都是泛尼托一人完成。

In the 2018 Buddha Day event, the local volunteers in Ormoc Great Love Village composed a script for a stage performance on "*The Gate of Hell*." All the props were prepared and completed by Juanito.

幸福是彼此關照、支持，如草皮的根相互纏繞，織夢深入泥土，變成一張不易碎裂的網。

海燕風災發生之前，泛尼托做過醫院的警衛、賣電動摩托車……不管做什麼事都極為投入，每一個工作都讓他學習頗多。在醫院擔任警衛隊長時，很多推銷員會給他健康食品，他就帶回去分給村裡需要的人，還有人因此稱呼他為「醫師」。他掘了一口井，並不占為己有，人人都可以來取水。

他的寬大與善良、勤奮、正直，成為許多人的倚靠。

後來轉行賣電動摩托車，他的努力忠誠深獲老闆信任，老闆娘還認泛尼托的兒子傑森（Jayson）做乾兒子。

海燕風災來襲，泛尼托失去了家，沒了電，無法再賣電動摩托車。他幫老闆把摩托車送到宿霧，老闆在那邊重新起家，

Happiness is to care and to support others, like intertwining grassroots burrowing deep into the land to form a strong network.

Before Typhoon Haiyan hit the Philippines in November 2013, Juanito Suco had worked as a hospital guard, sold electric motorcycles, among other jobs. No matter what kind of work he finds himself in, he gets extremely involved, and he learned a lot from his jobs. As the captain of the guards at the hospital, sales agents would often give him sample medicines which he would then dispense to the needy people of his village for free. As a result, some would call him "doctor". He is the type of person who, if someone ever needed help, would be there to extend a hand. Many people trust his generosity, kindness, diligence and integrity.

Later, he switched to selling electric motorcycles. His efforts and loyalty were deeply valued by his boss. His lady boss also recognized Jayson Suco, the son of Juanito, as a godson. When Typhoon Haiyan occurred, Juanito lost his

他自己一無所有地回到萊特島。有人送了捕魚的小船和魚網給他，有段時間他以此維持一家開支。後來政府設了收容所，他帶著全家等待奇蹟，冀望再次擁有一個安定的家。

離開海邊時，即便他極為窮苦，依然不貪求，那些人家贈予他的捕魚工具與小船，他不是轉賣獲取錢財，而是再送給別人，令其得以維生。他有善良的心靈，亮節的身教。

在收容所，當他接獲慈濟在奧莫克「以工代賑」的機會，馬上自收容所帶了十位朋友來幫忙，最終落腳在奧莫克大愛村。傑森的乾媽也決定把經營的美髮店讓給泛尼托的妻子瑪利貝思（Maribeth），瑪利貝思變成美髮店老闆，泛尼托成為慈濟職工，一家人終於安定下來。

有時候歷經某些不順遂，走過波折的時光旅程，那麼多的孤單與磨練，都是為了未來所需的鍛鍊。在慈濟，泛尼托學習做環保，也陪慈青去家訪和勸募，並協助需要醫療的長者。他不在乎賺錢多少，只想著要完成證嚴法師交託的事。

有一天，大愛臺來訪問他：「慈濟對你而言是什麼？」

泛尼托回答：「慈濟好比一個『金屋』。」意思是證嚴法師給他的不只是生命的方向，更重要的是法師教育他的「法」不間斷。他感恩能成為慈濟的一分子，有力量幫助自己的同胞。

人生就像一直在彩排，他每一天都很認真；每一天的彩排，都不能重來，因此他珍視著每一天。陽光與風陪著他，懷著一顆虔誠的心，穿越時間一次又一次嘗試，流著汗，從習慣到漸漸成為教養。泛尼托每天回到家裏，都會與家人分享他在慈濟的工作和喜悅。

home. It also became very difficult for him to sell electric motorcycles without electricity. He helped his boss ship the motorcycles off to Cebu where the latter rebuilt the business from the ground up. Afterwards, Juanito returned to Leyte, empty-handed. For a time, he supported his family by fishing using a donated boat and fishing equipment. Later, after the government set up temporary shelters, he moved with his family there and waited to build a stable home again.

Although he was extremely poor when he left his home by the beach, he did not let greed consume him. Instead of selling the boat and fishing equipment for cash, he chose to give them to the families who stayed behind to help them survive. Juanito has a good heart, and he lives his life as a good role model to others.

While staying in the government-built temporary shelter, he heard that Tzu Chi Foundation was offering a "Cash-for-Work" program in Ormoc. He immediately recruited ten friends from the shelter to join in the program and help in putting up the Ormoc Great Love Village. Eventually, they became among the recipients of the houses in the new village. Jayson's godmother decided to give her beauty salon to Juanito's wife, Maribeth Suco. Today, Maribeth runs the beauty salon while Juanito is a staff at Tzu Chi. Their family situation has finally began to stabilize.

Sometimes we may experience difficulties. But after we have been through all the ups and downs in life, we come to realize that all the loneliness and suffering were only preparing us for the future. In Tzu Chi, Juanito learned how to be an environmental protection volunteer. He accompanies Tzu Chings in conducting home visits, raising funds and assisting elders in need of medical care. He did not care how much money he made. He only wanted to accomplish the missions that were entrusted upon him by Master Cheng Yen.

One day, a Da Ai TV reporter arrived to interview him, "What does Tzu

兒子傑森接受慈濟助學金也加入慈青，但一開始並不很投入。直到二〇一七年卡南加發生地震，很多災民無家可歸，他看著父親為災民奔忙的身影，深受感動，決定跟隨父親的腳步。

　　傑森自初中就愛拍照，並探求每一張照片背後的故事。

　　有一次，他看見一位八十幾歲的老奶奶流落街頭，在街上討錢維生。他拍下老奶奶的照片，附上故事貼在臉書，希望藉此啟發人們的善念，並進一步去助人。他想用攝影，將慈濟在菲律賓的所有善舉拍下來，分享給全世界。

　　這許多照片讓他重新上了一堂課──月亮總是在黑夜中仰著頭，弦月以一半徹底的光亮保護著另一半的黑暗，就像慈濟，大愛的明輝撫慰災難的暗潮。

　　女兒潔索（Jaycel）在奧莫克大愛村遭逢一次大水災時，跟著志工去清掃，意識到慈濟從沒有離開，自始至終陪伴他們度過風風雨雨。潔索常聽父親轉述證嚴法師的教導：「法並非只是口裏說，而是在『做中學、學中覺』。」慈濟人付出無所求的精神令她感動，她終於能體會父親如此揮汗投入是為什麼了。那是一種行動，是一種回饋。

　　瑪利貝思雖在美容院上班，但她的心與全家人同在，每天早上還會叫他們趕緊起床做慈濟。她努力克服了困難，如今全家茹素。鄰人尊重他們家茹素，有時分享菜餚給他們時，都會說：「這是沒有加肉的菜。」

　　浴佛節將至，泛尼托一家冒著高溫，在房子裏繪圖做準備。泛尼托專心繪著一尾大魚，女兒潔索坐他右邊，兒子傑森坐他對面，一個畫著一頭豬，一個畫著一隻雞，那情景像是大樹伸

Chi means to you?" Juanito replied, "Tzu Chi is like a 'Golden House'." It means that Master Cheng Yen gave him not only a direction in life, but more importantly, taught him the "dharma" (the law of life). He is grateful to be a part of Tzu Chi and help his fellow countrymen.

Life is like an endless rehearsal. Juanito lives each day seriously. He cherishes every single day like a performance, knowing that each rehearsal cannot be repeated. He has a pious heart, so he is always embraced by sunshine and the wind. He sweated in every daunting task, yet time and again, hard work has become his lifestyle. Every day, when he comes home, Juanito shares with his family the joys he got from doing Tzu Chi works.

His son Jayson received a Tzu Chi academic scholarship and joined Tzu Ching. In the beginning, Jayson was not very involved in Tzu Chi's activities. But when an earthquake occurred in Kananga in July 2017 and left many victims homeless, he watched his father rush to help the victims. He was deeply moved and since then, he decided to follow in his father's footsteps.

Ever since junior high school, Jayson has loved photography. He explores the story behind each photo. On one occasion, he saw an 80-year-old woman strolling on the streets, begging for alms. He took pictures of her and posted her story on Facebook. He wanted to use his camera to document the charity works of Tzu Chi in the Philippines and share them to the whole world.

Many of these photos brings him back to one lesson: The moon would eventually show up in the dark night, just like Tzu Chi. The radiance of its Great Love brings relief to the tides of darkness triggered by disaster.

One time, when a big flood occurred in the Ormoc Great Love Village, Juanito's daughter, Jaycel, joined the volunteers in the clean up. She became aware that Tzu Chi never left at all! Tzu Chi is there from the beginning and will stay until the end, accompanying them through various hardships. Jaycel often listened whenever her father shares about the teachings of Master

展著樹枝，又長滿了青綠的新芽！浴佛當日，心臟不很好的泛尼托撐著把《慈悲三昧水懺》裏的「夢歷六道」演完，又將他與孩子們製作的道具都收好，才稍事休息。

什麼是堅強？堅強是複數的忍耐，未來式的柔軟，被動態的勇敢！即便鐵漢也有脆弱時，當全家都以爸爸為榜樣為榮，都認同他所珍愛的慈濟，當全家齊心並盡那分責任，他也會像個小孩，因感動而淚眼潰堤。泛尼托那麼至情至性的率真，珍惜著與任何人相關的，每一片段記憶。

泛尼托做事勤勉認真，自我要求嚴格，一人抵萬夫，是李偉嵩身邊最倚靠的助手。
Juanito is diligent and conscientious, with strict self-expectation. He alone can take up the work of several people. He is one of the most reliable assistants of Alfredo Li.

Cheng Yen. "The dharma is not just words, but a learning from doing, and an awareness from learning'." She is moved by the Tzu Chi volunteers' spirit of unconditional giving. And she finally realized why her father was always so sweaty at the end of the day. It's an action; it's also a way of giving back.

Although Maribeth works in the beauty salon, her heart is with the whole family. Every morning, she will wake them up and together, they will attend to their respective Tzu Chi duties. She had overcome her difficulty in adapting to the family's transformation, and now the whole family is vegetarian. Their neighbours respect their vegetarian lifestyle. Whenever a neighbor brings them food, he will reassure the family: "This is a dish without meat."

Buddha Day Ceremony is fast approaching. Juanito's family braved the heat inside the house as they prepare the materials for the upcoming event. Juanito concentrated on drawing a big fish. Jaycel sits to his right. Jayson sits opposite him. One draws a pig; another paints a chicken. The scene resembles a big tree with outstretched branches, each full of green sprouts!

On the day of the event, though Juanito's heart is frail and he struggled, he managed to finish the stage performance of "The Dream into the Six Destinies" from the "Compassionate Samadhi Water Repentance". Then, he retrieved the props he had made with his children and finally took a break.

What is strength? Strength is a relentless endurance, an extended gentleness and courageous motivation. But even a strong man has his moments of weakness.

When the whole family looks up with pride to the father as their role model, concur to his love of Tzu Chi and come together in fulfilling their responsibilities, that father would be like a child sobbing with joy.

(Translated by BT Lin)

艾莉莎 Alyssa Candela
被祝福的女孩
The Blessed Girl

二〇一九年國際人醫年會，身為社工的艾莉莎演說自己的改變，以及奧莫克大愛村的醫療狀況。
During the 2019 TIMA Annual Convention, Alyssa, a social worker, talks about her own transformation and Tzu Chi's medical assistance in Ormoc Great Love Village.

窗外的鳳凰木開滿了紅豔豔的花，萊特島鄉間小徑常見的花樹，引來昆蟲鳥雀，鳳凰花開，又一批莘莘學子要畢業走入社會。

二〇一八年入夏，艾莉莎從大學社工系畢業，取得證照，等待工作機會。她的同學在獨魯萬當慈濟志工，告訴她十月需要人手協助義診服務，心地善良的她想著，待在家裏等工作掉下來，還不如去當志工！

她收到慈濟的來信，需要一名志工進行白內障患者調查，並列出清單。

之前她已經知道慈濟，因為她的家曾經在海燕風災後，收到慈濟的救濟金一萬五千披索，沒想到慈濟還長期陪伴受災的萊特島居民。

The Fire Tree outside the window is thick with red blossoms. These trees are very common in the Philippines. When the Fire Tree is in full bloom, its flowers attract insects and birds. Because it blooms only once a year, it reminds me of another group of graduates who are entering into society and the workforce.

In the early summer of 2018, Alyssa Candela had just graduated from the University with a degree in Social Work. After taking and passing the licensure exam, she began sending out job applications to different institutions. While waiting for a job opportunity, one of Alyssa's classmates, who is a volunteer in Tacloban told Alyssa that they needed help in a medical outreach in October. Alyssa, being a naturally helpful person thought, "Why not go and volunteer?" It is certainly better than staying home, and being idle.

Later, Alyssa received a text message from Tzu Chi Foundation informing her that a volunteer was needed to handle different aspects for

艾莉莎來到義診地點，她的瀏海遮住了眼睛。眼科史美勝醫師注意到了，問她：「你為什麼要隱藏一隻眼睛？」這個問題讓艾莉莎十分不自在，那是她二十年來的痛！

艾莉莎自出生便右眼斜視，父母因為愧疚對她特別寵愛。上學以後，雖然她的功課名列前茅，卻有同學叫她「duling（鬥雞眼）」。她漸漸懂了自己是「不正常的孩子」！

家人的寵愛無法彌補她內心深處的自卑與遺憾。

她嘗試了各種髮型，以側邊瀏海掩飾眼睛斜視，但愈是隱藏，愈是有新朋友好奇問她：「為什麼要覆蓋那隻眼睛？」即使她戴上帽子掩蓋，盡力想讓自己像一個正常人，但依舊有人取笑她，他們說：「你真的為自己的外表感到羞恥嗎？」她聽了心裏總是滴血！

那一年，她喜歡上一個人，卻擔心眼睛的狀況不被接納。儘管也有些人追求她，但她都因這個「瑕疵」而拒絕，一心專注於學習，只因害怕受傷。

內心充滿沮喪、寂寞，她常與自己的影子坐在樹下或安靜的河邊，獨自沈思流淚。

高中時，父母曾帶她去找光學專家配眼鏡，但那完全是一種心理補償，對她的斜視並無助益，她把父母的心意收好但不曾使用它。

她很清楚這一切不是父母的錯，但又在心底不斷吶喊，希望能接受真正的治療，卻不敢說出口，因為她深知那是父母無法承擔的金額！

河旁的樹長得更高了，像她一樣，隨著歲月成長變得愈發

cataract patients. Alyssa is already acquainted with Tzu Chi because she had received 15,000 pesos in disaster relief from them. However, she never expected that Tzu Chi would continue keeping track of Typhoon Haiyan survivors's recovery.

When Alyssa arrived at the medical outreach, her bangs were covering one of her eyes. One day, the volunteer ophthalmologist Dr. Antonio Say noticed her and asked, "Why do you want to hide your eye?" Upon hearing the question, Alyssa became very uncomfortable for she was reflecting on the last twenty years of her life and all the pains she had endured.

Alyssa was born with strabismus in her right eye. As a result of this condition, her parents often spoiled her, believing that this would somehow make up for her condition. When she began attending school, she was called 'duling' (cross-eyed) even though she ranked among the best students. That was when she began to realize that there was something out of the ordinary about her.

Despite her family's attempts to help her cope with her condition, Alyssa developed a low self-esteem. Alyssa tried several different hair styles in an effort to hide her strabismus. But the more she disguised her condition, the more her new friends would grow curious and ask: "Why do you cover that eye?" Even if Alyssa wore a hat designed to cover her eye in an effort to look normal, someone would inevitably make fun of her. They would ask: "Are you really ashamed of your appearance?" Hearing it always pierces her heart.

One year, she found herself having a crush on someone. However, she doubted that he would feel the same way toward her because of her eye condition. And so, even if he was pursuing her, because of her "blemish", she chose not to pursue him. Instead, Alyssa devoted herself to learning and avoided getting involved with anyone in order to protect herself from getting hurt. Frustrated and lonely, she often sit under a tree or beside the quiet river accompanied only by her shadow.

美麗，但是斜視的陰影從未遠離她寸步。

到了秋天，樹葉漸漸變了顏色，東一葉西一葉絮絮飄落，好像在風裏漫天灑著美麗的金箔，葉子落入河水閃著光，艾莉莎渴望有奇蹟出現，為她帶來一絲光亮的消息。

「你為什麼要把一隻眼睛隱藏起來？」她排斥著不想回答，但是史美勝醫師看著艾莉莎，她知道醫師已經明白她的問題所在，無以迴避，又或許這是一個好機會，是「神」聽到她的祈禱了嗎？

天大的好消息降臨，但她擔心萬一不成功，父母反而失望，所以拖到手術前一天才告知父母。

慈濟借用獨魯萬聖言醫院，由美國醫師凱斯・奎・麥肯瑞格（Cathy Qui Macanraig）執刀，半個小時手術完成，奇蹟似地改換了艾莉莎的人生。

術後，艾莉莎的斜視不再如影隨形，二十年的孤寂與等待、自卑與脆弱，一瞬間她被拉回正向而積極的路上，原來那些綠綠的草地，在她心裏靜靜生長著，從未棄她而去。

她在大學念的是社工系，社會工作是一門助人的專業，焦點在於人類與環境的互動，目的在協助個人、家庭、團體、社區能適應所在的社會環境，增強或恢復社會功能，是有利於達成社會條件的一種專業，可預防或舒緩社會問題。

艾莉莎最終在奧莫克大愛村工作，發揮社工長才。她將整個大愛村居民資料詳細建檔。村子裏發生什麼狀況，村民來通報，她就立刻放下手邊工作前去了解。

比如安娜考瑞特（Anacorita Cuyos）奶奶與爺爺兩人，年紀

When Alyssa was in high school, her parents brought her to an optical specialist to buy a pair of eyeglasses. Unfortunately, the eyeglasses did not hide nor help with her strabismus. Alyssa appreciated her parents' efforts to help her cope with her condition, but she chose to never wear the glasses. She understood that her condition was not her parents' fault but it did not stop the anguish she felt. Alyssa would always pray that her parents would one day find someone who can treat her condition. But she never mentioned this out loud because she knew her family could not afford the cost of such treatment.

With each passing year, the trees along the river grew taller and taller and Alyssa grew with them. Alyssa also became more and more beautiful. But the shadow of her strabismus was not fading away. As autumn came, the leaves gradually changed colors. They began falling off the limbs and dropping here and there. It seemed as if a beautiful golden foil was sprinkled throughout the sky whenever the wind blew. The leaves that fell into the river were flashed with light. Alyssa became more and more eager to see a sign of hope.

"Why do you want to hide your eye?" Dr. Say asked, looking at her. Alyssa chose not to answer. She believed that the doctor had noticed her because she stood out like a sore thumb. But Alyssa also thought that Dr. Say noticing her could be a good opportunity as well. Has God finally heard her prayers? Soon, the good news that Alyssa had waited so long to hear finally came. However, anxious that her parents would be extremely disappointed and saddened if her treatment did not succeed, Alyssa opted not to tell them about the offer until the day before her surgery.

The Divine Word Hospital of Tacloban City allowed Tzu Chi to use one of their operating rooms. Dr. Catherine Qui-Macaraig spent only about half an hour in performing the surgery. Miraculously, the operation was a success and suddenly, Alyssa's life is forever changed. After her surgery, Alyssa's strabismus was no longer a shadow that follows her everywhere she goes. The twenty years of loneliness, insecurities and vulnerability have all disappeared. Within only a few hours, Alyssa could already look forward to a more positive

都七、八十了，膝下沒有子嗣，靠著幫人修剪庭院，賺取微薄工資。

有一天，奶奶為了跨過一個小圍籬，跌入溝渠，右手斷了兩截。艾莉莎接到通報，立時前往關懷，並且安排住院，她與慈青傑森（Jayson）一起照顧了三天三夜。

還有一次，是七十四歲的雷梅姬（Remegia Sabelino）奶奶在自家後院燒柴烹煮時，不小心往後滑倒，背部擦出一個大傷口，也是通報到辦公室。艾莉莎送她去醫院做了各項檢查，確定脊椎沒有受傷，純粹是傷口疼痛，才安心陪伴她回家靜養。

每當成功完成了一件事，艾莉莎心裏總是感到舒緩和寬慰喜樂。

她為自己能在別人需要時幫上忙，而覺得人生變得有滋味、有意義。她深覺要照顧好一個村子的平安，非常具有挑戰性，需要善用大智慧，這是她要再精進學習之處。

從小因斜視受到欺凌的艾莉莎，漸漸明白善良是留給受過傷的人，過往的一切都是良藥！

七月下旬，我們散步於大愛村的河廓，穿梭於幾畦小農田綠秧，繞過一家庭院整齊潔淨，有著美麗花圃，並把門外泥地鋪上草皮，修剪得平整，以利雨季沖刷而下時吸收雨水之處。

那時，我看見被父母攙扶著的女孩喬娜琳，她面容憔悴、神情憂鬱。我問艾莉莎，女孩怎麼了？艾莉莎說，女孩為愛受傷很深，在諾伊醫師看診下，已服抗憂鬱藥一年餘，卻依舊不見起色。

那幾晚，想到女孩為愛糾結，在幽暗隧道裏走不出來，心

and proactive path in life. It turned out that those green meadows were growing quietly in her heart and had never abandoned her.

She studied social work at a University. Social work is a profession that helps people, and it focuses on the interaction between people and the environment. Its purpose is to help individuals, families, groups, and communities adapt to their social environment, and to strengthen or restore their social functions. It is a profession that could help people achieve better social conditions by preventing or relieving social problems.

Eventually, Alyssa accepted a job at Ormoc Great Love Village. Here, Alyssa could prove her capabilities and boost her self-confidence by excelling at her chosen career as a social worker. She set up and filed a great deal of data representing the Great Love villagers. Whenever an occurrence was reported within the village, Alyssa would immediately get involved to learn what was going on. An example of the kind of help Alyssa provided is shown by this event: An elderly lady named Anacorita Cuyos and her husband are almost 80 years old. They do not have children. They earn a meagre income by trimming gardens. One day, Anacorita intended to cross a creek, but she fell into the ditch and broke her right hand. Once Alyssa received notice, she immediately arranged for Anacorita to be admitted to the hospital. Alyssa, together with a Tzu Ching, Jayson, tended to her for three days.

There was another time when a 74-year-old grandma, Remegia Sabelino, was cooking over an open fire in her backyard when she accidentally slipped and fell backwards. Remegia sustained bruises and a large wound on her back. Luckily, this incident was also reported to the Tzu Chi office. Alyssa had Remegia sent to the hospital to conduct several diagnostic procedures to make sure her spine was not injured. Fortunately, the wound was only painful but not life-threatening. After Remegia's treatment, Alyssa peacefully accompanied her home to rest.

Whenever Alyssa successfully completes a task, she always feels satisfied

就沈痛不已。

離境前一日，我為喬娜琳做藝術治療，把艾莉莎找來幫忙翻譯成米沙鄒語，配合畫面，傳達文字的力量。

從清晨忙到傍晚，事前準備終於完成，抵達喬娜琳家，藝術治療影音檔的音樂才剛流瀉而出，喬娜琳已泣不成聲、全身顫抖，母親為她遞來手帕，我們都圍著她，等她慢慢停止流淚，再繼續把藝術治療完成。

艾莉莎把我們演練了一個下午的句子，非常耐心地一則則翻譯給喬娜琳聽，用溫暖的語言和愛，撫慰了她。

來自臺灣的慈青大學長潘信成，買了一本圖畫紙和二十四色的蠟筆，在首頁畫了荷，傑瑞醫師（Jery Esperance）寫上「Great Love From Tzu Chi（大愛來自慈濟）」，把這兩樣物品送給她。

我們圍著喬娜琳，請她先挑一個顏色。她露出淺淺微笑，把微顫的食指在蠟筆上來回尋找，最後取出「紅」色蠟筆，那代表著希望與熱情，她用它在圖畫紙上畫了一顆紅色的「心」。

不可思議的一刻開始了，她的心繼續跳動，麻木已久的感覺再度回來，好比星沙在水波裏緩緩飄流開來，喬娜琳從迷失中回首，重新定義自己與世界的距離。

艾莉莎有時獨自去探望喬娜琳，有時找慈青一起去，最後連大衛、泛尼托都一起去了喬娜琳家，用手語歌表現無數祝福。喬娜琳在艾莉莎日日奔走下，畫更多美麗的圖，也嘗試走出家門散步，微笑裏揮別了憂鬱。

幸福離我們並不是真的很遠，它那麼真切地存在，如果你用簡單的心去碰觸。接受往日的每一個決定，你的經歷，決定

and relieved. For her, life becomes more meaningful when she helps people. She considers her job a challenge because she is responsible for the safety of a village. It is necessary to use great wisdom to fulfill such heavy responsibility. And this is where Alyssa is taking efforts to learn. Being bullied because of her strabismus since childhood makes Alyssa realize that kindness should be given more to those who are hurt. Her past experiences have become Alyssa's valuable medicine in life.

Late in July, we were taking a walk by the river in the village. We went through several farmlands with fresh green sprouts, bypassing a neat and clean courtyard, which was planted with beautiful flowers and paved with trimmed turf that could absorb rain waters when the rainy season comes.

I saw Jonalyn L. Rubia, gaunt as she stood up, supported by her parents. She looked melancholic and pale. I asked Alyssa, "What happened to the girl?" Alyssa answered, "She is heart-broken." After undergoing medical treatment under Dr. Noel Maico, she took anti-depressant medicine for over a year. But her condition had not improved much.

During those nights, I stayed up feeling sad every time I think of the girl who got tangled in love, groping in the dark tunnel, unable to find the way out. One day before I left Ormoc, I did an art therapy for Jonalyn. I asked Alyssa to help in translating the video to the Visayan dialect, matching the scenes to bring out the power of words.

The preparation started at dawn. By dusk, we were finally done and ready. When we arrived at Jonalyn's home and played the art therapy video, Jonalyn trembled as she wept. Her mother handed her a handkerchief as we surrounded her until she stopped crying. We then proceeded to finish the art therapy.

With love and a gentle voice, Alyssa patiently translated to Jonalyn the phrases she had rehearsed all afternoon; and it soothed Jonalyn.

你豐富而美麗的種種特質。

當我們把晚餐盛在飯盒裏，帶上水果走著大愛村的小徑，送到安娜考瑞特奶奶家，這一對無依的老夫妻臉上露出靦腆感恩的微笑。回程途中，艾莉莎緊拉著我的手，依偎我的肩膀，滿足地笑了。星斗閃爍的夜空，映著我們澄明而滿足的心。

我告訴艾莉莎：「像星星一樣，我們都是自己心裏最亮的那一顆。而你是被祝福的女孩！」

艾莉莎二十年來受斜視所苦，義診手術改變了她的人生，應用在大學讀社工系所學，進入奧莫克大愛村工作。
Alyssa suffered from strabismus (crossed-eye) for over 20 years. The medical outreach's free surgery in 2018 has changed her life. She is practicing what she has learned in the university as a social worker in Ormoc Great Love Village.

Apollo Pan, who used to be a Tzu Ching member from Taiwan, bought a coloring booklet and 24 colors of crayons. He drew a lotus on the front page. Dr. Jery Esperance wrote down Great Love From Tzu Chi'. They presented the gifts to Jonalyn.

We formed a circle around her, asking her to choose one color. Jonalyn smiled slightly. With trembling index finger, she picked a red crayon and drew a red heart, symbolizing her renewed hope and enthusiasm for life. Then, that amazing moment happens. Jonalyn smiled. Emotions from a heart that was numb for a long time came back, like reflections of star dust in the water ripples gradually drifting apart.

Sometimes Alyssa would visit Jonalyn by herself, sometimes with the Tzu Chings. In the end, even Tzu Chi volunteers David and Juanito will pay Jonalyn a visit and bring her blessings through sign languages. With assistance from Alyssa, Jonalyn drew more and more nice pictures. From time to time, Jonalyn would try to step out of the house to take a walk. Today, there is no more trace of depression in Jonalyn's smiles.

Happiness is not actually far away. As long as you touch it with a pure heart of simplicity, happiness truly exists. By embracing every decision we have made in the past and every life experience with open arms, they will mould your character to become a person of abundance and beauty.

We packed dinner in a lunch box, and with fruits in hand, walked down the alley to bring to Anacorita's house, the dispossessed old couple smiled shyly with gratitude upon seeing us. On the way back, Alyssa pulled my hand tightly, snuggled against my shoulder and laughed with satisfaction.

I told Alyssa: "We are like stars. We are the brightest star inside our hearts. And you are the blessed girl."

(Translated by Celia Chang)

亞當 Adam Sumaljag

鼓動生命樂章

Drumming up Enthusiasm for Life

亞當是奧莫克大愛村的鼓樂老師，村裏若有需要，他總勤快地幫忙，以身為慈濟志工為榮。

Adam is the musical drum band teacher of Ormoc Great Love Village. If there is a need in the village, he will always be diligent to help out. He takes pride in being a Tzu Chi volunteer.

天是陰沈的，雲層裏懷滿貴金屬一般沈甸甸的水氣。奧莫克早晚總會下場雨，讓草原顯得一絲絲陰鬱。曲折的丘陵罜起在大愛村外的平原外緣，山丘深沈質地堅硬，遠遠看它，有著淡淡的寂寞。

亞當每晚訓練奧莫克的慈青慈少鼓樂隊，甚至到夜間九點星空滿布，還沒有休息。孩子們配合著他的教導，認真而耐心地一再反覆同一首曲子與腳步，迴轉變換著各種動作。而他呢？亞當每天啞著音聲，毫不厭倦，也不生氣或埋怨。

兒時家庭經濟不好，父母經常為了亞當的升學問題爭論不休，亞當只讀到中學二年級，便到奧莫克市當建築工人，也到馬尼拉工作很長一段時間，並且取得焊工技術證書。

海燕風災後，亞當的母親住進甘恩杜收容所（Bunkhouse

The day has been gloomy with thick dark clouds hanging low over Ormoc City. Day in and out, it always rains in this part of the country.

The winding hills rise behind the Great Love Village. From afar, the ground appears desolate.

Only the sound of drums can be heard in the evening.

Adam Christopher Sumaljag rehearses the Ormoc Tzu Ching with their drum band often until 9 o'clock every night.

The children follow his instructions, learning earnestly and patiently by repeatedly playing the same songs in time with their corresponding footsteps, turns and other movements.

As for Adam, he is always full of energy. He never complains nor lose his

Can-untog），因此他從馬尼拉又回到奧莫克當焊工，慈濟興建大愛村時，他就接了焊接工作。

人的興趣，總隨著人生旅程和際遇不斷變換。

亞當八歲就很喜歡打鼓，當他在奧莫克中央學校（Ormoc Central School）學習時，加入了學校樂隊，學會了管絃樂器等。二〇一八年八月開始，他教導慈青慈少鼓樂，鼓勵年輕孩子們不要沈迷電腦遊戲，他明白每個孩子都有演奏樂器的天賦。

一開始只有少數人，之後李偉嵩發現了，覺得這是能讓孩子們發洩精力也凝聚情誼，很有意義的一件事，於是提供了樂器。亞當因此有了一個好機會回饋慈濟。

鼓樂隊每週練習三次，若逢活動像是浴佛節，就必須每天練習。孩子們表現得好，他們會產生信心，亞當為孩子們築起的自信，感到無比喜悅。

奧莫克大愛村的孩子們很幸福，在精力旺盛無處發洩的年紀，有籃球場、足球場，有樂隊、讀書會，有語言班、手語班，還有許許多多藏書……讓孩子們廣學興趣，從中尋找自己未來的出口。

草地在奧莫克孩子們的心裏靜靜成長，自信也逐漸在他們心中高築。

亞當讓孩子們學習演奏每一種樂器，他教他們基礎樂理，讓孩子們專注於音樂和節拍。

看到孩子們在音樂中得到療癒與自信、快樂，這些改變同樣回饋給亞當，成為他每日精神上的可貴資糧。

村裏有些孩子曾失去人生的道路方向，透過演奏樂器，他

temper even if his voice would become hoarse after hours of practice.

Adam came from a poor family. In his childhood, he witnessed how his parents struggled to pay for his school fees.

Adam dropped out of school after his second year in High School. He went to Ormoc City to do construction work and later moved to Manila in search of greener pastures.

After Typhoon Haiyan destroyed their house in 2013, Adam's mother moved into the government-provided temporary houses in Can-untog, Ormoc. Adam, who was then in Manila, decided to return to Ormoc. He used his skills in welding to help build the Great Love Village.

Throughout people's life journey, things happen that will lead them to another path, but they will always go back to their interests.

Adam was eight years old when he first played the drums. When he was still studying in Ormoc Central School, he joined the school band and played the string instruments.

In August 2018, with firm faith in the musical talent of Ormoc youth, he formed the Ormoc Tzu Ching band.

He encouraged the young people to get involved with the band instead of spending their time playing computer games.

In the first few weeks after the band was formed, only a few people joined in. Alfredo Li recognized the significance of this band among the youth so he supplied the musical instruments. Adam was cheered. He realized this will be a good opportunity to give back to Tzu Chi.

The band practiced thrice a week. During special events, like the Buddha

們重燃對生命、生活的渴望，再「專心一點，少想一些」，亞當希望孩子們集中精神於演奏中，他願他們擁有自己的夢想和目標。

從這些孩子們身上，他回想起自己還是那個十七歲的孤獨少年時。

當時他生活錯亂，總是遇見麻煩、與父母爭吵，懷疑父母是否真的在乎他？他在外四處闖蕩，常想：「慢慢來，等等心裏的那個小孩。」

當他受到欺凌，他盼望心靈的壯大，就如一顆小小的金桔子，盼望能成為一棵碩大而飽滿多汁的橘子樹一般。

如今，亞當在大愛村已有家庭，有個可愛的三歲兒子，雖然如此，他感覺學習並沒有結束的時候，他認為人生就是終身學習。

在不同的領域裏，他想成為一個更好的人，而他心底還有一個想法，他想當一名警察，感覺那是他曾任少尉的父親在呼喚著他：「孩子，跟上來吧！」

從兒時到高中畢業，從建築工人到焊接工到鼓樂老師，如今的安定，每一件事都是一個成長的契機，在任何一個領域必定有它的意義。

亞當甚至覺得鼓樂隊的孩子們彷彿把他當成第二個父親，他肩負了證嚴法師賦予他的職責，他要引領孩子們去發現人生的價值。

二○一九年十月，史無前例地於奧莫克市舉辦獨立義診，由本土人醫會醫師與馬尼拉人醫會醫師合作。

Day celebration, the band will be there to perform. Its young members would work very hard in rehearsing every day.

Seeing how he has helped build the children's confidence makes Adam very happy.

The children at the Ormoc Great Love Village are quite blessed. In their growing years, when they are bursting with youthful energy, they have a basketball court, a football field, a musical band, a study group, language and sign language classes, and a vast collection of books.

As a result, they always have something new to learn and are able to envision their future.

Like grasses that grow silently in the field, the confidence of these young people are reinforced as they grow up.

Adam encouraged the children to learn how to play any instrument that they like. He taught them the basic musical notes. Each time he sees the improvement in each child, he feels proud and happy.

These children used to have lost their path in life. Through music, they have found life's meaning.

Adam fervently prays that they will keep on doing music. He believes that it will help them shape their dreams and steer them towards their goals.

Adam sees himself in these kids. When he was 17 years old, he used to constantly argue with his parents and wondered whether they really cared about him. He ran away from home, wanting desperately to be on his own.

Now, Adam has a family of his own, a 3-year-old son and a house at the Great Love Village. While it may seem like he has a settled life now, in his

為了鼓舞大家的士氣與自信，義診日一早，亞當便帶著鼓樂隊走在隊伍行列最前面，之後是所有參與義診的醫護與志工，鼓樂氣勢磅礴的聲音響徹雲霄。

　　亞當雖尚未當上警察，但他挺直的腰桿，告訴我，他已踏出自己生命的價值。

　　雨停了。陽光漸漸探出頭來，反射的光線投射在亞當晶亮的瞳孔，他每每一晃動，光點便從他身上的汗珠發亮著。

　　參與世界是如此美麗，你有沒有全心相信的事情呢？

亞當就像一個孩子王，每當有活動來臨，他總會帶領著大愛村的孩子們勤練鼓樂，毫不倦怠。

Adam is like a father to the children. Whenever there is an upcoming event, he would always lead the children of the Great Love Village to practice the musical drum band, without slacking.

heart, Adam knows that he still has so much to learn.

Adam hopes he can be a better person and dreams of becoming a policeman someday. He felt he was being called to follow the footsteps of his father, who was a second lieutenant.

From his childhood, to becoming a construction worker, a welder, a music teacher, to finally settling down with his own family- every step that Adam took had been an opportunity to grow. Every stage of his life is valuable. The children in the drum band take Adam as their second father. He happily bears the duty of guiding them to discover their life value.

In October 2019, Tzu Chi International Medical Association (TIMA) doctors from Manila cooperated with the local doctors to conduct their first ever medical outreach in Ormoc City.

During the opening ceremony, Adam's drum band led the doctors and volunteers to the venue, uplifting everyone's morale and confidence. The majestic sound of their drums resounded to the clouds.

Adam has yet to become a policeman but seeing him standing tall and upright as the leader of the band tells me that he is living a life of value just the same.

The rain has stopped.

The sun has come out and reflected into Adams' bright eyes. When he moves, the sun illuminates his crystal sweat spots.

Belongingness is always filled with wonders. Is there something that you wholeheartedly believe in?

(Translated by Emily Chu)

艾維斯 Ives Famador

水資源的收放閉鎖

Making Every Water Drop Count

奧莫克大愛村有一千五百八十五戶人家，艾維斯與三位隊友日夜維護村裏的水資源運作。

There are 1,585 households in Ormoc Great Love Village. Ives and his three team mates are in charge of the daily maintenance of the water supply in the village.

風一來，堤岸蘆葦發出窸窸窣窣的聲音，奧莫克大愛村晚間七點，亮起 LED 燈，有些地方密集一排排，有些地方少數幾盞。

光束照不到的地方，眼前一片黑暗，雙腳踩過河邊的曠野，長草與蔓藤交錯，若非水資源管理處的燈光投射過草葉彎刀似的葉緣，一路上是多麼容易被絆倒。

水資源管理處外有鐵絲網籬笆，鐵絲網邊緣圈綁木條，形成一扇門，門邊是菲律賓常見的錦帶花，儘管黑暗，那桃紅色的花朵簇簇盛放，依舊繽紛。

這樣隱密處，表示這是一處重地。

艾維斯與另三位隊友在水庫旁搭設多用途小屋，廊下一方小桌，微燈在夜色裏晃動，他們圍坐著聊天，等著每日開水閥

As the wind blew, the reeds at the embankment hissed continually. It is seven in the evening, and the LED lights are switched on. There are some areas densely packed with rows of LED street lamps, while others only a scattered few.

The Water Resource Management Office of Tzu Chi Ormoc Great Love Village is located in an area where there are no street lights. Going there is difficult as there is nothing in front of us but total darkness. Along the side of the river, tall grasses and vines lined the way towards the office. If not for the light coming from the office that illuminated the sharp grasses, anyone could easily trip along the way.

Ives, together with his three companions, works at the Water Resource Management Office. The office is close to the reservoir and surrounded by a wire fence. Under the dim light in the middle of the night, they sit together chitchatting, awaiting for their daily schedule to open the gate valves.

的時刻到來。

　　水庫的白牆上，書寫著大大的英文字：「Say good words. Have good thoughts. Do good deeds and help make a world of difference.（口說好話，心想好意，身行好事，讓世界更好。）」醒目提醒著每日路過的人，這是一個充滿鼓舞又美好的警語。

　　進了鐵網門，兩隻小白狗奔跑著過來爭寵，艾維斯看到我們來很開心，他說稍胖的那隻叫「小慈」，略瘦的那隻叫「小濟」！我開心地蹲下來逗牠們玩，可見他有多愛慈濟。

　　我們走著小徑到小方桌的路上，又是一棵高大的醋栗樹，高到我的手摘不到它紅色的小甜果，白色的花瓣隨風飄飛的景色，是我在奧莫克大愛村最享受的氛圍。

　　艾維斯是水資源管理小組四人中的領隊，他介紹著他們此地水資源的運作：「於深夜兩點，會有一人先將斷路器打開，讓水湧進水箱內充滿，另一人再將水閥門轉開，讓水流往大愛村三間房的住戶去供應用水，直到早上十一點鐘，再關閉水閥門與斷路器，約三十分鐘，讓潛水泵得以休息，使之不會過熱。下午一點三十分，再次打開斷路器與另一組水閥門，讓水再度流出，這次是供應給兩間房小單位的村民使用，直到晚上九點再度全部關閉。」

　　一整天的程序，看似簡單，然而要精確俐落地完成，卻是一種無聲的考驗。比如下大雨刮大風的日子、整頓檢修儀器與用具、調整水量與流速、定期清理管線……每個步驟都需要專注與專業。

　　乍看不過是開開關關水閥，讓水彷似一條河流的旅行，穿

Posted on the building wall of the water reservoir is a large sign written in English: "Say good words. Have good thoughts. Do good deeds and help make a world of difference."

These words are intended to inspire people to create a better world.

As we enter the building, two small white dogs rushed over to Ives to play with him. Ives tells me their names – the fat one is called "little Tzu" and the thin one is "little Chi". I can just imagine how much Ives loves Tzu Chi as I play with the dogs.

Ives is the leader of the four-person water resources management team. He explains the daily operations his team is responsible for: supplying water to the village on a set schedule. From two o'clock until eleven o'clock in the morning, water is allowed to flow. Between eleven in the morning and one thirty in the afternoon, the water is turned off to allow the submersible pump to cool. By one-thirty in the afternoon, the water supply resumes until nine in the evening. It seems like a simple task, but it must be performed carefully and meticulously every day. Each step of the complex operation requires concentration and professionalism. On days of heavy rains and or strong winds, the water volume and flow rates must be adjusted. Pipes must also be regularly cleaned, etc.

One may think that a day in the life of Ives is quite simple because of the routine. But each day brings a new test to the system and the daily work that needs to be done requires a person's full attention. The water supply is like love... too much supply or insufficient provision would not bring happiness.

Ives said, there used to be a villager who complained about the excess cost of the water. After tracing the problem, they discovered that it is the meter-man's mistake in jotting down the wrong information, causing them to be harshly scolded. There are times when his companion were attacked and bitten by the villager's dogs.

越水管輕暢地在早晨流往一處去旅遊，回家後稍事休息，下午又出門到另一方雲遊，然後晚間就回家睡覺了。

簡單的面，往往有著繁瑣複雜的後背。水的供應也像愛，太多與不及都會不愉快。艾維斯說，曾有村民抱怨水費太貴，追查結果，是記表員登錄錯誤，害他們遭了一頓罵！有時去收費遇到大狗咬人而受傷，有時收不到水費……

水資源的管理收放閉鎖之間，彷彿反覆陳訴不盡那些鑽牛角尖的陳年往事。遭到誤會也像細小的螺絲，要非常細心地計較，不能鬆懈只記錄那些重點而忽視細微，寫下不完整的故事。

你必須在別人不相信的時候，耐心說話，別人相信的時候，唯有耐心傾聽。即便是再小的狀況，都要善用智慧來解決，才能一一破解。

艾維斯聲音清亮而沈穩，他曾在聖彼得學院讀電腦科系，受到鄰居和叔叔的影響，後來中輟轉入軍事領域受訓。

軍人背景，造就艾維斯英氣勃發、果敢嚴謹、自律守諾的印象。海燕風災發生時，他的房子全毀，奧莫克要蓋大愛村，他被推出來當領隊，蓋第一批大愛屋時他就來了，因此已經住了近五年。

過去他曾待過奧莫克市政府水利局（Ormoc water Authority, ORWASA），習得管控水的技術，因此又被委以重任，在二○一七年一月接下水資源管理工作。

整個奧莫克大愛村有一千五百八十五戶，他一個人忙不過來，丹特（Dante）、傑瑞（Jerry）與基瑞（Gerry）這三位老實脾氣好的農夫被請來幫忙，丹特負責水閥門的開放，基瑞負責

In order to perform the job correctly and to successfully deal with different situation, patience and wisdom are essential.

Ives speaks with a clear masculine voice. He used to study computer science at St. Peter's College. Inspired by his neighbors and family, he joined the military. His military training mould him to a figure of a fine gentleman, a bold and rigorous character, and a self-disciplined image.

When super typhoon Haiyan hit the Philippines in 2013, his home was completely destroyed. When Tzu Chi Foundation is building its Great Love Village in Ormoc, he was recommended to be a leader of a pre-fabricated houses installation team. Therefore, since the start of Tzu Chi's project in building the first batch of houses, he was already with Tzu Chi. And he is living in the village for five years now.

In earlier times, he worked at the Ormoc Water Authority (ORWASA) under the city government, and learned the technology of water control. With this knowledge and experience, in 2017, he was eventually assigned to manage the water supply of the Great Love Village.

There are 1,585 houses at the Ormoc Great Love Village. Supplying water to these homes is a challenging task. To help him manage, Ives assigned three good tempered farmers: Dante, Jerry and Gerry as his assistants. Each of them has a specific task to perform every day: Dante will open the gate valves, Gerry will close the valves, while Jerry is assigned in the operations of the breaker.

Ives takes his responsibilities seriously. After the gate valves were opened at 2AM, and his three companions have gone home to sleep, Ives would sit alone at the side of the small square table, reminiscing on his past. He thinks about Tzu Chi and how different and unique it is from other organizations, its inspiring teachings that allowed him to experience charity works that he had never experienced before.

水閘門的關閉，傑瑞負責斷路器的操作。

艾維斯做事認真負責，深夜兩點水閘門開啟後，其他三人回家休息了，他仍獨坐小方桌旁，想著住在奧莫克大愛村的生活瑣事，回想往日艱辛。他留意到慈濟與其他組織不同，有許多獨特與鼓舞的教誨，讓他體驗過去未做過的善事。

烏茲曼風災時，馬米尼（Mabini）是重災區，它位於卡塔曼市（Catarman）的一個很偏僻的里，那裏地勢很高，倖存者自山頂走五個小時的路，方能下得山來到卡塔曼發放地點。

當時那裏是新人民軍駐守，所以馬米尼人來到卡塔曼就怕被政府軍抓走，但艾維斯本著純潔而真誠的心去幫助他們，因此並不害怕。

當他發給他們每人三千菲幣，平時僅靠著香蕉等作物維生的他們，從未看過「錢」，不知道這是什麼東西和作用，只是呆呆地望著他。

終於了解祝福金用途的災民不斷道感謝，艾維斯意識到自己是如此幸運，難耐胸臆苦澀，他哭了！淚水一直滴下來，擋也擋不住，只能轉過身去極力掩飾。

這世界沒有百分之百完美，水資源管理團隊面對細如牛毛的抱怨，和不懂得「錢」的災民比起來，什麼事都沒那麼重要了！他覺得自己能加入慈濟這種以幫助人為目的的團隊，是多麼美好的事！

如今他在靜靜的大愛村有妻兒相伴，無比幸福，他笑了。

讓艱辛模糊一點，幸福就清楚一些，他想成為更好的人，醞釀至誠的信念，孵化希望。

For instance in December 2018, when Typhoon Usman hit, the barangay of Mabini in Catarman was heavily affected. It is located in the remote area of Northern Samar, high up in the mountains. Survivors had to walk for more than five hours to get help, going through areas where the New People's Army (NPA, the armed branch of the Philippine Communist Party) operated.

Survivors were often afraid that they could be mistaken as militants by government forces. Fortunately, Ives was there to help them. He was sincere and fearless. Tzu Chi provided 3,000 pesos to each individual as a form of relief. Since the people there only relied on bananas and other farm products for food, most of them had never seen money before, and had no idea of the value of this 'money'. As Ives handed them the cash assistance, the people simply stared back at him, bewildered!

As he reflected on this, he began to weep. He realized how lucky he was as a Tzu Chi volunteer.

Finally, the recipient of the cash assistance realized the value of what they were given. They endlessly expressed their thanks. The scene that unfolded before him pulled at Ives' heartstring. He turned around to hide his tears.

There is nothing perfect in this world. Faced with the petty complains that they encounter in their water resource operation and the disaster survivors who do not even know what "money" is, everything has become insignificant. For Ives, what matters now is that he is part of Tzu Chi – a group that aims to help people.

Now, living with his wife and children in the Great Love Village, he is happy and content. Life is hard, but difficulties fade in his mind as he strives to be a better person, developing sincere faith and nurturing hope in his heart.

(Translated by BT Lin)

靜靜琢磨自己的成色

The Shepherd Blowing Flute

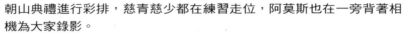

朝山典禮進行彩排，慈青慈少都在練習走位，阿莫斯也在一旁背著相機為大家錄影。

During the rehearsal of the three steps one bow pilgrimage, Amos carried a video camera to document the event.

人生多變悲喜交加的過程，彷如一首跳躍起伏的音韻。音樂是生活，歌詞是故事，每人每日都在為自己的生命譜曲，假使那音韻一成不變，必定會是單調的曲子；倘若曲子抑揚頓挫，就會變得悠揚而蕩氣迴腸。

這一天，燠熱依舊，一場大雨過後，綿綿小雨猶未絕，衣服溼黏裹住身體，煞是難耐，但本土志工們臉上全是歡喜，認真聽聞證嚴法師《人間菩提》開示。阿莫斯坐在螢幕左側的電腦前，拿著遠鏡頭相機伸縮取景，捕捉大家凝聽法音的各種動人表情。他的眼睛不大，但雪亮敏銳。

阿莫斯的父親是一位三輪車夫，在他大學三年級時，突發嚴重中風，之後雖然還能說話及緩步行走，但失去了聽覺，家人之間的溝通變得困難。孝順的阿莫斯思忖著，父親無法再工

Life is an unpredictable journey that is full of joy and sorrow like an undulating melody. If life is music, then our story is the lyrics that we sing about. We compose our own special music everyday. When life is plain, the music is flat and unadorned. When life is swaying and rocky, the music is melodious.

It was a hot day even after a heavy rainshower; although it seemed as if the rain never really stopped. Our clothes were soaked with sweat yet the local volunteers' enthusiasm to listen to Master Cheng Yen's *"Life Wisdom"* never wavered. Amos was sitting in the right side of the screen, documenting the event with his camera. He was doing his best to capture the audiences' expressions as they listen to the Master's words of wisdom. His eyes were not big, but these were bright and sharp.

Amos's father used to earn a living as a pedicab driver. When Amos was a junior in college, his father suffered a stroke and lost his hearing. As a result,

作，家裏經濟不穩定，他決定中輟學習去工作。雖然在大學讀的是電腦相關知識，可是阿莫斯的第一份工作卻是當一名麵包師傅，很難想像阿莫斯為何找了與本科性質相去甚遠的工作？未久，轉換跑道擔任保全人員，身材中等但是壯碩精悍，精確理性的分析能力加上敏捷的手腳，讓他十分稱職。

父親中風事發突然，他並未因此慌亂，明快決定行動並伺機尋找適合自己的工作。阿莫斯最後在奧莫克網路電腦商店任職，從拖地清潔雜工被提升為銷售服務員，然後是倉庫管理員，最後成為電腦技術員。不計較工作卑劣，直視心中想望，不斷進取而沒有埋怨，這種胸襟並非人人能有。

才放下父親中風帶來的陰影，孰料海燕風災又瞬間降臨！家沒了！幸好家人都還在一起。原來，失去也還有幸福的滋味！

萊特島進駐許多非政府組織，他試圖加入那些組織，但無緣繼續。在所有非政府組織相繼離開後，他重拾舊業，在商店為人修理電腦，並租住於獨魯萬市，這時他發現慈濟人依舊於萊特島救助他的同胞，建蓋了大愛村。這是慈濟留給阿莫斯最初的美好印象！二〇一五年，阿莫斯的父母親幸運地搬入奧莫克大愛村，他的父親是首位在那塊土地上種植木薯等作物的人。

好景不長，阿莫斯的父親再度中風，這次身體右側癱瘓，起初完全認不得人，後來母親耐心引導，終於慢慢認得出家人。父親努力運動身體，隨著時間推移，又能夠走路了。如今大愛村裏每有重要事件，幾經磨難的父母一定都去做志工。放晴的天空逐漸爬上星斗，隱隱約約，不同顏色，深深淺淺閃爍，像河中的卵石在波浪裏各自發光，偶爾飄浮起來，有時沈沒下去。

Amos had to quit school and work in order to support the family. He was a computer engineering student. The first job he got was as a baker. It might be difficult to comprehend why Amos would choose a job that is completely unrelated to his course but at that time, he did not have the luxury to pick a job he likes. He was the family breadwinner and he was determined to provide well for his loved ones. The next job Amos had was as a security guard. He has a medium built, is strong and does not speak much. He is also quick on his feet, which makes him very qualified for the job. Amos did not panic when his father had stroke.

Later on, he left his security guard position and joined the Ormoc Net Computer Store. He began with cleaning the floors, then moved to the post-sale service department. Afterwards, he became a warehouse clerk and finally, a computer technician. As Amos climbed up the ranks at the computer shop, not a single complaint was heard from him. He always did his best in order to advance to the next position that will give him more challenges. He has unparalleled consistency and persistence that are not found in everyone.

As Amos and his family was starting to recover from his father's stroke, Typhoon Haiyan devastated Leyte. His house was blown to pieces and their life was suddenly turned upside down again. Despite the tragedy that befell them, Amos managed to keep his family intact. For the first time in his life, Amos understood what it means to be blessed despite their loss.

In the wake of the super typhoon, various non-government organizations (NGOs) worldwide extended a helping hand to Leyte. Amos wanted to volunteer with them but did not have the chance to join. When the NGOs left, Amos went back to his old job in the computer shop and eventually rented his own place in Tacloban City. There, he witnessed how the Tzu Chi volunteers built the Great Love Village. It turned out that, unlike most NGOs, Tzu Chi Foundation had not left the province. They continued to help Amos' fellowmen and this left a favorable impression to the locals. In 2015, Amos' parents moved to the Ormoc Great Love Village. His father became the first

阿莫斯有著母親的靈活頭腦，又具備父親勤勞不怕吃苦、發掘先機的能力，他靜默一如處子，開始在時間的窗外窺測著他與慈濟的距離。二〇一七年，他與妻子史黛拉（Stela）和女兒也幸運入住奧莫克大愛村，一邊還是在商店裏為人修電腦。

　　艾達和阿莫斯過去是奧莫克市里納歐（Linao）區的鄰居，因緣際會進入慈濟辦公室當職工。這時他們重聚在大愛村，艾達就向阿莫斯提起慈濟正在招聘文件歸檔人員，於是阿莫斯成為慈濟辦公室的資料庫總管理人。

　　星斗在空中一一擁有自己的名字，它們並非漫無目的地徘徊，除了發出微光似乎一無所有，靜靜被人發現又遺忘，好像捉迷藏，最後總能躲起來，再也尋不回它！

　　二〇一八年四月，阿莫斯可敬的父親，在最後一次中風時，永遠離開了他。父親往生時，慈濟支付了醫藥帳單，風災後幾無存款的阿莫斯，對慈濟無所求的資助，心底翻騰著無盡的感激之情！他想用一輩子作為一名工作人員，來回饋慈濟，他所負責的影片、照片等資料，歸檔和編碼都做得特別好。

　　母親原是大愛村非常活耀的環保志工，失去丈夫後依然不變初衷。阿莫斯探索著如何達成慈濟的工作任務，他上 YouTube 搜索及學習相關資訊，配合大學時期所學，認真用心地把任務達成，為慈濟保留歷史。雖然沒有共同的宗教，每當他在《人間菩提》節目畫面中見到證嚴法師，還是不由自主地悸動想流淚，看到感人的真實故事，他更加見苦知福。

　　他像星斗在空中旋轉著，靜靜琢磨自己的成色。他的妻子史黛拉即將參加二〇二〇年《慈悲三昧水懺》的手語演出，他

farmer to plant cassava in this new community.

But not all good things last. Amos' father suffered another stroke, paralyzing the right side of his body. Initially, he could not recognize anyone. But with his mother's love and care, his father gradually remembered them all. With continuous exercise, his father was able to walk again. At the Great Love Village, Amos' parents would always volunteer whenever Tzu Chi Foundation has disaster relief missions.

Amos got his wits from his mother, and his diligence from his father. In 2017, Amos, his wife Stela and their daughter moved to the Great Love Village. At that time, Amos continued to work in the computer shop.

Amos remembered watching the colors change as the sun rises and sets. He can also vividly recall how the stars seem to look like floating pebbles.

As time passed, his mother saw how enamored Amos has become of Tzu Chi Foundation.

One day, Amos met Aida Cornito, a staff of the Tzu Chi Foundation Ormoc Office. They are both neighbors from Barangay Linao in Ormoc City. From her, he heard that the Tzu Chi office was recruiting staff and volunteers to work at the Great Love Village. Aida informed Amos about a job opening for a document filing clerk position. He sent an application and eventually got the job, handling the Great Love Village database.

Stars have names and identities. They don't just wander around, merely being forgotten.

In April 2018, Amos' father suffered another stroke and died. Tzu Chi Foundation paid for all his medical bills. Amos felt deeply indebted to Tzu Chi and intended to work for the foundation as a sign of gratefulness. He took charge of its video and photo documentation, as well as the filing and coding

們全家也正努力茹素，不再為口欲而進食那些有感情的動物。阿莫斯自己也想成為一名慈誠，將慈濟所做的慈善事與人分享，生生世世勸募善款，為無家可歸的人們付出愛。

學位並非成功的基石，慈悲才是最寶貴的，而時間對我們總是靜靜地理解，來洗滌那原本明淨的心靈。

阿莫斯的心奏過一曲頻率變換極大的生命音韻，如今奧莫克大愛村的寧靜生活，使他好似一名有情而善良的吹笛者，綿延不絕的夏日野草在細細傾聽，他將成為一位吹笛的牧羊人。

為記錄在奧莫克大愛村首次自行舉辦的義診，阿莫斯深入手術間拍攝醫者父母心的鏡頭。
In order to document the first medical outreach program organized in Ormoc, Amos went inside the surgery room to film the doctors as they attend to the patients like loving parents.

of databases.

After her husband's death, Amos' mother continued to be an active environmental protection volunteer in the Great Love Village. She never missed a day of helping out at the village's recycling center.

Amos tried to find innovative ways to help Tzu Chi accomplish its mission. He searched online for videos and photos. And then using the skills he learned in college, he told Tzu Chi Ormoc's story through documentaries.

He appreciates how Tzu Chi helped the villagers without asking for anything in return. Not a religious person himself, Amos would always tremble and weep whenever he listens to Master Cheng Yen in the "Life Wisdom" program. He came to understand that there is a blessing in pain.

Amos is like a star wandering in the sky. He quietly evaluates himself and appreciates his life. Stela, Amos' wife, will participate in a sign language performance of "The Compassionate Samadhi Water Repentance" in 2020. Amos and Stela are striving hard to become vegetarians, sincerely avoiding meat in their daily meals. Amos hopes to be a member of the Tzu Chi Faith Corps someday to share the good deeds of Tzu Chi, to help raise fund for the Foundation, and to give love to those who were homeless.

An academic degree does not always bring true success; kindness and compassion are a person's most precious virtues. We are given ample time to quietly acknowledge the deeper and clearer side of our hearts.

The tune in Amos' heart has gone through extreme ups and downs. Now, he enjoys a peaceful life in the Great Love Village. Amos is like a kind and passionate flute player, performing religiously to the endless summer grass. Eventually, he will become a shepherd who plays the fantastic flute.

(Translated by Joanne Lee)

理芝莉 Lizly Fuentes
如飄飛的種子落土壤
Flying Seeds Fall into the Land

理芝莉最大的安慰就是可愛的兒子，她常說：「兒子好幸福，從小就能跟著慈濟走。」
The greatest consolation of Lizly is her lovely son. She often said: "My son is so blessed. Because he met Tzu Chi at a young age."

不動產，是人世間沒有誰能輕易帶走的東西；而人生在世，一如蒲公英的種子，隨風四處漂泊在未知的空間。

時間是一條彎彎曲曲的長河，人好似在長河裏，頃刻流蕩，這如微塵般的生命。

理芝莉來自宿霧，放棄了大學三年級的學習機會。具有語言天分的她，當時選修英文和德文，但她愛玩又一直渴望掙錢，欲求買到她想要的物品。父母不斷規勸，希望她能完成學業，遺憾的是，最終她還是選擇放棄。

回想那段日子的魯莽，她知道自己浪費了上天曾經賜予的一個美好機會。

儘管曾努力當一名銷售員，但她無法忍受一成不變的工作，再度放棄。之後，她試圖運用德文專才，管理朋友的貸款業務，

Tangible items are something we cannot take with us to our next life. However, people are like dandelion seeds, drifting in the wind to the void. Time is like a long winding river, and humans seem to flow along this river for only a brief moment, like dust.

Lizly Fuentes is talented in language. She was in her third year in the university as an English and German language major when she quit studying. Despite her parents' pleas for her to finish her studies, Lizly was adamant. Instead, she went to Cebu to work. She was very eager to make her own money so that she could buy all the nice things she wanted. Looking back at it now, she realized she had let a wonderful opportunity slip through her fingers.

In Cebu, Lizly worked as a saleswoman. But she could not stand the drab job and eventually gave up. Afterwards, she tried to help manage a friend's loaning business. She thought her language skills would come in handy in this new job. But after some time, Lizly got bored and left again.

一段時間後依舊覺得無味。

　　理芝莉，像一隻飛得高高的蝴蝶，在花叢間東飄西盪尋來覓去，對自己的工作始終不滿意，一直在尋找別的東西。隨著時間推移，即便她曾經跟理想靠得很近，最終卻在猶疑、等待中，被風吹開跌落在地！種種挫敗讓她覺察到自己的心高氣傲與不沈著。

　　一日，她結識了一名男子，並決定與他步入婚姻。婚後，她想到馬尼拉找工作，先生則希望回到家鄉奧莫克，雖然他已離鄉背井許久，而且家鄉的兄弟姊妹和父母都懶散不工作，極為貧窮。

　　唯獨理芝莉的先生勤奮，是一名水電建築工人。初回奧莫克沒有人脈，難以找到工作，少有進帳卻不斷耗盡房租等費用，夫妻倆盤纏用盡，生活得貧窮艱難，三餐常常只能以香蕉果腹。

　　然而皇天不負苦心人，先生終究找到一份好工作。

　　二〇一三年六月，理芝莉生下兒子，因為流血過多險些死亡。她向上蒼祈求，讓她能夠活下來照顧兒子，先生也花錢購買營養品給她喝。終於，她醒來了，看到了一盞燈，解除了生命危機，深感上蒼的慈悲眷顧。

　　但憂慮並未停止，同年十一月海燕風災突發，他們的租屋受損，斷垣殘壁無可安身，小嬰兒哭鬧著，理芝莉緊抱著襁褓中的兒子，掩不住心中焦慮而淚水雨水分不清。

　　她於年輕時想遇見人間盛放的火花，如今有了兒子，又在風災中保住了生命，她從信仰記取教養與愛的規訓，再重新回到生活裏，理芝莉對人生的想法也有了轉變。

Lizly, like a butterfly flitting from flower to flower, was constantly in search of something that will fulfill her desires. But she could not find a job that would suit her skills and satisfy her needs. As time passed, although she was earning money, she found herself still wanting more. Eventually, her discontent led her to stumble hard and hit rock bottom. This made her realize that she had been too proud and had always wanted an easy life.

One day, Lizly met a man whom she eventually decided to marry. After they were married, Lizly tried to find a job in Manila, while her husband wanted to return to his hometown in Ormoc. His absence from the family took a toll on their finances. His parents and siblings refused to work, so their expenses eventually drained their savings.

On the other hand, Lizly's husband is hard-working and specializes in plumbing, electronics and construction. On their return to Ormoc, they both realized that it was hard to find a job when they are not connected to anyone. Being jobless exhausted their savings. To stretch their budget, they only ate bananas for every meal.

The family struggled until Lizly's husband finally found a job. In June 2013, the couple was blessed with a son but Lizly faced complications and almost died during childbirth. She prayed earnestly to God to let her survive so she could take care of their growing family. To help her recover, her husband bought her vitamins and provided her other needs. Not long after, she recovered and thought that their suffering must have ended.

But destiny had other plans.

Later that year, Typhoon Haiyan devastated Ormoc.

The house that Lizly's family was renting was not spared from the destruction. Once again, they were homeless. Lizly recalled how, during the onslaught of the typhoon, she was holding her child so tightly that she could

曾經，她熱心幫助過鄰居一位老太太，在生活仍然窮苦時，只要擁有什麼，便會和老太太分享。老人家有一塊地，重建房子時，留了一小塊給理芝莉當作回報，於是先生想蓋一間尼帕小屋。

　　尼帕小屋是用椰子細長的葉子、密密綑綁做屋頂，撿拾來的木材為支架，有人很講究地建有美麗條狀的窗戶，有收納的椅子在室內，當作民宿出租，然而理芝莉家的尼帕小屋，只能勉強用來遮風蔽雨。

　　尼帕小屋尚未蓋好，他們發現慈濟和政府同時在蓋屋。於是先住進了政府收容所的十一區，同時理芝莉和先生領了一批人投入蓋大愛屋，眼看著住房漸漸成型，他們欣喜若狂！

　　陽光帶著輕輕的甜味穿透建物隙縫，寬容地照著理芝莉美好的側臉。她的先生用福竹磚砌房時，她一邊照看兒子，一邊負責裹上水泥。

　　人生三十幾，她的雄心在命運的作弄裏反覆出錯、反覆練習，如今，那些挫敗都變成甜蜜資糧，這裏才是她踏實生活的地方，望著先生認真工作的身影，那麼幸福，那麼安心！

　　二〇一六年，兒子三歲了，他們開心地搬進奧莫克大愛村。

　　她開始學習美甲和按摩，賺取微薄工資，減輕先生的負擔。先生回到奧莫克市工作，建設公司為他租了摩托車，由於路途遙遠，方便他來往大愛村與奧莫克市。後來公司不再付錢租車，他只好放棄工作。

　　這讓理芝莉感到心力交瘁，又兼職當洗衣工，有一陣子家裏甚至買不起煮食用的木炭。

not tell if the wetness she felt was from her tears or the rain.

In her younger years, Lizly sought to experience the wonders of this world. But now that she has a son, her mindset has shifted. Lizly remembered the teachings of her religion and came back to her senses.

When an elderly neighbor had needed help, Lizly had gladly extended a hand. Even though she had very little, she shared what she had. Now, this elderly neighbor owned a piece of land. As she was rebuilding her house, she gave a portion of the land to Lizly to repay her kindness. In this new land, Lizly and her husband built a nipa hut.

The roof of their nipa hut is bundled densely with slender leaves from coconut trees and its brackets are made of wood that they have collected. Some people are very particular in designing their windows with beautiful strips, installing retractable chairs inside the house and then renting it out. But Lizly's nipa hut was only good for sheltering the family from the elements.

They learned that Tzu Chi Foundation and the government were building houses at the same time that they were building their nipa hut. They first moved in the 11th district of the temporary shelters that the government had built. From there, Lizly and her husband led a group of people to help build the Great Love Village. Seeing the houses gradually being built, Lizly and the others could not hide their happiness.

The rays of the sun peered through the gaps of the building, caressing Lizly's beautiful face. While her husband was laying the floor bricks, Lizly was responsible for putting cement and taking care of their son.

Although she was only 30 years old, she already had her fair share of misfortune because of several wrong decisions that she had made. Soon after, she realized that the Great Love Village is where she should live. The series of unfortunate events had become the catalyst that she needed to continue

生命的激流原來仍有淺灘，輕快跳過平坦的卵石，不意又再度掉進另一個漩渦，她意識到自己點燃的微光，只是如一盞昏黃的紙燈籠！蠟燭燃盡一切都暗下來，又或者手輕微顫抖，火苗便將紙燈籠燃燒殆盡……

　　她想起生產時大量出血，生命面臨危機，醒來看見的那盞燈，使她堅信恩典必有其深意，決定自告奮勇向那盞光明的大燈推薦自己，成為了一名慈濟職工。

　　她的工作是守衛會的成員之一，每晚在村子裏巡視，維持大愛村的和平與秩序。為此，每當慈濟有大型活動，比如佛誕日、歲末祝福等，她總是志願承擔。

　　時間是易被淡忘的日用品，裝在日日頂著的腦袋，卻不是最好的行李。

　　理芝莉的生活稍微輕鬆一點，就又放縱起來。

　　有段時間，她老和大愛村一群同齡人出去玩，喝了酒，彷彿重回十幾歲的年輕時代，那些細瑣音聲誘惑著她。直到午夜夢迴醒來，想起每日進出慈濟辦公室，聽著證嚴法師的《人間菩提》開示，心中滿是懊惱與懺悔！

　　喝酒的人怎能守護大愛村的安全呢？辦公室牆上貼著「慈濟十戒」，雖然她不是佛教徒，但她特別記取法師的教誨，為自己的不負責任流淚了！

　　想著自己的人生轉啊轉的，因為慈濟的幫助生活才過得平安，她望著窗外模糊交錯的樹葉與月影，決心不再像蒲公英的種子飄飛不定。

　　如今，除了成為守衛會的一員，她也是水資源系統的抄表

living her life. Watching her husband work, she was reassured that this time, everything will turn out fine.

In 2016, when her son was already three years old, Lizly's family finally moved in to Tzu Chi's Great Love Village in Ormoc City. She learned to give manicures and massages to earn a meager income and augment her husband's salary. Her husband went back to Ormoc. The construction company where he used to work rented a motorcycle so he could travel to and fro the Great Love Village and the city proper. But after a while, he quit the job because the company was no longer willing to pay the motorcycle rent. Lizly realized she had to help, so she took a job as a laundry woman. Money was tight that they could not even afford to buy charcoal to cook their meals.

In life's raging current, there are always shallow shores. As we jump across the rocks, we may fall into a swirl if we are not mindful. Lizly realized that she is like a feeble candle light inside a paper lantern. If the candle burns out, everything goes dark. A gentle trembling of the hand could also burn the paper lantern down.

She remembered the time when she was giving birth to her son and almost bled to death. Her life was put at risk, but after recovering, she knew that her life was spared for a reason. She decided to do something worthy: she became a Tzu Chi volunteer.

She is now a member of the Peacekeepers team of the Great Love Village. Her job is to patrol the village every night and help maintain peace and order. As a volunteer, whenever Tzu Chi Foundation would conduct a large-scale event, such as Buddha Day, Yearend Blessing Ceremony, etc, she is always willing to participate.

But after some time, Lizly found herself going back to her old ways. She would gamble and drink alcoholic drinks. When the brief moment of pleasure has passed, she would realize that she has done something wrong. Once, she

員之一，更是慈青三位領隊之一。她也協助健康中心，每個月三次的孕婦產前檢查。她拍照、錄影，然後把訊息傳給負責人，以掌握整個大愛村的利益與安全。

　　月夜下巡視大愛村，她在心中對尊敬的法師說：「當我遠遠拍照，衡量著自己與慈悲的距離，過去總是得理不饒人，現在即便別人說我的謠言，我也會靜靜觀照自心，不再做無意義的爭辯。因為有您，我理解到湖面的寬度只是肉眼的境界，如果我真正去尊重、感恩並愛惜別人，便不會再有淺薄的計較！」

浴佛節將至，理芝莉與志工一同練習〈呷菜上蓋讚〉推廣素食的閩南語歌謠，跳得笑呵呵！
As the celebration of Buddha Day draws near, Lizly and the other volunteers cheerfully practice the Taiwanese song entitled "*Veggie is the Best*" to promote vegetarianism.

woke up in the middle of the night, remembering everything that she has learned from Tzu Chi Foundation as well as from listening to Dharma Master Cheng Yen's "Life Wisdom". Lizly knew in her heart that she had to change for the better.

How could she safeguard the safety of the village if she is drunk? The Ten Precepts of Tzu Chi Foundation were posted in their office. Although she is not a Buddhist by faith, she clearly remembers the teachings of Master Cheng Yen. She was disappointed with herself and began to cry because she has, for a time, become irresponsible.

Thinking of how her life was changed with Tzu Chi's help, she stared outside the window, reflecting. She decided not to become a dandelion seed that drifts in the wind, with no direction.

In addition to being a member of the Peacekeepers, Lizly is now one of the meter readers for the village's water resources service. Besides that, she is among the three supervising volunteers of the Tzu Ching Group. At the village's health center, Lizly is also responsible for assisting in the monthly prenatal health checks for pregnant villagers. She also took photos and videos, and then send these to the person in charge to communicate the developments and activities in the Great Love Village.

Under the moonlight, while patrolling the village, Lizly said of the Dharma Master, "As I take pictures from afar, and gauge my distance to compassion, I would recall how I used to disregard other people, believing that my decision is always right. But now, even if I hear rumors about me, I would just let it pass and look deep into my heart and stop making petty arguments. Because of the Master, I understand now that the width of the lake is often perceived based on the limited view of the naked eyes. If I truly respect with gratitude and cherish others, I will not get involved in shallow disputes."

(Translated by Celia Chang)

大衛 David Lumacang

尋找一葉葉幸運草

Dreams Made of Clover

大衛（前排左一）與泛尼托、理芝莉一起領導慈青做家訪、急難救助等，也深入經藏演繹，並深深感動。

David (first from left in the front row), together with Juanito and Lizly, led the Tzu Chings in the home visitations and emergency relief aid distributions. They also focused on the sutra adaptation performance and were deeply touched.

如夏夜的晚風一般溫柔，傍晚的天空，深深的紫中帶有橘黃雲彩，美麗交織的互補色，為何大自然什麼都懂？

奧莫克的潔淨天空，如少女穿著顏彩的裙擺飛揚，又如隨風撒上鮮豔的一幅沙畫，夜晚時，感覺星子們都還在彩布上閃爍著。

一位美麗的女孩咯咯淺笑，挽著父親的手輕輕私語，談笑著在曠野草長中悠哉悠哉漫步。他們與幾隻羊兒打了招呼，往回家的路上慢慢游移，我低頭取出手機想拍下那美麗的畫面，但手腳總是溫吞，不知不覺已經落後一段距離。

拍照時，少了一頭羊兒，就少了一點故事；雲朵色澤被吹散了，便聚不出初見時鮮濃的模樣，於是那分恬靜淡了幾分。

小小幾個因素不再，味道就變了；要在合適的季節，遇見

The wind is gentle in the summer night. Late in the afternoon, the sky turns purple and the clouds become orange. The colors complemented so well, it made the sky look even more beautiful. How can nature express all the pretty things in the world? Each day, it is as if a girl wearing a colorful dress dances across the skies of Ormoc, or a sand painting with bright colors is spread out in the sky.

A beautiful girl held her father's hand and giggled. Smiling and whispering to each other, they walked slowly through a grass field towards their home. Along the way, they found themselves greeting a goat that they have encountered as if it were an old friend. I tried reaching for my phone to take some pictures. I wanted to share this touching moment later but I was too clumsy and missed the chance. The goat must have been spooked and walked away. With just some elements missing in a photo, its message would be entirely different. Perfection is achieved only with the coming together of proper timing, encountering the right person or the right incident, and it is

合適的人或事，都要即時掌握，才能湧現美好。

　　皮膚黝黑、鼻梁上架著黑框四方眼鏡的女孩父親，體格高大挺拔，給人的感覺像位學者，那是今年六十歲的大衛，他與家人是奧莫克大愛屋的首批入住者，兩男一女三個孩子均已成年，步入社會工作。

　　大衛與泛尼托、理芝莉三人是慈青的領導小組，大衛總管財務。

　　海燕風災來襲時，大衛住在滂塔（Punta，西班牙語岬角之意），三層樓的家被海嘯沖得只剩一樓部分勉強能作臨時避難，但是一下雨，水便氾入屋內，地板全溼，使人無法安眠。

　　他們只好住進政府收容所，超過一年，五口之家擠在一個小單間，實在不是辦法。大衛的小兒子想著要修復滂塔的家，這時，大衛聽聞慈濟招聘以工代賑者來建造大愛屋。

　　他從未想過，投入建造大愛屋，並遵守「三好：口說好話、心想好意、身行好事」與「三不：不抽菸、不喝酒、不賭博」，便能住進親手建造的大愛屋裏，這使得他欣喜若狂！

　　「非常高興，因為我們建造的慈濟房屋狀況良好，有完整的設施，如衛浴間、廚房、二至三間臥室和客廳，這跟過去住在一個小單間的收容所相比，簡直是天堂！慈濟的房子如此美好，不僅保有隱私，還有空地可種植蔬菜、開出美麗花朵。」

　　這麼好條件的房子，本以為只是鏡花水月、金色泡沫隨水浮沈的夢境，如今，大衛用雙手捏塑出堅實的碗，盛出一朵朵希望。

　　災難發生前，大衛一家人生活艱苦。他曾受僱於一家電信

seized instantly.

The father who was walking with his daughter is David Lumacang. He has dark skin and wears a pair of black-rimmed rectangular glasses. He is 60 years old, tall and casts the appearance of someone who has a vast knowledge. His family is among the first batch to move into the Ormoc Great Love Village. David has three children - two boys and a girl. They are stepping into society to begin working.

Along with Juanito Suco and Lizly Fuentes, David leads the Ormoc Tzu Ching Group. David is in-charge of the group's finances. His family was living in Barangay Punta when Typhoon Haiyan struck Leyte in 2013. "Punta" is a Spanish word that means "a cape point" in English. Due to its proximity to the sea, David's three-story house was smashed by the typhoon. In the aftermath, only the first floor remained, though it also sustained significant damage. Despite this, the family remained in that house after the storm has passed. However, the roofs leaked when it rained, swamping the floor with rainwaters. Under such conditions, it was impossible to get a good night's sleep.

Eventually, they moved into a government-provided temporary shelter where they stayed for over a year. For their family of five members, they were given a single small room. Inside, it was too crowded that five people could not sleep comfortably. David's youngest son decided to repair their home in Barangay Punta so the could move back there. While the family was struggling under the situation, David heard about Tzu Chi's "Cash-for-Work" program which invites typhoon victims to help out in building the Great Love houses from the ground up. David did not expect that by joining the program, and by abiding by the Three Goods (Good words, Good intentions, Good deeds) and Three Nos (No smoking, No drinking, No gambling), they would be among the beneficiaries of the houses. Nonetheless, he was ecstatic!

"I am satisfied. The Great Love house is perfect for our family. It is complete with the essential facilities. It has a toilet and bathroom, a kitchen,

公司，負責維持無線電設備，後來被迫辭職。他失業了，妻子是單純家庭主婦；大女兒每週三次家教，收入微薄；小兒子經營一個互聯網小咖啡店，每天所得僅約一百披索，家庭經濟頓時陷入困境。

還在發愁，海燕災難旋即來湊熱鬧，讓他愁上加愁。

在最大的悲傷之前，僅能眼睜睜望著眼前的痛苦，空洞無淚的眼睛盡是黑暗，卻忘了要堅定生活的信念，去相信背後必有光亮降臨。

住在政府收容所那一年，他幫一個政府組織美化房子、修理樓梯、建造長椅凳，很受組織肯定，但那畢竟是暫時的工作，每天賺一百五十披索。是慈濟在人生最低潮時給了他希望，他在大愛村以工代賑建屋，一天是現金兩百五十披索，這才足夠解決一家五口生活所需。

心上掛著一個大問號，大衛很擔心這些是否也只是暫時？那些承諾有一天會消失嗎？因為所有的 NGO 都已離開。

「後來，我從慈濟得到啟示，當時我們還在修建村屋。每天清晨八點，聽志工講述證嚴法師創立慈濟的歷史，我拿到許多法師的開示文影本，一份份珍惜收藏。」對於證嚴法師的教導，他萬分珍重，尤其喜歡《靜思語》，每當感到沮喪或疲乏時，一句法語就能給他無限的力量！

下午四點收工時，換以工代賑者分享付出後的心靈感受，大衛會把早上聽法做成的筆記，和鎮日心得對照，再說出看法。透過聞法與自省，他從中得到生命的沈澱與感動！

很遺憾的，之後啟德風災氾濫大愛村，大衛丟失了所有影

three comfortable bedrooms and a living room. Compared to the small unit in the government shelter where we had stayed, our new home is a paradise. The house that Tzu Chi had built for us are beautiful and gives us our privacy. It even comes with a yard, allowing us to plant vegetables and beautiful flowers," David shared. David never thought they would own a house very suited to their needs. And for now, David is using both of his hands to build their future that is filled with hope.

David's life was filled with suffering even before Typhoon Haiyan hit. He used to work as a maintenance man at a telecommunications company. However, the company forced him out. His family had faced severe financial difficulties after he lost his job. His eldest daughter, a tutor, worked three times a week and earned very little. David's youngest son owned a small coffee shop and usually earned around 100 pesos a day. Collectively, their incomes could not support the family. At this difficult period in their lives, Typhoon Haiyan struck, further compounding their situation. At that time, they could not see yet where those challenges will take them. They were only focused on their sorrow. They could only see darkness ahead of them. They forgot to believe in their strength and that there is hope awaiting them at the end of this dark tunnel.

During his stay at the government-provided temporary shelters, David worked for an organization that helped remodel houses, repair the stairs and build a bench and stool. They did a wonderful job with the remodeling and David liked the work, but it was only temporary and paid only 150 pesos a day. In his darkest time, Tzu Chi came and gave him hope. David and his family were granted a house unit at the Great Love Village and as he helped build his home and his fellow typhoon survivors', David was also receiving 250 pesos daily allowance from Tzu Chi. This was enough to provide for his family's needs.

Our life is simple and happy in our youth. But as we grow older, things get more complicated. In our minds, we always carry a big question mark

本，這讓他心碎。天黑時最接近夢想，樹葉飄落時渴望堅強，大衛更加奮發在下午三點收看《人間菩提》，重新記錄法師的談話。

住進大愛村時，從星期一到星期五，大衛被指定做資源回收。他從證嚴法師的談話裏，深深理解到環保的重要性，因此賣力不懈地做得很歡喜。星期六，他們有個出售二手衣稱作「TABU-TABU MARKET」的小店，他將小店所得充入菲律賓慈濟慈善基金。

「海燕風災發生之前，我的生活很艱難，沒有工作，如今我成為慈濟志工，這些工作為我帶來許多快樂，因為我不僅改變了自己，同時也能幫助其他人。」大衛閃亮的眼神充滿動人的真誠，發出肺腑之言。

他的心中有一個巨大的希望，「證嚴法師讓我比過去更具同情心，教會我成為一個善良的人，我學習到付出無所求，這讓我常保一顆無欲無求、自在與快樂的心。」

大衛是奧莫克青年助學金的主持者，他還陪伴卡南加的助學生人文班，處理他們的交通費、學校各項雜支與學費、伙食費、學習用品、制服開銷等。若是學生家庭狀況改善，可以自己支付，就不需要再由慈濟基金會提供。

每當助學金付款時，學生必須先簽署，然後才能支付學費。

「證嚴法師常說：『我們做人要誠、正、信、實。』誠實是最重要的事情，這樣你才能獲得別人的信任。」大衛被委以如此重責大任，是因為他遵循著這分崇高的教導。

大衛好比那小小鳥兒，他開始學飛，過程中或許有挫敗，

for things that we do not understand. And as we become more and more suspicious, our life becomes one of suffering. So it goes for David. He was worried that their happy state will not last long. All the non-government organizations he came across with have left after the initial phase of their disaster relief operations. David was convinced Tzu Chi will be no different.

"I used to get inspiration from Tzu Chi. We learned about the history of Tzu Chi and Master Cheng Yen's teachings while we were building the houses," he said. Every morning at 8 o'clock, David would receive several copies of a single-page teaching materials. He kept each page as if it were a treasure. Jing Si Aphorisms are his favorite. Each Jing Si Aphorism seems to nourish his strengthen in his moments of weakness.

Every afternoon at 4 o'clock, the workers would share about their experiences and how they feel about being part of the "Cash-for-Work" program. David would use the teaching materials he had received that morning and would add his own thoughts when his turn to speak comes. David had learned a great deal from the Master's teachings. Unfortunately, he lost all the teaching materials he had collected when Tropical Storm Kai-Tak flooded the village in December 2017. David was saddened.

When the sky turns dark, it is the time we are closest to our dreams. A tree that sheds its leaves is only preparing itself to grow bigger and stronger. So instead of moping over his loss, David became even more diligent in his cultivation. He listened to the Master's "Life Wisdom" every afternoon at 3 o'clock. And, he began to keep a record of the Master's teachings again.

When he moved into the Great Love Village, he was assigned to help with Tzu Chi's recycling work. He recognized the importance of environmental protection from the talk of Master Cheng Yen, so he worked very hard and thoroughly enjoyed his task. Every Saturday, David would sell second-hand clothes at the "TABU-TABU MARKET". He would donate all the proceeds to Tzu Chi to become charity fund.

各種氣流干擾他學習飛翔，但在被啟蒙與醞釀的慈悲中，大衛逐漸成熟，帶領著慈青們尋找一葉一葉的幸運草。

他時時將法師的教誨放在心裏，並將其應用在日常生活中。他從法師那兒學習到最重要的一點，是「多用心」。

他的面部表情看似冷峻嚴格，但心卻是那麼熱那麼柔軟。所謂「冷暖自知」的生活裏，大衛不再有憂慮，有再多的困惑攤在眼前，他相信只要抱著用心學習的角度面對，任何事都會明明了了地展現它的存在，必有其恩典。

每天下午三點證嚴法師《人間菩提》時間，大衛總是非常認真勤做筆記，並反覆思索法師的開示。

Every day at three in the afternoon, the program "Life Wisdom", which is delivered by Master Cheng Yen, comes on TV. David would pay serious attention, diligently take notes and review the Master's teaching.

"My life before Typhoon Haiyan was very difficult because I did not have a job. Now I have a better life as I have become a Tzu Chi volunteer. Tzu Chi works have brought me a lot of happiness. I am not only changing myself but I am also learning to help others," David's eyes are shining with moving sincerity. His words came directly from his heart, which is also full of hope. "Master Cheng Yen has made me more compassionate than before. She taught me to be a kind person and I have learned to give without expecting anything in return. This helps keep my mind happy and free from desires."

David helps manage the accounts payable of the educational assistance program for the Ormoc youth. He also helps with Tzu Chi's Humanities class for the scholars in Kananga. His responsibilities are handling their transportation, school miscellaneous, food and uniform expenses, as well as tuition fees. If the students' financial situation improves, and they can shoulder their own expenses, then Tzu Chi does not have to subsidize. Whenever a scholarship grant gets approved, David must get the signature of the concerned student in order to release the tuition fees. Master Cheng Yen often said, "We must have sincerity, integrity, honesty, and be trustworthy." Honesty is the most important thing in gaining people's trust. David was commissioned for his job because he closely followed this noble teaching.

Like a little baby bird, David is continuously learning how to fly. He may have encountered setbacks and frustrations as he tried to navigate his way against the airflow, which interfered with his learning. But in terms of enlightenment and compassion, David is gradually maturing. He is leading the youth to find leaf after leaf of Clover.

He always keeps the Master's teachings in his heart and will put them into practice throughout his life. Master Cheng Yen has changed his life. David believes the most important thing he has learned from the Master is- "to be mindful".

(Translated by Audrey Cheng)

III. 夜再黑永遠有光的線索
Light at the End of the Tunnel

快樂向前行

Happily Moving Forward

雷伊（左一）和妻子雙雙加入慈濟做志工，也認真地和大家一起練習手語歌。
Rey (first from left) and his wife joined Tzu Chi as volunteers. They practiced sign language with the team.

正午時分，豔陽白花使我的眼睛幾乎睜不開，這裏的原野一望無際，好似有神的眷顧，即便乾旱連年，從近處的黃土望去，卻是綠草綿延。

　　我走到一條清澈的河邊，聽人說這兒上游的許多大樹遭人砍伐，有一回下了一場大雨，河水淹上了岸，沖入民宅。但如今，淌淌流水穿過芒果樹與美洲合歡交錯的葉子，與河面親暱地映在一起，卻是如此安靜！和風吹來的時候，一起懶洋洋地晃動。

　　雷伊以前的工作是幫人布置結婚典禮場地，身材高大帥氣，很愛打籃球。一年，三月杜鵑花開時節，正是寂寞十七歲的他，開心地與同村的孩子打籃球，左腳不慎踩到一顆尖石，腳底筋膜發炎、瘀血，痛得厲害。但那時年輕不以為意，他依舊行走自如，慢慢地也就不覺得痛了。

At noon, the sun shines as the whitest of flowers, that one could barely open his eyes. Here, the wilderness is endless. Even though the drought continues, the green grass, as if blessed by God, stretched across the fields. I walked upon a limpid riverside. People said there was a large area of trees being cut down upstream. Not long ago, a heavy rainfall occurred and the river flooded over the banks, crashing into the houses. But nowadays, the turbulent water is flowing beneath the interlaced leaves of the mango trees and American acacia, which reflection on the river looks tranquil. When a gentle wind blows, the trees sway together sluggishly.

Rey is tall and handsome. He loves playing basketball. His previous job was assisting in decorating wedding venues. One day in March, when azaleas were in full bloom, Rey was happily playing basketball with kids from his village when his left foot accidentally stepped on a small sharp stone, inflaming his sole with blood stasis. Despite this, he would still walk as if he was not in pain.

二〇一三年底，二十歲的雷伊已婚並育有二子，海燕颱風引發的海水倒灌，把家園摧毀，而他的腳泡在水裏兩天，左腳底出現傷口，發炎的情況逐漸往上爬到小腿的一半。即使大水已退，但泥濘髒汙仍繼續侵蝕他的痛腳，並開始潰爛，形成蜂窩性組織炎。尋訪醫師多次，但都無人能治癒他潰爛益發嚴重的左腳。他既不方便走路，潰爛的腳也發出惡臭，便再也無法做原本的工作，改為客人理髮。身痛病苦及家園受損重重壓力打擊下，雷伊脾氣變得不好，生活消極沮喪。

　　臺灣慈濟人醫會有次來到村裏義診，雷伊的妻子幫忙做志工，她鼓勵並勸服雷伊出來給慈濟醫師看看。妻子一句：「相信我！」雷伊彷彿抓到茫茫大海裏的一根浮木，來到義診處，醫師建議馬上去馬尼拉大醫院處置。

　　慈濟志工李偉嵩立即陪伴雷伊搭機前往馬尼拉。醫師判定他的腳必須截肢。一聽到「截肢」，雷伊無法接受，返回奧莫克。細菌不但造成傷口潰爛嚴重，更沒日沒夜不停地侵蝕神經，雷伊痛苦難當，陷入憂鬱。

　　李偉嵩再度關懷並陪伴他赴馬尼拉大醫院，此時醫師告知病菌已侵入骨頭，病情嚴重危急，隨時都有可能失去性命。

　　想到妻子與兩個稚齡的兒子，雷伊這回不再堅持，他必須留著生命看孩子長大啊！

　　於是，在百般無奈下，雷伊接受了截肢手術。

　　住在河畔的雷伊，有時望著月亮飄浮於空中，有時又彷彿映在河上靠近他，靠得更近時，水波似乎讓月兒長了翅膀。

　　他知道那不是真的，但那張開的翅膀，好像勉力安撫著吹

In 2013, when he was 20 years old, Rey got married and had two kids. The same year, Typhoon Haiyan came and caused storm surge that destroyed his house and his neighbors'. Rey's feet were soaked in the murky water for two days. Later on, a wound appeared on his left sole and the inflammation slowly spread up to his calf. Even after the water had receded, the infection continued and his foot started to fester, eventually causing severe cellulitis. He consulted with many doctors but no one could treat his foot, which was only getting worse as the days passed. It had become difficult for him to walk, so he was left without a choice but to stop working. He decided to do haircuts instead. Suffering from the pain on his foot and the effects of the typhoon, Rey became ill-tempered and fell into depression.

One day, a team of Tzu Chi International Medical Association (TIMA) from Taiwan was conducting a medical outreach at the village where Rey's wife was also volunteering. She told Rey to have his foot checked by the TIMA doctors. It took some time to persuade Rey to go to the outreach but he eventually did. The doctor advised him to go to a hospital in Manila immediately. Tzu Chi volunteer Alfredo Li accompanied Rey in a flight from Leyte to Manila. There, the attending physician told him that his foot needs to be amputated. Rey could not accept this. Heartbroken, he decided to go home to Ormoc. Later, the bacteria caused serious ulceration and continued attacking his nerves. Rey was in so much pain and fell into serious depression.

Alfredo Li came to visit him again and persuaded him to come back to the hospital in Manila. There, the doctor informed them that the bacteria had already invaded the bones in his foot. The situation was so critical that it was possible to lose his life any moment. Thinking of his wife and two young sons, Rey gave in, "I have to keep living so I could see my children grow up." He eventually agreed to undergo an amputation surgery. Rey, who lives beside the river, sometimes watches the moon slowly drift across the sky. Sometimes, he can see the moon's reflection on the river and it looked like it was growing its own wings. Even though it was not real, the outstretched wings seemed to bring a gust of wind that soothes his heart, giving him courage and inspiration.

過的每一陣風，也包括他的心，這帶給他勇氣與鼓舞。

他開始拄著助行器走路、工作。

三年的光陰如此匆匆，有一天李偉嵩又來探望他，將心比心，不捨他才二十二歲卻要跛著腳一輩子，又想到他為人理髮，如此拄著個助行器總是不便，於是鼓勵他裝義肢。

雷伊的經濟並不寬裕，他知道自己絕對付不起這筆費用。幸運的是，當時扶輪社資助了費用，李偉嵩來來回回陪伴雷伊奔波於奧莫克和馬尼拉之間。一個月而已，雷伊已經適應了義肢，不但走路靈活，工作更是方便，他找回失去已久的自信。

水就是水，參與各種可能，譬如雨、河流、湖泊、海浪、露滴，在這些成為什麼的改變過程中，它都是一個個的故事。

雷伊接受了恩惠，心頭先是一顆晶瑩剔透露滴般的感恩，藉由這露滴，漸漸地開展慈濟之路；而這改變，正如水的演出，一種經驗的總和。雷伊反覆想著，從一切即將落空，到有人陪著他追回自己，這漫長的過程，慈濟人的大愛到底是什麼？怎麼辦到的？

為了找到大愛的答案，雷伊開始與妻子一起當志工。他漸漸發現，大愛就是快樂、滿足、施予、自信。他終於明白李偉嵩不求任何回報地幫助他，是為什麼了……無爭無求的奉獻，才是真快樂！

人生的美麗是一種試探，是為打起精神、勇敢並願意努力站起來的人作準備。在燠熱的奧莫克，就算坐著也能出一身汗，更別說做事了；即使渾身溼透，他和妻子也要跟隨著，連同家裏三歲、四歲的兒子們一起，跟著慈濟往下一個目的地前進。

With this, he started to walk with crutches, and went to work. Three years flew by and Alfredo Li came to visit him again. Alfredo Li was worried that Rey would be walking with crutches for the rest of his life. Rey was only 20 years old at that time. Alfredo Li saw that it was very uncomfortable for Rey to do a haircut, so he encouraged him to consider wearing a prosthetic leg. But prostheses are quite expensive and Rey is not well-off. Luckily, Rotary Club offered to fund his prosthetic leg. Alfredo Li continued to accompany Rey in traveling between Ormoc and Manila. In just one month, Rey had adapted to his new leg until one day, he was able to walk and work again. Rey finally recovered his confidence.

Water is still water even it may take different forms—as rain, river, stream, lake, wave, and dew drop. But all they really are is a story on the process of becoming. Rey had received an act of kindness that filled his heart with gratefulness, like crystal dew. And with this dew, the path of Tzu Chi gradually became clear before his eyes. This transformation is just like how the water undergo change. It is the sum of experiences. Rey kept thinking back to when he thought his life was about to fall apart and then suddenly, someone extended a hand to help him get back on his feet. It had been a long process. Rey was curious, "What is the great love of Tzu Chi? How did they achieve it?" To search for the answer, Rey started to volunteer at Tzu Chi with his wife. He gradually realized that Great Love is bringing happiness, being content, giving willingly, and filled with self-confidence. Rey began to realize why Alfredo Li helped him without expecting anything in return. To give unconditionally brings real happiness.

The beauty of life is an exploration. It is prepared for those who can cheer up, is brave and willing to stand up. In Ormoc, it is so sweltering that sweat covers the whole body even if one is just sitting still. Despite soaking in sweat, Rey, his wife and their sons, who are three and four years old, all began to follow Li to their next destination.

(Translated by Celia Chang)

馬克 Mark Mendoza

最驕傲的事

The Most Glorious Moment

浴佛節當天，馬克將母親以糯米與巧克力、黑糖做的兩百多個傳統點心送給慈濟，以示感恩。

On Buddha Day, Mark's mother made more than 200 traditional snacks for Tzu Chi, which made by sweet rice, chocolate and brown sugar to show their appreciation.

奧莫克大愛村慈濟中小學動土儀式，與二〇一九年五月十二日浴佛大典僅相隔十四天，慈青與慈少都在加緊練習手語。我瞧見一個長髮小女孩，眼睛大而圓亮，也跟著認真比著手語，肢體動作柔軟。小女孩是馬克的妹妹，馬克是大愛村的慈青，二〇一八年十二月曾經到臺灣參加生活營。

馬克的父親在他十二歲時，自房子二樓墜下，摔斷了胳膊，媽媽一出生便沒了雙腿。通常孩子還不懂事時，可能會因為父母親殘疾，在同學的閒言閒語中感到不舒坦，但馬克卻覺得驕傲，因為他的父母勤勞，雖然勞累，依然打起精神工作提供生活所需。同學笑他時，他會捍衛父母，完全不改變對父母的愛和尊重。他感恩父母對他的付出，他接受上帝這樣的賜予。

馬克回憶去臺灣時，觀察到很多慈青在做資源回收，他問

The Buddha Day ceremony on May 12, 2019 and the groundbreaking ceremony for the Tzu Chi Primary and Secondary Schools in Ormoc Great Love Village were only 14 days away from each event. Both Tzu Ching (Tzu Chi Collegiate Youth) and Tzu Shao (Tzu Chi High School Youth) members were stepping up their sign language performance rehearsals. During the practice, I saw a long-haired little girl who has a pair of big round eyes. She was closely following the performers' every hand gesture. The little girl is Mark Mendoza's sister.

Mark is one of the Tzu Ching members in the village who went to Taiwan in December 2018 to attend a retreat camp. Whenever his sister would practice a sign language lesson, she would always ask him if he can teach her Chinese songs.

When Mark was 12 years old, his father fell from the second floor of their house, breaking his arm and leaving him physically challenged. His

自己：「為什麼我不嘗試加入這樣一個組織？」他發覺資源回收不僅為自己，同時改善整個社會與地球環境，抵禦地球暖化。

當他懂得這些道理，便不再害羞去拾取寶特瓶。他了解這不僅是在幫助其他人、幫助環境，最重要的是自己變成一個好人。於是他加入慈青，記取證嚴法師的教誨，也從去臺灣學習到時間管理，目睹證嚴法師二十四小時努力散播大愛，「時間不空過」這句話讓他意識到早起可以做很多事，而不是遲到。

他也參與醫療任務，以及村里老人和病人的家訪。他與其他慈青越過山，去尋找年長而有眼疾的患者，將他們送到醫院讓菲律賓眼科中心的史美勝醫師進行篩檢，並動手術恢復光明，這讓他感到助人的喜悅。他也在大愛村家訪年長獨居者，為他們打掃環境，看到他們露出微笑時，他覺得自己好比一隻輕盈的蜻蜓，用著近乎透明的翅膀，舞動了自己美好的生命。

如果一個人確實有一顆誠摯的心和奉獻的精神，便能毫無猶豫地去助人。如果一個人總是有決心，無論遇到什麼阻礙，都能有辦法去克服。命中注定的事情儘管殘酷，只要相信自己值得被愛，我們便能足夠勇敢去追求生活。

一個驟雨的午後，我們走過泥濘去探望馬克兄妹及其父母，家裏雖只有幾張小椅子、一張小桌，地板卻十分乾淨。馬克的父母露出淺淺微笑，用雙手將糯米、巧克力和黑糖揉成糰，放在抹了層油的香蕉葉上，包成長條狀，再將香蕉葉兩端綁緊。馬克的妹妹偎在父親懷裏練著手語，馬克將母親綁好的香蕉葉剪齊，五個一包裝好，這樣一包甜糕可賣三十五披索。他們會搭三輪車到碼頭去賣，來往宿霧的人們總會買來當伴手禮送人。

mother, on the other hand, was born with stunted legs. Despite his parents' disabilities, Mark was never ashamed of them. Instead, he is grateful that they were his parents.

Gossips may dishearten any child. However, Mark is proud of his hardworking parents. He understands that they do their best to provide for the needs of their family. Whenever his classmates would tease him, Mark would defend his parents. He does not waver in his love and respect for them. He is eternally grateful towards them. For him, his parents are gifts from God.

Recalling his trip to Taiwan, Mark had observed that many Tzu Chings were engaging in the recycling mission. He asked himself, "Why don't I try to join such an organization?" Eventually, he found out that Tzu Chi's recycling effort aims not only to raise funds for the needy and disaster survivors but is preserving the environment and helping the earth withstand the effects of global warming.

When he realized this, Mark was no longer ashamed to pick up discarded plastic bottles. In addition to doing charity and loving Mother Earth, this campaign is also teaching the volunteers on how to become a better person. Because of all these, Mark joined the Tzu Ching group and took to heart the teachings of Master Cheng Yen.

Mark also learned to manage his time wisely during his visit in Taiwan. He watched the Master work 24 hours a day to spread Great Love around the world. "Do not let time slip by vacantly" is the phrase that made him realize that getting up early every day will help him to become more productive. Together with other volunteers, Mark had also gone to the mountains to find older patients with eye problems and help send them to the hospital for screening by Dr. Antonio Say of the Tzu Chi Philippines Eye Center. The surgery helped the patients to restore their eyesight, much to Mark's delight.

Mark had also visited a number of elderly who live all alone in the Great

那個夜晚，他們一家和樂的印象始終仍縈繞我心，想著他們夫婦在碼頭熙來攘往人潮中緩緩匍匐著行進；在豔陽下揮汗賣著甜糕，生活如流水。馬克的母親說：「孩子們在慈濟那兒學習到孝順，也懂事乖巧，我們不僅深深感恩，也寬慰安心。」

　　那些個長長、流下眼淚的日子，最終也有幸福的句點。馬克說，他的志願是當一位將善行報導的主播。夜晚的醋栗樹白色花瓣隨風飄落墨色中，像暗夜裏的星辰點點，與天上一彎上弦月相映，除了寧靜，還有一種善待歲月的美麗心情。

「母親節、佛誕日、全球慈濟日」三節合一慶祝會上，馬克帶領村裏的孩童比手語。
At the three-in-one celebration of "Mother's Day, Buddha Day and Global Tzu Chi Day", Mark led the children in a sign language performance.

Love Village and helped clean their homes. When they smiled, Mark felt as if he was a dragonfly, dancing with near-transparent wings.

If a person has a sincere heart and dedication, he can help others without hesitation. If a person is determined, there is always a way to overcome the obstacles he will encounter. Destiny sometimes can be cruel, but as long as one believes that they are worthy of love, they can bravely pursue life.

One rainy afternoon, we went through the muddy road to visit Mark's parents and siblings. Although they only have a few small chairs and a small table at home, their floor was very clean. Mark's parents gave us a shy smile. They mixed rice, chocolate and brown sugar in a clean and coated layer of oil on the banana leaves, and then wrapped it up with strips and tied both ends of the banana leaves.

Mark's sister snuggled up against her father's arms to practice the sign language. Mark trimmed banana leaves and tied together his mother's rice cakes, five pieces in one bundle. Each can be sold at Php35. They would take a tricycle to the dock to sell these snacks. People who travel to and from Cebu would always buy this as gift for their loved ones.

The joy and harmony in Mark's family that night still lingers in my heart. Mark's mother said, "The children learned filial piety and have become well-behaved in Tzu Chi. We are not only deeply grateful, but also relieved."

Those long and sad days have finally come to an end. Looking ahead, Mark's goal is to become a news anchor who will broadcast people's good deeds in society. The white petals of gooseberry tree fly at night with the wind. They are like the glittering stars in the night sky that complement the moon. Aside from its tranquility, it brings a beautiful ambiance of cherishing our days.

(Translated by Christine Fisk)

羅伯特 Robert Ejada

有個蝴蝶說

The Butterfly Theory

浴佛彩排預演，羅伯特掌鏡頭留下歷史，任務圓滿後，臉上露出滿足的微笑。

During the rehearsals of the Buddha Day ceremony, Robert took pictures to document this historic event. He can be seen smiling, satisfied for another completed task.

奧莫克大愛村附近一個小廣場裏，蔡昇航正在臺上向來參與浴佛的民眾解說《慈悲三昧水懺》的涵義，並為非洲東部水患復甦的艱難而募款。

小廣場外有人賣花生，有人賣冰，也有人賣炸物沾糖，基本上菲律賓人很喜歡吃炸物與甜食。雖然小廣場外美食誘惑多，但是在廣場內學習浴佛的民眾卻極為虔誠，專心凝聽蔡昇航的引導。在為東非水患募款之前，大家沈靜虔誠地雙手合十默禱，然後紛紛踴躍捐款，即便是口袋羞澀的只有五元、一元，沒有一個人坐在原位上不動，不論錢多錢少，愛心是一樣滿滿。

羅伯特是奧莫克大愛村辦公室負責攝影的年輕人，他掌握著不同角度，全神貫注在雙眼的目視鏡裏，把自我置之度外。羅伯特拿到攝影機，自己摸索如何使用，不知是前世他留下來

In a small square in Barangay RM Tan, Michael Siao explains on stage the meaning of "The Compassionate Samadhi Water Repentance" to the attendees of the Buddha Day Ceremony and to also raise funds for the flood victims in East Africa.

Outside the venue, some vendors are selling peanuts, ice cream bars and fried snacks with sugar. Filipinos basically love to eat fried and sweet foods. Although there are many mouth-watery foods outside, the people attending the ceremony attentively listen to Tzu Chi volunteer Michael Siao. Before the donation drive for the East Africa flood victims, everyone prays silently and piously with both palms joined together. Then everyone voluntarily steps forward to make a donation even though they have little money in their pockets. No matter how much the donation is, each contribution is filled with love.

Among the crowd is Robert Ejada, a young photographer from the

的印象？抑或者他是攝影的天才？他如此熱愛攝影，那已經融入成為他生命的一部分。

回程的路上，羅伯特吃著炸物沾糖，他是一位十六歲的慈青，濃濃的眉下一雙虔誠的雙眼，嘴邊總掛著一抹微笑，已經素食五個月。我問羅伯特為何想素食呢？他說在臺灣那段時間，他了解到素食的真正意義是為了拯救地球。

然光是這個觀念應該還不足以撼動他，另有一位慈濟志工分享：「即使你知道助人是多麼美好的事，可是你仍然為了自己的欲望不斷吃肉，有人為了讓你能吃到肉，就會去殺動物，你的肚子其實好比動物的墳場呀！你在助人的同時，卻沒有慈悲心地在吃動物的肉，這是很矛盾的！」

羅伯特才升上高二，他在臺灣見過證嚴法師，由於羅伯特一出生便沒有見過自己的奶奶，因此他把證嚴法師當成了自己的奶奶。證嚴法師受所有人敬重，他愛天底下所有的生命，連走路都要輕踩，怕地球會痛。

這深深讓羅伯特感動，於是他決定用嘴巴救地球！可是羅伯特又遇到一個困難，那就是他的父親是奧莫克公共市場的一名魚販，而母親賣著燒烤，似乎完全素食對他而言十分艱難。為了實踐自己內心的渴望與對自我的承諾，他力勸父母跟著茹素，當然一時半刻要讓雙親改變飲食習慣很難，於是他決定自己做飯。只要是羅伯特自己做飯，就會炒大量的蔬菜，但若是父母做飯，他就只好挑著蔬菜吃。這讓他感到十分焦急與無奈。

有一天，他告訴父母：「有一種說法，提到當你的家人或是愛人往生之後，會變成一隻蝴蝶飛來家裏，我們不會殺了蝴

Ormoc Great Love Village office. He holds the camera with full concentration, focused on capturing images of the people and scenes around him. Since the first time he got hold of a camera, Robert had learned how to use it on his own. Is it a skill that he had learned from his previous life? Or does he just happens to be a photography genius? Since then, Robert has integrated his love for photography in his daily life.

On the way back to Tzu Chi Great Love Village, Robert is seen eating a fried food coated with sugar. He is a 16-year-old Tzu Ching with a pair of pious eyes under his thick eyebrows, and often wears a lovely smile. Robert has been following a vegetarian diet for five months now. When asked why he adopted a vegetarian diet, Robert answered that during his stay in Taiwan he learned that the true essence of vegetarianism is saving the planet.

But this is not the only reason why Robert shifted to this lifestyle. According to him, a sharing from a Tzu Chi volunteer had left a deep impression on him. "The volunteer had said that even though you are creating goodness by helping others, when you still eat meat and other animal products to satisfy your desires, you are turning your stomach into a cemetery. Why? It's because your action is actually against what you believe in, you are still eating animal meat and there is no compassion in that!"

You may know how wonderful it is to help others, but you still eat meat to satisfy your own desires. Animals are killed so you can eat that meat. You are making your stomach a cemetery for animals! It is very contradictory that you are helping others out of compassion while you forgot your compassion when you eat animal flesh!

Robert did not have a chance to meet his own grandmother so when he was a sophomore student and he met Master Cheng Yen, he has considered the Master as his own grandmother.

Master Cheng Yen is well-respected by many people. The Master loves

蝶，因為我們相信那蝴蝶是我們剛剛往生的所愛。所以如果我們相信我們的所愛有可能變成那蝴蝶，也有可能我們的所愛會變成一隻豬呀！因為動物都是有生命的，牠們能感受到痛，也會對人類有感情，當我們要殺牠們的時候，牠們會害怕也會流淚啊……」

自那以後，父母便慢慢開始少吃肉了。

我們需要練習，注視自己敏感、多慮、難以控制的心，才能培養那可貴的慈悲。

在綠樹婆娑花影處處的大愛村裏，羅伯特等志工對村民進行採訪，認真地捕捉畫面。
In the Great Love Village, under the shadows of the trees, Robert and fellow volunteers are interviewing a villager. Robert is always attentive in shooting footages.

all living beings. When she walks, her steps are very light, not wanting to hurt the earth.

The Master's teachings deeply moved Robert, so he decided to follow the Master and help save the Earth by curbing his desire for meat.

But that decision did not come without challenges. Robert's father is a fishmonger at the Ormoc Public Market while his mother sells barbecue. With his parents' jobs, how could he follow a strict vegetarian diet?

Fortunately, Robert is firm and resolute. He requested his parents to also follow a vegetarian diet. But he also understood that it would be difficult for his parents to change their eating habits immediately so he decided to cook his own meals.

Whenever he cooks for the family, Robert would serve a lot of vegetables. But when it is his parents' turn to cook, he had no other choice but to carefully pick and eat only the vegetable ingredients in the dishes they make.

Eventually, he told his parents that, "Catholics believe that if someone dies, their spirit turns into a butterfly. This is why we don't kill butterflies because we somehow believe that they are our loved ones. So if we believe that our loved ones can turn into butterflies, it is also possible that they can turn into pigs. All living beings have feelings and they feel pain. When we try to kill them (pigs), they will feel frightened just like humans would..." Shortly after this, his parents gradually started to eat less meat.

We must make it a habit to reflect on our sensitive, worrisome and uncontrollable minds in order to bring out the compassion we all innately have.

(Translated by Christine Fisk)

維曼 Vicmar Casil

大愛雜貨店

Great Love Grocery

維曼改掉惡習，與妻子在村內開設雜貨店，提供新鮮蔬果給村人選購，滿足如今於大愛村的恬靜生活。

Vicmar and his wife owned a grocery store in the village where they sell fresh fruits and vegetables to the villagers. Nowadays, the couple is satisfied with a quiet life in the Great Love Village.

奧莫克大愛村的家家戶戶前後，都有個能種花種樹的小騎樓。那天，我們在村子裏散了一會兒步，我已經數不完總共有多少樹種和花草了。村民非常愛惜這得來不易的家，想盡辦法讓自己的家園適得其用。

村裏的小朋友看見我們走來，便紛紛從家裏奔出來，恭敬地一一牽起我們的手，搭在他們的額頭上。「這是孩子們對我們表示的一種敬意。」當他們的小手拉著我的手貼近額頭時，我的心有一種怦然的恬靜與感動，於是脫口說：「乖，感恩。」

遠處一戶人家的屋前，正煙灰濃濃地燒著落葉、廢紙，甚至是塑膠，「這是他們的習慣，怎麼勸都勸不住！」「家家戶戶這一天你燒，明天我燒，那豈不是天天都在聞這些戴奧辛的毒氣？」「就是啊！但是我們怎麼宣導還是這樣！」這是大愛

Surrounding every house within Ormoc Great Love Village is a little space for each family to do their own landscaping.

We walked around the village one day. I could not count how many trees, plants and flowers were planted in the neighborhood. Villagers love their hard-won homes, trying their best to make it suitable for their use.

When some young kids in the village saw us, they quickly ran to us and took our hands to their foreheads because this practice is a customary way of showing respect among Filipinos.

My heart skipped a beat and was very moved when my hand touched a young kid's forehead. I said: "Good boy, thank you!"

In the distance, I noticed a fire in front of a house. Someone was burning leaves, papers and other trash. "Regardless of how much effort we put

村的頭號問題。

就在此時，我們站在一棵高大的醋栗樹下，醋栗多毛的綠葉伸展得很長，彷彿秋香綠的長袖般，風吹時整株樹隨著幾百條舞袖搖動起來，綠袖上的白花與成熟了的紅果子紛紛落下。紅果子很甜，白花如雪，煞是美麗。如此簡單的幸福感，在過去，奧莫克大愛村的村民們是不曾有過的。

醋栗樹下的人家開了間雜貨店，貨品從家裏的客廳滿滿地一直擺到騎樓，再以木板伸展到醋栗樹的兩側，雜貨、大米、木炭、木柴甚至電腦的出租，看似應有盡有。男主人維曼，身強體壯，眼睛雪亮。

李偉嵩說：「這是奧莫克大愛村最大的雜貨店。」維曼的妻子狄蘭（Dayline）露出微笑禮貌地拚命點頭，李偉嵩用萊特島的方言與夫婦倆寒暄，不久他們的兒子馬爾（Mar Vincent）從屋內走出，向李偉嵩恭敬地點頭後，羞澀地笑了。

李偉嵩回頭用中文說：「維曼的好友給他電腦，讓他出租，然後從中賺取百分之三十的利潤。這人很會打算盤。」我笑一笑，因為我是最不會打算盤的那個。

李偉嵩看見他家後院用竹籬笆圍了起來，那是違規的，因為會影響他人的出入。狄蘭一直解釋，李偉嵩給她建言，最後她妥協了。

奧莫克大愛村能維持秩序，多半靠著大家信服李偉嵩的恩威並濟，另方面也靠著愛惜家園的那分自律。唯獨市政府鋪路的承諾尚未能兌現，一下雨，泥濘難行，車過留下深深的凹痕。

離開前，李偉嵩與馬爾寒暄了幾句。我好奇地問李偉嵩剛

forth to persuade them not to, the residents still burn their trash in the yard."

"The residents here would be exposed to dioxins if many families take turns in burning their trash." This is the number one problem in the village that I see.

Meanwhile, we stood under a tall gooseberry tree, the long, yellowish, hairy green leaves extended out as if they were long sleeves! When the breeze blew, hundreds of leaves began dancing with white blossoms and red fruits. This made such a beautiful scene in front of us.

Before the villagers moved into the Ormoc Great Love Village, such a simple happy life was an impossible dream for them!

One family lives nearby the gooseberry tree and owns a grocery. His products were laid out from the living room to the outside, stretching towards the wooden boards beside the gooseberry tree. Whatever one needs, the store seems to have it for sale: groceries, rice, charcoal, wood, even computer for rent.

The owner, Vicmar Casil, is a well-built man with bright eyes.

Alfredo Li said: "This is the largest grocery in Ormoc." The owner's wife, Dayline, nodded with a smile. Alfredo chatted with them in the Leyte dialect.

Later, their son, Mar Vincent, walked out of the house and nodded at us with a shy smile.

Alfredo turned around and told us in Mandarin: "A good friend of Vicmar offered him computers for rent and gets 30% commission from the sales. This friend is good at calculating."

I laughed for I am not good in that.

剛聊了什麼？

李偉嵩說：「這是一個翻轉人生的故事。」

「維曼尚未住進大愛村時是扒手，跟著壞朋友到宿霧、馬尼拉行竊。他要是不如意、心情不佳，就抽菸、喝酒，跟妻子吵架。壞朋友一來找，他就出去玩不回家，也不告訴家人行蹤，脾氣暴躁，使家庭陷入愁雲慘霧中。

海燕風災後，他們被分配到奧莫克大愛村居住，這裏環境安靜，也沒有那些誘惑；而他的兒子數學很好，參加國際數學比賽，非常優秀。

因為維曼以前不學好，馬爾的同學就會取笑他、評論他的父親。他把父親的不好轉為一種讓自己更好的動力，獲得學業、體育的好成績，他總是努力學習達到自己期望的目標，但願將來不會再受苦。

維曼發現兒子這麼優秀，在大愛村裏和平的生活，也不似過去住的地方總是吵雜，他想讓自己的兒子得到好教育，努力想成為孩子的好父親。

以前的壞朋友再來找他，他都會推說必須照顧雜貨店，要和妻小在一起。維曼改變了生活的態度，從壞變好，脾氣也從暴躁變得平靜；夫妻倆不再吵架，感情愈來愈好，生活很幸福。

現在他那些壞朋友，有的被政府通緝，有的被抓進牢服刑，而朋友們的孩子總共有九位，都是他在濟助，還接了其中三位來同住。」

古代「孟母三遷」，意喻住的環境、參差的生活，像一個巨大的齒輪在運轉。維曼被不良的事物、朋友林林總總追著逃

Then, Alfredo saw the bamboo fence at the back yard and mentioned that the fence is illegal because it blocks the neighbors' pathway. After contemplating what Alfredo had said, Dayline agreed with the suggestion of adjusting the fence.

Ormoc Great Love Village maintains its order with the guidance of volunteers like Alfredo while also relying on each other's love.

The only regret is that the government has yet to fulfill their commitment of paving the road.

Whenever it rains, the wheels leave deep tracks on the muddy road.

Before leaving, Alfredo talked to Mar for a while. Curious, I asked him what they talked about and he said: "This is a story of turning over a new life."

Before he moved to the village, Vicmar used to follow some of his friends to Cebu or Manila to pick-pocket. Whenever he was in a bad mood, he smoked, drank, fought with his wife, went out with friends without informing his family where he was. The whole family fell into this hell-like situation due to his ill-temper.

After Typhoon Haiyan, they were relocated to the Ormoc Great Love Village. It was a nice, quiet environment that presented no temptations. Additionally, his son, being so outstanding in math, was chosen to participate in an international competition.

In the past, the children used to tease and laugh at Mar because of his father's bad records. However, Mar turned that ridicule into a source of power and spared no effort in school and sports so as to reach his goal for a much brighter future.

Vicmar finally realized that he had such a wonderful son and a lovely

亡，他的心真的累了。隨順因緣來到奧莫克大愛村，這裏的樸實讓他漂泊的心定了下來。他思考著人生最重要的是什麼？是他的家，是行善。所謂積善之家必有餘慶，永恆不變的是一個信念的倚靠。

　　傍晚了，彩霞由黃到深橘、紅豔，美到讓人發呆。許多的美好保護著我們，但一開始也許不是美的形式，所有滿布驚惡的細節，有如天黑的時候，要勇敢一點，選擇一個值得苦苦追求的目的地，去努力翱翔！翻轉出一片自由而美善的天空！

維曼（後排左三）過去的損友入獄後，他不僅收留他們的孩子，還供應他們念書，努力成為讓兒子引以為傲的好父親。
When Vicmar's (third from left at the back row) friend was imprisoned, Vicmar took in his friend's children and sent them to school. He promised himself that he would be a good father and do his best to make his son proud.

living environment. He wanted his son to have a better education than himself and he wants to be a much better father.

He began changing his life and got rid of old friends who were bad influence. He now wants more time with his family. He changed his attitude towards life: no more ill temper, no more fights with wife.

He began to cherish everything that he has and he actually feels happy!

As to his old friends, some have been among the police's "wanted" list while others are serving their time in jail. Vicmar now takes care of these friends' nine children. Three of whom are even living with his family.

Vicmar's story echoes an old, historical Chinese story titled "Mencius's Mother Moving Three Times" that talks about a parent finding a better environment for her children and their future.

The drastic change in their lives after moving into the Great Love Village put Vicmar's mind at peace.

He began setting new priorities and preferences in life. The answers he found are: his home, his family, and doing good deeds! These will be his life-time beliefs!

As the sun started going down, the color of the sky began to change from yellow to deep orange to bright red! The stunning beauty of the sunset is too spectacular to stare at! When surrounded by beauty, do not ignore it, there may be something under or behind it.

Be brave and courageous in the dark! When the target is set, go for it! You may turn over a new leaf! A free and beautiful blue sky lies ahead of you!

(Translated by Helena Lin)

莎德拉娜 Sandrane Pepito

遇見美麗人生

A Beautiful Life

情人節當天，莎德拉娜參與孝親活動，跪在黃土石礫上，為從事木工
的父親洗足、按摩。
On Valentine's Day, Sandrane Pepito was kneeling down on the loess
gravel, washing her carpenter father's feet and giving him a massage.

有時我覺得好奇，渴望知道有誰會在哪裏與我相遇，也許在
某個轉彎處是一隻小花貓？或是一隻可愛的狗兒？或是一
片花海？樹林？活在這個人間，每一刻總是充滿驚奇。尤其在
奧莫克大愛村裏散步時，常常驚喜地遇見不知名的美麗花朵。

莎德拉娜個頭小小，長髮綁了兩條馬尾，笑起來很甜美。
她有個當木匠的父親，和替人幫傭的母親，兩人不曾受什麼教
育，因此對家裏三個孩子懷抱希望，夫妻倆齊力奮鬥著。當莎
德拉娜被診斷出腎臟有問題，他們非常焦慮卻束手無策，直到
慈濟幫助莎德拉娜就醫，讓她恢復了健康。因為莎德拉娜體弱，
起初父母不贊成她加入慈青，但是她覺得「受人點滴，當湧泉
以報」，堅決投入。

柔順的草，反而更有韌性毅力，白色的花朵看似樸素，卻

Sometimes I am curious and eager to know who or what I will meet. Maybe it will be a kitten? Or a cute dog? Or a sea of flowers? A forest, perhaps? Living in this world, every moment is filled with little surprises, especially when walking in the Ormoc Great Love Village. I am often surprised to encounter beautiful flowers which are not familiar to me.

Sandrane Pepito is a little girl who wears her hair in pigtails. She has a very sweet smile.

Her father is a carpenter. Her mother is a domestic helper. The two had never received any formal education. Although they struggle, they have big dreams for their three children.

When Sandrane was diagnosed with a kidney problem, they were very anxious but were unable to do much for her. It was the Tzu Chi volunteers who helped Sandrane to seek medical treatment.

更能發出香氣！莎德拉娜到臺灣參加生活營，此行共有四十位菲律賓本土慈青參加，由愛心人士為他們籌措來回機票等費用。

營隊期間，她看到一個影片，關於犧牲動物性命以滿足人類的口欲，她發覺動物和人類一樣有感情也有恐懼，因此深感難過而流淚、不捨，決定茹素來拯救動物。

莎德拉娜身體不好，父母擔心素食營養不足，但是莎德拉娜決意再也不吃肉，她不想讓牠們充滿靈性的生命消失。自從素食之後，莎德拉娜不但不似以往老是發燒、咳嗽、感冒，還變得強壯，讓父母也放心，接著她又影響姊姊開始素食。

在慈濟，她學習把心交在手裏，再交付出去，她不讓自己的歲月空懸，比過去更長智識，也不再脆弱了。

莎德拉娜的祖父母住在蘇里高（Surigao），距離她住的地方很遙遠。每當她跟著慈青去做家訪，幫獨居的長者打掃，感受到年長者內心的喜悅，就好像與自己的祖父母相處一般，備覺安慰。她意識到，整個奧莫克大愛村就像一家人那般親近；滿滿的喜悅，迴盪在她的心間。

助人的日子裏，陽光晒著她的頭髮和頸項，微微發燙，彷彿有人撫著她的頭說：「你真好！」風從山谷吹出，聲音聽著像是透明的，她的心情也是澄澈通透。

自己曾經歷病苦，莎德拉娜立願成為一名醫師，隨著身體的強健，她的心志也更加堅定。她想學中文，想到臺灣讀醫學院，想了解讓人健康的要素在哪兒，她的使命是探求恢復健康的密碼，去造福人群。

莎德拉娜對證嚴法師有滿滿的話要說：「感恩您給予我們

Since Sandrane is sickly, her parents did not approve of her joining Tzu Ching at first. However, Sandrane felt indebted to those people and she is resolute to repay what they had invested in her.

The supple grass seems especially resilient and persevering. The white flowers look simple, yet emit a sweet fragrance!

After joining Tzu Ching, Sandrane had an opportunity to attend the retreat in Taiwan in December 2018. On this trip, forty Filipinos participated. Caring people raised money for the Tzu Chings' round-trip airfare tickets and other expenses throughout their stay in Taiwan.

During the retreat, Sandrane watched a film about how animals are being sacrificed to satisfy human's palate. From the film, she witnessed that animals, like humans, feel fear and wish to live.

She felt sad and cried during the session. In that moment, she decided to become a vegetarian to save animals' lives, slow down the effects of global warming and mitigate natural disasters.

But her parents were woried that a vegetarian diet will harm her health, especially since she was too sickly. However, Sandrane was determined not to eat meat anymore.

Surprisingly, a vegetarian diet kept Sandrane healthier. She rarely gets fever, cough or cold after she made the shift. This put her parents's hearts at ease.

In Tzu Chi, Sandrane learned through hands on experience. She would not allow time to pass by idly, and has become wiser and is no longer vulnerable.

Sandrane's grandparents are in Surigao, which is quite far from where

所有的祝福和愛，我將繼續將您的愛散播，完成您的任務，我要成為一名醫師在醫療任務中去解救那些受傷的災民，撫平他們心中的傷痕。因為您改變了我的生活，讓我成為善良的人，讓我意識到即便我不富裕，一樣能用一顆真心和雙手，給予愛、分享生活，這些才是生命中最美好的事！」

此心安處不再有一絲猶疑，正午陽光傾入窗口，靜靜亮在莎德拉娜微笑的臉上，她與「希望」靠得好近好近。也許莎德拉娜就是我在奧莫克大愛村散步時，驚奇遇見的一朵美麗小花。

莎德拉娜（右一）加入慈青後，不但有很多志同道合的好朋友，同時愛上中文，並努力學習助人。
Sandrane Pepito (right) joined the Tzu Ching Association and met many like-minded friends. Simultaneously, she loved the Chinese language and tries her best to learn how to help people.

she presently lives. Each time she joins her fellow Tzu Chings in visiting and helping the elderly villagers who live alone, it is as if she is visiting her grandparents. She realized that the entire Ormoc Great Love Village is as close as a family, full of heartfelt joy.

During the days she participated in charity missions, the sun bathed her hair and neck making it warm. It was as if someone was stroking her head and telling her: "You are so good!" A breeze blew from the valley, and she heard the voice distinctly.

Her experiences as a patient led Sandrane to dream of becoming a doctor someday. As her body grows stronger, her mind gets even more determined.

She wanted to learn Chinese and to attend a medical school in Taiwan. She's looking forward to understand the elements of human health, by exploring the key to revitalizing health, and bring blessings to mankind.

Sandrane has nothing but kind words for Master Cheng Yen: "Thank you for giving us your blessings and love. I will continue to spread your love and carry out your mission. I want to be a doctor and be part of Tzu Chi's medical outreach to treat injured disaster victims and to heal the scars in their hearts."

"Because you changed my life and made me a kind person, I realized that even if I am not wealthy, I can give love from my heart and hands. Sharing compassion and love are the best feelings in life!"

There is not a trace of hesitation in Sandrane's heart. The mid-day sun pouring through the window falls quietly on her smiling and hopeful face. Perhaps Sandrane is one of the beautiful flowers that I saw during my walks at the Ormoc Great Love Village.

(Translated by BT Lin)

瑪恬 Marithel Valiente

志願報導美善

Reporter in Action

浴佛節當天，村裏孩童要表演手語歌「人間有愛」，一早瑪恬陪著孩童們在樹蔭下練習。

For the Buddha Day ceremony, the children will be performing the sign language "*Love in The World*." In the morning of the event, Marithel and the children were rehearsing the performance under the shade.

近傍晚的交易市場，遠看像一艘翻轉的船掛在空間裏，因為天色漸漸暗下，支撐的細長柱子隱隱約約。孩子們還在那艘「船」下練著手語，影子隨著音樂整齊擺動，另一處操場則鼓樂聲鏗鏘不斷。

彩霞布滿天空，油彩般的許多顏色，以非常緩慢的速度轉換著，下沈，漸漸消失。

地球是圓的，我常想那沒入的遠方是否有河流，有不知所終的下游？

瑪恬突然從背後抱住我說：「Auntie SUSU，我想您一直待在奧莫克。」

這個直心的女孩看起來這麼瘦小，卻已經二十歲，高三畢業，申請臺灣慈濟大學想念傳播系，但因為語言問題而無法如

In the late evening, the village market looks like a boat that had flipped over. Its supporting slender pillars flicker when the sky gets darker. The children were practicing sign language songs under the "boat". Their shadows were moving in time with the music while drum beats can be heard in the distance.

The sky, stained with glamorous colors, seemed to cast an image of an oil painting in the sky. Since the globe is a sphere, I wondered if there are rivers flowing downstream at the farthest ends of the world, or is there no end to the downstream?

While basking in the beauty that surrounded me, someone suddenly embraced me from behind. It was Marithel Valiente, a thin fragile 20-year-old girl who was pleading: "Auntie SuSu, I hope you can always stay in Ormoc." Marithel has such a pure heart. She just graduated from senior high school and her dream is to apply to the Tzu Chi University in Taiwan and study Communications. Although the language barrier is a challenge, Marithel

願。她並沒有因此而放棄，對自己的信念很堅強。

瑪恬的母親生了六個孩子，父親很早往生，她從未見過父親。母親以雙手為人洗衣撐起一個家，度過很長一段缺米缺糧的日子。

在這樣艱難的環境下，瑪恬怎麼長得高？她能這麼美好地活著已是萬幸。

幾隻飛鳥停在一旁的路燈頂端，再過不久，所有的風景都將轉暗，路燈就在牠們腳下亮起了。

我反手抱瑪恬拍她瘦小的肩，深深呼吸，想像風在我的體內透過那手掌安撫孩子的孤寂，願她的心在痊癒與傷害兩種力量的彼此耗損中得到調息。

她告訴我，以前不認識慈濟時，曾對母親是洗衣婦而不屑一顧，常與母親吵架，因為她的心稜角處處。母親說她不是時，她總是一再頂嘴，容不得任何一粒沙。

她無法用心體察那雙支撐一家的手，每日在洗衣時可能有過多少傷痕，那些傷痕在失去伴侶後，心裏的無依又是多麼脆弱？但為了六個孩子，母親告訴自己沒有脆弱的理由，她比過去光著腳走更多的石子路，去洗更多的衣服……

海燕風災發生之後，他們失去了房子，受到慈濟的庇護而住進奧莫克大愛村，那是二〇一六年五月的事。

她看見慈青逐漸組織起來，穿著整潔、紀律嚴明，作為一個年輕人，她不想花時間在家裏賴在床上，她希望跟著慈濟做好事，於是她加入了慈青。

證嚴法師說：「天底下有兩件事不能等，一是孝順，一是

remains confident and determined to achieve her goal.

Marithel lost her father when she was very young. She cannot remember ever meeting him. Her widowed mother raised six children by doing the laundry for the rich people. The family faced financial hardships throughout Marithel's life. In such a poor family, it is a blessing that she survived.

As evening descends, one sees birds resting on nearby light posts. Then, as it becomes dark, the only thing that becomes visible are the streetlights under the birds' feet, all lit up.

I held Marithel in my arm, patted her slender shoulders, and took a deep breath. I imagined that the wind, through my palms, was consoling her from her loneliness and wishing that she would get some calm in the tug-of-war between the healing and damaging forces inside her.

Marithel told me that before she came across Tzu Chi Foundation, she despised her mother for being a laundry woman. She often fought and talked back whenever her mother would reprimand her. She just could not stand anything that her mother would say.

Marithel had never paid attention to her mother's hands. She had never cared to count the scars that her mother had sustained from doing laundry works every day, or to consider how helpless and heartbroken she had felt when she lost her husband.

On her part, Marithel's mother had told herself that for the children who rely on her, she just could not afford to be vulnerable. She must keep walking forward through roads paved with stones and wash more strangers' clothes than she had in the past.

Marithel's family lost their home when Typhoon Haiyan occurred. In May 2016, they were lucky to be relocated to the Ormoc Great Love Village,

行善。」

一家子沈重的負擔，母親很努力地扛著，用勞力的方式愛著她的孩子，三餐雖羞澀艱難，靠的也是母親的一雙手。

母親為了孩子們犧牲掉自己的青春，她心靈的高貴，應該要被愛與尊重才對。

瑪恬開始有了無盡的懺悔。

二〇一八年五月，瑪恬進入慈濟滿兩年，在佛誕日、慈濟日、母親節三節合一的日子，她有了一個機會向母親懺悔。

在浴佛典禮中，她請母親坐下，拿出裝了水的小臉盆，母親危顫顫地伸出因長途跋涉、走過石子泥濘路的瘦腳，首次仔細凝望那坑坑疤疤長出粗繭的腳，所有的前塵往事一古腦兒讓她悲從中來。

她哭泣著幫母親輕柔地洗腳，忍不住撲向母親，有生以來第一次說：「我愛您！」

母親因女兒遲來的感謝和擁抱，一時無語凝噎，淚水不斷自眼角流下，她伸出滿是厚繭的手回抱著女兒。珍惜著孩子說出的每一個字，因為每個字裏都隱著他們共有的回憶與說不盡的故事。

奧莫克熏熱的微風吹拂著，掀起淡淡的金色灰塵。

愛的表達有許多型態，當愛還很小的時候，只能分作討厭和喜歡。

隨著歲月拉長，愛有感傷、也有疲乏，又充滿深深的憂慮和希望。

最後，愛會穿梭在人群，一片一片，撿拾無人打掃的落葉，

which is a project of Tzu Chi. In their new village, Marithel began to see life differently. Suddenly, her interest and attention was caught by the emerging local Tzu Ching, or youth group. In the youth group's inception, Tzu Chi provided accountability and direction to the members. This includes uniforms to wear along with rules and regulations to follow. Marithel, tired of being idle, joined the youth group and began doing good deeds for others.

She learned from the teachings of Dharma Master Cheng Yen that: "There are two things in life that cannot wait: one is fulfilling filial piety, and the other one is doing good deeds."

Marithel came to see that she was not on the correct path of life. Suddenly, her mother's sacrifices became clear to her. Although raising six kids all alone is a heavy burden, Marithel's mother willingly and happily shouldered the task, tirelessly working as a laundry woman, day in and out and showering her children with unconditional love. Realizing this, Marithel was filled with pride, love and respect towards her mother. She began to repent her behavior in the past and vowed to do better.

In May 2018, on her second year with Tzu Chi, Marithel joined in the celebration of the Buddha Day, Tzu Chi Global Day, and Mother's Day. That special day gave her an opportunity to express her repentance and gratefulness towards her kind and loving mother.

During one part of the celebration, Marithel, holding a basin of water, knelt in front of her mother to wash her feet. Her mother slowly extended her feet, which were weary after walking along stony and muddy roads, towards Marithel.

In that moment when she held her mother's feet in her hands, Marithel felt the rough calluses that had developed from years of hard work. Her heart welled up with pity, regret and anxiety. Crying, Marithel embraced her mother and for the first time in her life, she told her: "I love you."

小心翼翼去拼湊破損，讓它得以完整。

　　瑪恬在慈濟大愛薰陶下學會感恩、尊重、愛。六個兄弟姊妹，只剩下她和弟弟兩人還在念書。

　　加入慈青的她，很幸運地得到慈濟助學金，弟弟則在一戶有錢人家裏幫傭，並想方設法讓自己成為班上的佼佼者，努力獲取學術獎金。

　　優秀的姊弟兩人，雖然在不同的情境下求學，但都各自勤勉自律。瑪恬未來希望成為記者，而弟弟希望成為機械工程師。

　　慈濟希望能幫助瑪恬的弟弟，他們總是敞開雙手援助懂得上進、肯吃苦的孩子。但弟弟覺得姊姊已受慈濟資助，便想自食其力。

　　二〇一八年暑假，瑪恬的弟弟得了登革熱，瑪恬原本好想參加慈青的活動，但因弟弟生病，她選擇去打工，把賺來的錢用來醫治弟弟的病。

　　姊弟倆都有著可貴的自尊，不輕易因生活的匱乏而提出更多要求。

　　蔡昇航教導孩子們《慈悲三昧水懺》經文，裏面談到「業力」、「因緣果報」。

　　瑪恬領悟到若只會手語而不解其意，無法運用於生活中，那一切便失去了意義。

　　她認真地去了解經文的涵義，後來深受經文感召開始茹素。她了解到素食能減少地球暖化，也擔心自己變成一頭豬，因為豬對人類唯一的貢獻，就是被殺來變成盤中飧。

　　瑪恬領悟力極高、反應敏捷，學習與表達能力都很好，令

Wrapped in Marithel's embrace, her mother was tongue-tied as their tears flowed together. Her hands are also full of calluses but her hug was warm and comforting.

At this very moment, Ormoc has a warm breeze and golden dust. Expression of love comes in many forms. When our love is narrow and small, it is merely a distinction between liking and disliking. As time passes, love hurts. It grows weary, and may even be filled with worries and expectations. But in the end, love permeates among people, like gathering the scattered pieces of fallen leaves, and carefully piecing them back together.

As Marithel spends more time with Tzu Chi Foundation, she begins to practice the ideals of gratitude, respect, and love in her daily life. Among the Valiente kids, only Marithel and her younger brother are still in school. Marithel manages to continue her education through a scholarship grant from Tzu Chi Foundation, while her brother supports his studies by serving a rich family as a helper.

Despite the challenges, the siblings are excelling in their academics. Both are well-disciplined and very diligent. Marithel dreams of becoming a journalist someday, while her younger brother hopes to become a mechanical engineer.

Volunteer Alfredo Li, who is always supportive of students who are diligent in their studies despite life's difficulties, wanted to help Marithel's brother. However, Marithel's brother did not want to add another burden to the Foundation. With Marithel already under Tzu Chi's scholarship program, her brother chose to strive on his own.

In the summer of 2018, Marithel's brother contracted dengue fever, forcing Marithel to work in order to pay for her brother's hospital bills. Because of the situation, Marithel missed several Tzu Ching activities.

我驚訝的是她最愛《慈悲三昧水懺》經文裏的「一性圓明自然」。這句話給她的感受是明淨的心靈與善良，能用平靜的心態不對任何人生氣，不對負面的事情過度思考。

　　瑪恬就要離開這裏到馬尼拉上大學、學中文。她說，要透過當記者來幫助慈濟，一生奉獻給慈濟。

　　我告訴她：「遇到困境、覺得傷心的時候就去看海，讓海千篇一律地告訴你，沒有關係、沒有關係……直到你真的相信，然後對每一個承諾認真。」

人文課堂上，教育小組教導孩子們進食禮儀，瑪恬敲著小木魚，引領大家唱供養歌。
In the humanities class, they taught the children the proper etiquette in eating. Marithel tapped the little wooden fish to lead everyone in singing the Offering Verse.

Both siblings value their dignity and do not easily request for assistance upon encountering shortcomings in life.

At the Ormoc Great Love Village, Tzu Chi volunteer Michael Siao willingly spent his time expounding on "*The Compassionate Samadhi Water Repentance*" to the village children. In this sutra, the Buddha expounds on the topics of karmic retribution and the law of cause and effect.

Marithel seriously studied the meaning of the sutra and simultaneously learned the corresponding sign language in order to use it in her daily life.

Inspired by the teachings she had heard, Marithel decided to become a vegetarian in November 2018. She understood that vegetarianism would be the fastest way to slow down the effects of Global Warming and save our planet. But apart from that, Marithel was also terrified of the idea that if she eats meat, she might be reincarnated as a pig in her next life and will be slaughtered to be made into pork dishes to satisfy people's palates.

Marithel is a wise girl who learns pretty fast and is also quite articulate. In the sutra, "*The Compassionate Samadhi Water Repentance*", she mostly appreciates the topic on "Pure Radiant Buddha-Nature." She learned that our pure intrinsic nature is a calm mindset, avoiding anger and not lingering on negativities.

Marithel is leaving Ormoc to learn the Chinese language in Manila. This is in preparation for her college education in Taiwan. She wants to become a journalist for Tzu Chi and to dedicate her life to this organization.

I sincerely advised Marithel, "Please look at the vast sea when you are sad. Let the sea remind you over and over again, that everything will be okay. Keep on believing this, then fulfill your every vow seriously."

(Translated by Carmen Sy)

羅梅爾 Romel Aseo

三個寶貝女兒

Three Baby Girls

羅梅爾只是一位三輪車夫，但他對女兒們的教養甚為重視，雖然臉上沒什麼笑容，但心比誰都柔軟。

Romel Aseo is a humble pedicab driver but he takes his daughter's education seriously. Although he rarely smiles, he has a soft heart.

羅梅爾是三輪車夫。菲律賓的三輪車長相可愛，又被稱為「嘟嘟車」，招呼滿六個座位就開車，一人要價十披索。它被限制在巷弄口招攬乘客，不能行駛市區幹道。

羅梅爾略微害羞，卻是一位有智識見地、內心柔軟的人。他與妻子瑪吉（Margie）有六個孩子，原本住在「新人生（Bagong-buhay）」地區那兒，用木頭和膠合板搭的小房子裏。

海燕風災發生，小小房子被毀，他們逃到阿姨家避難。慈濟讓他們落腳奧莫克大愛村，他們深感幸運而不可思議，家中口數多，分配到三房的建築，有電也有水，孩子念書還有助學金，慈濟樣樣都貼心地設想周到。

羅梅爾夫婦看到慈濟人行禮如儀端莊，可讓孩子們學習為人處事、通情達理，於是鼓勵孩子們參與慈青，貢獻自己。他

Romel Aseo is a pedicab driver. The appearance of the pedicab in the Philippines is lovely and are also called "Tricycle". The car will start moving once all six seats are occupied. The fare for a pedicab ride is 10 pesos per person. This car is authorized to drive in the small alleys but not allowed in the city's main streets.

Romel is timid but he knows a lot of things and has a soft heart. He has six children with his wife Margie. They used to live in a small house that was made of wood and hardiflex boards in Barangay Bagong Buhay.

That house was destroyed when Typhoon Haiyan hit Leyte. Romel evacuated his family to his aunt's house. Eventually, they moved into Tzu Chi's Great Love Village in Ormoc. They felt very lucky to have received a three-bedroom house, equipped with all the utilities such as water and electricity. In addition, their children also received scholarship grants from Tzu Chi, allowing them to receive a good education. Romel was grateful that Tzu Chi

們的三個女兒，就這樣來到慈濟學習。

　　起初，羅梅爾起床了若看孩子們還在睡，就會問：「你們今天要當志工嗎？」孩子們說：「要啊！」「那你們為什麼還躺在那裏？現在應該準備好了！」他比孩子們還認真。

　　夫妻倆災後愁著的心事，都在慈濟的幫助下迎刃而解。他們知道慈濟來自臺灣，又不同宗教，可是慈濟從來不談這些，只是幫助他們愛他們。

　　他們一家人有時站在屋前的小徑，就可以遠眺至山谷遠遠的起點。羅梅爾總感慨，歲月在永恆面前，我們永遠是學生，無常總是推著人往前走，「何其有幸，我們是被神選中的人！」這個神在他的心中已無任何分別。

　　二〇一八年，有個機會讓奧莫克慈青前往臺灣學習，菲律賓政府規定年滿十八歲才能出國。當時三姊妹裏只有上大學的夏拉（Shyla）滿十八歲，兩個妹妹萊卡（Lyka）、梅姬（Mhelgie）垮著臉很沮喪，她們分別是十六歲、十四歲。

　　後來，李偉嵩爭取放寬條件到滿十六歲的孩子，萊卡好開心，手舞足蹈。這下只有梅姬不能去，她滿心不情願地哭了。李偉嵩知道後，查看許多活動照片都有梅姬的身影，覺得這孩子這麼認真學習，不讓她去太可惜，於是破例讓她也成行，她才破涕為笑。

　　學習是日常，理想是一條河，河上自然有船，河裏有飄搖的藻荇。夏拉性格安靜，但為了保護弟妹，生起氣來像一隻老虎。如今，她在證嚴法師的教誨中學會思考，「生氣，就是拿別人的過錯來懲罰自己。」「嘴巴不好，心地再好，也不能算

had thoughtfully took care of their needs.

The Aseo couple, after observing the Tzu Chi volunteers's polite and well-behaved demeanor, decided that they want them to be their children's role models. Hence, they encouraged their three daughters to volunteer for Tzu Chi so that they will learn how to interact properly with people and how to contribute to society.

In the first weeks, the couple would wait for their children to wake up each morning and ask them, "Do you still want to volunteer today?" The children would answer, "Yes we want to!" "Then why are you still lying in bed? You should be getting ready now!" The parents were more serious about volunteering than the children. This was because the couple's problems have been solved with the help of Tzu Chi. They knew Tzu Chi came from Taiwan and practiced a different religion but Tzu Chi never mentioned anything about their differences. Tzu Chi just loved to help them.

Sometimes this family would stand by the small alley in front of their house, looking at the far end of the valley and ruefully say: "In the face of our future, we are always going to be a student, seemingly being pushed forward without a choice. We realized that we were so lucky that we have been chosen by God." At this moment, God to them has no difference.

In 2018, there was an opportunity for the Tzu Chings in Great Love Village to visit Taiwan and learn more about Tzu Chi's mission of education. However, according to the Philippine law, travel is regulated for people under 18 years old, and Tzu Ching is intended for collegiate youth only. Shyla was just 18, and Lyka and Mhelgie were 16 and 14, respectively.

Later, Alfredo Li made some arrangements so that 16 year olds will be allowed to travel. Lyka was so happy when she heard about this. Mhelgie, being the only one who could not go among the sisters, cried out sadly. Alfredo heard about this and seeing how serious Mhelgie participated in most

是好人。」她反覆再三地提醒自己，不去介意別人的挑釁，因為她不想成為傷害別人的人。

小時候她有芭比娃娃，由於對人體構造感興趣，經常將娃娃肢解以探究竟，但娃娃當然無法滿足她。現在她想當一名護理師，這樣就能透過解剖學了解人體，並在醫療團隊裏去助人。

萊卡有著快樂性格，不喜歡悲傷的事，然而世上必有艱難時刻，要能學會承受。「人要學習經得起周圍人事的磨練而心不動搖，並學習在動中保持心的寧靜。」

她學會正向思考，學會不去勉強，隨順因緣，因此現在擁有許多好朋友。她尤其喜歡房子，所以志願成為一名工程師，她要為家人蓋一個溫暖的窩，也為別人的幸福而努力。

梅姬擅長愛的表達，至今還會親吻她的父親，她了解父親表面嚴肅，其實內心有著巨大的溫暖。未來希望成為一名老師的梅姬，覺得能傳揚正確知識與人生信念，是一種使命。她喜歡學習中文，希望能在臺灣完成學業後，歸國擔任慈濟學校的校長。

二〇一七年卡南加附近十四個里再度發生強震。夏拉曾於海燕風災發生時，看到一個獨魯萬的孩子隻身倖存的消息，她無法想像，失去雙親的孩子要如何獨自面對未來的悠悠歲月？

當年徒有悲憫，卻沒有能力幫忙，這次她帶著兩個妹妹一起參與義診發放、家訪與資源回收。她們為善助人的強烈渴望，在慈濟人的帶動下不斷被啟發，她們說：「身體在全心全意的投入下雖然勞累，心靈卻是充滿喜悅與悸動。」

住進奧莫克大愛村，羅梅爾與瑪吉夫婦才開始能對孩子們

activities, and her eagerness to learn, he made exceptions and allowed all three to go to Taiwan. Mhelgie jumped with exultation!

Learning is a daily task; ideas are streams or rivers and boats sail on rivers, where seaweeds float.

Shyla has a tranquil character. But if any of her siblings are in trouble, Shyla would transform into a fierce tiger to rescue them. From Master Cheng Yen, Shyla learned that "Getting angry is actually punishing yourself with the mistakes of others" and that "If we are temperamental and used to speaking harshly, then we are yet to be considered decent people even though we have kind intentions." Shyla often reminds herself not to mind people's comments and to remain calm in dealing with everyone.

Shyla recalls an incident in her childhood when she dissected her Barbie doll. It was the earliest manifestation of her interest in the structure of the human body. Of course, this did not satisfy her pursuit of knowledge, so Shyla aspired to become a nurse or a doctor. If she becomes a nurse or a doctor, she will understand more about anatomy and will be able to help people.

Lyka is a cheerful girl who does not like sorrow or immense sadness. However, throughout life, one will always have to face difficult challenges. So Lyka must learn how to cope with those situations. "Learn to remain undisturbed in the tumult of people and events. Remain at peace within even when busy and occupied."

She is learning how to think positively and to not force herself to react to something she is incapable of accomplishing. Because of this ability, she makes a lot of friends. She likes houses so much that she wants to be an engineer. If she becomes an engineer, she would be able to build a warm house for her family and for many other people.

Mhelgie is fond of expressing her love towards her father with a kiss on

的未來有所憧憬。他們發現，原來愛不是那麼難，夢不是那麼遙遠不可追，愛是種自然的賦予，我們只需要學會跨出去！奉獻出愛的時候，雖不期待任何回報，但是它並非全然沒有回報，因為善良會來到你身邊。

　　生命像是一幢房屋，讓我們彼此成為房子裏對開的兩扇窗戶。孩子們，發了宏願，就應大步迎向前，要真心相信自己擁有那能力！

受慈濟助學的三姊妹萊卡（左起）、夏拉、梅姬，聊起兒時回憶和志向，眉宇間展現了信心。
Sisters Lyka (left), Shyla, and Mhelgie received Tzu Chi's scholarship grant. They share about their childhood and dreams, as well as expressed their confidence about what the future holds.

the cheek. Although her father is a solemn man, his heart is full of warmth.

Mhelgie wants to be a teacher someday so she can help spread knowledge. She believes that this is her calling. She enjoys learning the Chinese language. Hopefully, she will be able to complete her studies in Taiwan, and become the principal of Tzu Chi School in the Philippines.

After an earthquake struck the municipality of Kananga in 2017, Shyla met a child from Tacloban City who survived Typhoon Haiyan. The child lost his parents in the tragedy. Shyla could not imagine how an innocent and helpless child would face the future all by himself.

Back then, Shyla was unable to help. However, this time, she is accompanied by her two younger sisters in volunteering for medical outreaches, in visiting families and in promoting recycling.

Led and inspired by Tzu Chi, the siblings are determined to put forth their best effort and help people. Sometimes they would feel tired but then they would realize that their hearts are bursting with happiness and is in the right place.

After moving to the Great Love Village, the Aseos have begun looking forward to the future. They discovered that love is not too difficult to manifest, that dreams are not too far to reach and that love is innate in each person; we only need to reach out to show it and receive it. Although we do not ask for anything in return in doing good deeds, as we give love to the world, love comes back to us.

Life is just like a house. Let us be the windows in a house that open up across each other. Children, do not be afraid to make vows for the future. Believe in yourselves, for you are capable of giving love.

(Translated by Danny Tam)

終於戒酒了

Staying Away from Alcohol

魯迪吉利歐過去因喝酒惡習，讓妻子羅西塔很辛苦，參與慈濟活動後堅定戒酒，全家喜極而泣。

Ludegario was an alcoholic. His wife Rosita suffered due to his bad habit until he joined Tzu Chi and quit drinking.

沿著傍晚的河邊走一會兒，河流溫馴，此岸有玉米，對岸彷彿看到甘蔗，能夠傷人的葉緣，細細長長，使我想起弗洛雷斯（Flores）一家人。

緣分就是奇特，愛也通常不會公平，愛就是愛，沒有原因。

弗洛雷斯家的媽媽羅西塔（Rosita）讀到大學一年級，爸爸魯迪吉利歐才小學二年級的學歷。

魯迪吉利歐家境不好又不愛念書，在工廠上班時認識了美麗的羅西塔，兩人條件懸殊卻迸出愛的火花，奉子成婚生下兒子阿里爾（Ariel）和女兒克莉絲提美（Kristil Mae）。

有愛就不難，胼手胝足相互扶持，婚姻總還是美麗。

剛開始，夫妻倆幫一位大地主割甘蔗，烈日炎炎一直是菲律賓氣候的常態，甘蔗細長的葉刮著手，汗流浹背體力用盡，

I am walking by the riverside one evening. The river is calm. Cornfields stretched on my side while sugarcanes rose in the field across the river. The sugarcane leaves are slender and long around the edges. It can easily cut through the skin. It reminds me of the Flores family.

People's fate is peculiar. Love does not have to make sense all the time. You do not need any reason to love. Rosita Flores went to college for one year. Ludegario Flores was only able to attend grade school for two years. Ludegario came from a very poor family. He could not stand studying. While working at a factory, he met the beautiful Rosita. Despite their differences, they found themselves falling for each other. By the time they got married, Rosita was already pregnant with their first child. Today, the couple has a son named Ariel and a daughter named Kristil Mae.

Love helps overcome difficulties. By supporting and complementing one another, their marriage is a beautiful love story.

一人一天只能賺到一百披索。孩子沒錢上學，也一起幫忙割甘蔗，一家人生活拮据。

魯迪吉利歐想辦法轉業，到餐廳當主廚副手，習得烹調祕訣。羅西塔與先生分隔兩地，各自努力工作，賺來的錢終於能供孩子們上學，到學校得走二十分鐘，但總算能受教育了。

羅西塔與魯迪吉利歐彼此間並非完全沒有隔閡，魯迪吉利歐一直想努力去補平那缺口，因此他盡心盡力賺錢，讓自己在羅西塔的面前像個大丈夫。但外面的誘惑實在太多，而他總不夠堅定地再次沈淪。

心有時寂寞，魯迪吉利歐偶爾跟同事出去喝酒，不料愈喝愈多，慢慢有了酒癮，貪杯的結果就是供給孩子的教育費用變少了。

同時，酒癮問題也折磨著魯迪吉利歐的心志，他變得沒有耐性，出現戒斷症候群。

魯迪吉利歐想要改變卻無法控制，內心交戰，幸虧他掛念妻兒的心很強烈，決定回到老本行砍甘蔗。

羅西塔理解先生的內心，她決定更小心自己的言語，給予先生更多的自信。

夫妻倆借錢給孩子上學，羅西塔耐心地輔助魯迪吉利歐戒酒，有時魯迪吉利歐酒癮犯了，沒有酒，望著杯子哭泣，像個小孩子一樣，羅西塔的心很是煎熬，但她忍耐支撐下來！

天災來了，生活更陷入混亂。夫妻倆聽說大愛村需要人手鋪「福竹磚」（以竹子代替鋼筋，環保又便利），他們有了工資，還了債，之後又住進大愛村。

After they got married, the couple worked for a landowner, harvesting sugarcane. Under the sweltering afternoon heat, the couple worked outdoors. The sharp leaves of sugarcane cut their fingers and hands. It did not seem right that after a day of hard labor, each of them would only receive 100 pesos. With such a meager income, they could not afford to send their children to school. Eventually, the children would go with their parents to work in the sugarcane fields instead of going to school. The Flores family was living in poverty.

Ludegario decided to find a better-paying job. He eventually got a job as an assistant chef at a restaurant. There, he gained cooking skills. Although Rosita was not too happy to be separated from her husband, Ludegario was earning well from his new job, making it possible to send their children to school. The children walks 20 minutes each day to reach the school. Finally, they are on track to receive an education.

But as Ludegario worked harder to make more money to support the family and make himself a big man in front of his wife, he was also constantly being exposed to the temptation of drinking alcohol.

He would go out drinking with his co-workers whenever he feels lonely. The more he drank, the more he fell into alcohol addiction. His salary went mostly to his alcohol cravings so he sent less and less money to his family. At the same time, the alcohol had begun afflicting Ludegario's mind. He became more and more impatient as withdrawal symptoms affect him. Ludegario realized that he needed to stop drinking but he did not know how to quit. He constantly had an internal struggle because of his drinking issue.

Fortunately, he cared more about his wife and children so he decided to go back to work in the sugarcane fields. All the while, Rosita knew in her heart what was going on in Ludegario's mind. She paid more attention to every word she says to avoid hurting her husband's feelings and to encourage him even more.

兒子阿里爾與女兒克莉絲提美有慈濟的助學金，魯迪吉利歐與羅西塔成為環保志工，安靜安定的環境與過去的勞頓奔忙有著極大反差，他們心中感恩無限。

阿里爾身材高大，有一次發放大米，他幫忙送給一對老夫妻時，突然想到過去爺爺奶奶、父親母親曾有過長時間困頓辛勞的生活，有時家裏有一餐沒一餐，忽然悲從中來淚流不止！

魯迪吉利歐聽證嚴法師說：「不抽菸、不賭博、不喝酒……」他羞愧不已，想對自己一直以來的不稱職向家人懺悔。生性害羞的他非得藉酒微醺，才說得出口，此舉讓家人哭笑不得。最後，家和樂了，他也終於把酒戒了。

二〇一八年，夫妻倆搭船到保和島去交流環保，那是他們首次走出萊特島。而一對兒女也搭飛機到臺灣參與慈青生活營，那也是平生首次搭飛機。

從辛勞、欠債、困頓，不知明天在何處的黑暗生活，到今日什麼都擁有的光亮，這一家人所有的第一次都是因為慈濟，慈濟的愛讓他們翻轉人生。

慈濟對他們全家而言，有如一個火星子，點燃了他們心中溫暖的火炬，點燃了他們對生命的希望。他們開始能築夢，想齊心合力開一家餐廳……

有一回，村裏辦活動，借用奧莫克市小學廣場。正值雨季，近黃昏的奧莫克，路上來往行人少，廣場上慈青與本土志工仍為隔日活動努力排著椅子，練習手語，熱騰依舊。

魯迪吉利歐排好紅椅子，與太太羅西塔及幾位本土志工坐在後邊稍事休息，看慈青在臺上演練手語一遍又一遍。

The couple loaned money to pay for their children's school fees. Rosita even helped Ludegario to quit his drinking. Each time Ludegario's addiction kicks in, he would look at an empty wine glass and cry like a baby. Rosita suffered with him. But together, they made it through the hard times.

Life became even more challenging when Typhoon Haiyan hit. Fortunately, the couple heard that the Great Love Village was under construction and that they were looking for typhoon survivors to help out in making "Bamboo Bricks" (Tzu Chi had used bamboo in place of steel for the bricks to make sure the houses are built without harming the earth). The couple got the job, paid their debts and moved into the Great Love Village.

At the Great Love Village, Ariel and Kristil Mae received scholarship grants from Tzu Chi while Ludegario and Rosita became environmental protection volunteers. Tzu Chi has helped turn their lives around from one of suffering to peace. The family is grateful for their new lives.

Ariel, being a tall and strong young man, could not understand why one day as he was helping an elderly couple receive a sack of rice, he could not stop crying. In that moment, he was thinking about his grandparents and his parents and the difficulties they had encountered and are still faced with. No matter how hard they work, sometimes they just cannot put food on the table.

Ludegario learned that Master Cheng Yen teaches: "No smoking, No gambling, No drinking…" Ashamed of his past actions, he wanted to apologize to his family. But, being an introvert, the only way he could muster the courage to say all these was to become mildly drunk. Seeing him do this, Ludegario's family laughed at his ridiculous behavior. Finally, Ludegario quit his drinking and his family had never been so happy.

In 2018, the couple took a trip to Bohol Island to share about their environmental protection experience. It was their first time to leave Leyte. Their two children also flew to Taiwan to join the Tzu Ching retreat. It was the

我趨前拍魯迪吉利歐肩膀，請他跟著比手語看看！不料他竟一溜煙不見了！

　　四處張望不見人影，我納悶著走回羅西塔旁邊，正想開口問：「魯迪吉利歐怎麼不見了？」眼睛隨即掃描到蹲躲在羅西塔座位後面的他，赤著臉，兩手摀著眼，笑得不知所措，活像一個大男孩。羅西塔和其他人早已笑成一團，我不禁莞爾。

　　那樣真純樸實！我回想他倆過去的點點滴滴，忽然明白他們究竟是怎樣走過來的了！

魯迪吉利歐（蹲者）戒了酒，歡喜做志工，只要有活動，他總是勤快地幫忙，因為慈濟改變了他的人生。
Ludegario (squatted) quit drinking. He loves to volunteer for any Tzu Chi activity. Whenever there is an event, he would always offer to help as his way of showing gratitude to Tzu Chi for changing his life.

first time either child had flown on an airplane.

In the past, the family had suffered, was deep in debts, tired and could not even tell if they could make it to tomorrow. Today, they have fulfilled lives. Many of their best first experiences had to do with Tzu Chi. The love and care from the Tzu Chi volunteers have turned their lives around. Tzu Chi volunteers are like the fire that lit up the Flores family's lives and hopes. They inspired the family to dream again. Perhaps someday, the Floreses will open their own restaurant just like they wish they would.

Once, the village held an event at Ormoc Elementary School. As it was the rainy season, there were not many people on the street before sunset. At school, Tzu Ching and local volunteers were still arranging the chairs for the next day's event. While the Youth Group were practicing sign language, others carried on with the preparations.

After Ludegario arranged the red chairs, he sat down with his wife Rosita and other local volunteers to take a short break. They were watching the Tzu Chings practice their sign language performance. I tapped Ludegario in the shoulder, inviting him to join in the sign language. When I looked again, he was gone!

I looked around but could not find him anywhere. I walked back to Rosita, confused. Just as I was about to ask how it was possible for Ludegario to disappear just like that, I found him hiding behind Rosita's seat. His face turned very red and his hands went up to cover both of his eyes. He was smiling like a little boy. Rosita and the others laughed out loud. I could not help but smile.

He is just so pure and unpretentious! Recalling their story, I suddenly understood how they were able to walk through it.

(Translated by Audrey Cheng)

艾碧 Ivy Rose Godinez

變得更懂事

Becoming More Sensible

浴佛儀式中繞佛繞法練習，艾碧站在最前面為標兵，仔細聽著解說帶領大家走步。

During the Buddha Day ceremony, Ivy stood in front as a guide person. She listens carefully to the instructions in order to lead the participants in the event.

夜裏走了長長的路，來到大片草坪的中央。前些日子修整過的草坪，清新的草香彌漫在空氣裏，帶著淡淡的悠然，草葉上潮溼的雨珠，在黑暗中發光。

我站在星空下聽著鼓樂，孩子們廢寢忘食，努力地一次一次排練，樂聲、人影，深深感動著我。

艾碧看到一個哭泣的小女孩，即使她們彼此陌生，她還是走過去把小女孩抱在懷裏，安慰著她。那一刻，也許她覺得這小女孩就像是自己的妹妹一般。看著艾碧以輕柔又堅定的音調哄著小女孩，我肯定她有一顆善良的心。

十七歲即將升高三的艾碧，心裏有夢，她希望將來成為一位專業人士。現今社會新技術迭起，變革需求很高，她想成為電腦工程設計領域的佼佼者。

One evening, after taking a long walk, I finally arrived at a large section of lawn that had recently been mowed. The smell of cut grass still lingers in the air. The moisture on the leaves due to a recent rain seemed to sparkle under the moonlight. I was standing under the starry sky listening to the sound of the drums. The children were tirelessly practicing their drums and it touched my heart deeply.

Ivy Rose Godinez glanced at a little girl who was crying. Though they did not know each other, Ivy approached the girl, and then hugged and comforted her. In that moment, maybe Ivy saw her like her own younger sister. As Ivy soothed the girl with her soft but firm voice, I knew that she possesses a kind heart.

Ivy will be promoted to the ninth grade at the age of 17. With the advancement of technologies nowadays, she dreams of becoming a computer engineer someday.

艾碧從口袋掏出一顆糖果給小女孩，原來天色黯淡，小女孩的哥哥在練鼓樂，她在昏暗中看不見哥哥，就哭了。哥哥走過來，指著遠遠的山谷上空，有著一片灰藍，「不怕，你看，那像不像海？」

　　我笑一笑，走進廚房煮起一大鍋南瓜湯，先炒了洋蔥、蘑菇和高麗菜，炒軟了飄出香甜的氣味，水滾了，把它們輕輕放入滾水中，轉中火，再把從椰子殼內層刮出的椰子渣擠出椰奶，慢慢添加進入滾水中，最後再把南瓜泥一杓一杓放入，攪拌出金黃可口又營養的南瓜椰奶蔬菜湯。等孩子們練完鼓樂，就能給他們勞動的身子補充營養。

　　走出廚房，看見小女孩靠在燈下牆邊，看著艾碧、哥哥，還有許多大哥哥、大姊姊持續練習，臉上堆滿了笑，口裏含著艾碧給她的糖果。我們相視笑著。

　　艾碧一開始加入慈青，只單純想結識更多好朋友，但是當她愈是深入學習幫助別人的事，愈覺得原來自己是被需要的，自己的存在是有意義的。身邊都是如此奉獻愛心的人，她深深被感染了。世上有很多事會慢慢相互感染，比如微笑、善念、勤勞、自信心。

　　艾碧的父親是一位魚販，母親是家庭主婦。菲律賓與日本有一件事雷同，婦女婚後，多半成為單純的家庭主婦。

　　家裏有六個孩子，艾碧是老大，可能因為如此，她看見弱小總會習慣性地主動去呵護。她來到慈濟基金會當志工已經有一年，二〇一八年她幸運抵達臺灣見到證嚴法師，心裏十分悸動，因為證嚴法師創造的慈濟世界是奧莫克的希望，這一分恩

Ivy gave the little girl a piece of candy to calm her down. She found out that the young girl was crying because she could not see her brother, who was practicing drums in the dark. The little girl's brother noticed her crying. He came over and pointed to the gray-blue sky above. He told her: "Don't be afraid! Don't you see that looks like the sea?"

I smiled and walked inside the kitchen to start cooking pumpkin soup. I knew the children would be hungry after practicing the drums. I wanted to prepare something delicious and nutritious for them. Walking out of the kitchen, I saw the little girl leaning on the wall, watching Ivy, her brother and the others carry on with their practice. As their group played the drums, Ivy could see that the little girl was smiling because she was enjoying the candy that she had given her. The moment our gazes met, we broke into a smile.

When Ivy first joined the Tzu Ching, her intention was to make more friends. However, as she got more involved with the group, she realized the true meaning of volunteerism. The more help she extended to others, the more she felt needed.

Ivy's father is a fishmonger and her mother is a housewife. The culture of the Philippines is similar to Japan: after getting married, most women end up being housewives. Ivy's parents had six children and being the eldest, Ivy was responsible for helping out a great deal with looking after her siblings. Whenever Ivy sees someone who is young, weak and needed help, she would readily extend a hand. In 2018, after a year of volunteering for Tzu Chi Foundation, Ivy was lucky to have the opportunity to travel to Taiwan and meet Master Cheng Yen. There, she was very moved to see the birthplace of the Tzu Chi world that Master Cheng Yen had created and had become Ormoc City's inspiration. Ivy surmised that it would be difficult to repay the kindness that Master Cheng Yen has shown to her community.

Ivy carefully observed the Master and noticed that the Master was very friendly to everyone. She kept thinking back to the disaster that hit Leyte.

情很難報答。

　　她仔細觀察證嚴法師的身行，法師對任何人都非常友善。她不斷回想起二〇一三年巨大的災難突然降臨萊特島，臺灣距離菲律賓遙遠，證嚴法師也不認識萊特島上的任何一人，卻那麼寬容而大愛地指示志工到萊特島幫助他們。法師宏觀的氣度與無私大愛，深深折服艾碧。

　　艾碧好喜歡「生命的價值」那堂課，體悟到慈善是慈濟志業的根基，慈濟人以愛傳愛，為受災民眾安身、安心和安生之餘，進一步帶動他們成為助人者，發揮生命的價值。

　　過去一直都在浪費生命，在慈濟世界裏，她認知到我們來到這個世界，應該創造夢想的未來，為更多人的福祉而努力，切莫讓時光空過！

　　從前艾碧會與母親口角衝突，如今她了解生命是母親冒著生命危險給予她的，孝順都來不及，怎能再多方忤逆？她深感懺悔，現在不但親身奉行，也會教導弟妹要尊重父母、孝順父母，並且鼓舞弟妹也加入慈青。

　　「謝謝您為我們所做的一切，幫助我們。沒有法師您，我將無法擺脫錯誤的行為；您教會我成為一個好女兒，成為一個好青年；您改變了我的生活，讓我成為一個更好的人。」

　　人生旅程中，一路上布滿各種顏色，紅豔的喜氣可能最討喜，但它總是經不起一點灰塵沾染。而淡淡的灰雖不討喜，它所帶來的澄明與平靜，卻讓我們能明辨謙虛、自信或慚愧。

　　艾碧已學會真心分辨人生的對錯與價值，她懷著一個寬容尺度，丈量著自己生命裏的種種可能。

Taiwan is far away from the Philippines. Master Cheng Yen did not know anyone in Leyte and yet she was so concerned and loving towards its people. She instructed the volunteers to help the typhoon survivors. Witnessing first hand the Master's compassion and selfless love only fuelled Ivy's conviction to push for Tzu Chi Foundation's missions.

Ivy particularly liked the Master's teaching on "the value of life". She realized that charity is the core of Tzu Chi's work. Tzu Chi volunteers bring love and peace of mind to calamity victims and moreover, encourage them to help others to bring out their values in life, too.

Reminiscing about her past, Ivy remembered how she wasted her life by going against her parents' wishes. Ivy recalled how she and her mother used to always disagree on almost every subject. Today, however, she understands that her mother had risked her life to bring her into this world. How then can Ivy afford to be so rebellious? Instead, Ivy repented. Now, she does not only treat her parents with respect but also teaches her siblings to do the same and encourage them to join Tzu Ching.

"Thank you for everything you have done for us. If not for you, I would not have the chance to set my bad behaviors right. You taught me how to become a good daughter and person; you have changed my life and made me a better person."

As we journey through life, we discover all kinds of colors. The bright color of red may be the most pleasing to the eyes, but it cannot withstand a few dust. Meanwhile, the faint gray color may not look as pleasing but the clarity and calmness it brings allow us to distinguish between modesty, self-confidence, or disgrace. Ivy has indeed learned about the value of life and how to distinguish right from wrong. She carries a tolerance scale to measure every possibility in her life.

(Translated by Danny Tam)

阿爾貝托 Alberto Monteves

有地就有希望

Hope in the Land

阿爾貝托有塊地在火山岩上，土質肥沃，有了安心住屋，他與妻子勤快種菜，忘了身上的病痛。

Alberto has a piece of land at the foot of a volcano in Barangay Cabintan. Although he is suffering from leukemia, Alberto, along with his wife Lea, diligently plant and harvest vegetables in this piece of land.

車窗外，我瞧見那棵鳳凰木開著紅色的花朵，開得那麼燦爛，充滿喜氣、希望和豐收。

樹可以活得比人還老，看過比人類所見更廣大的世界，靜靜旁觀人們的生活，有時點點頭，有時搖搖頭，什麼都不說，卻毫不吝惜提供給人類使用！草木怎會無情呢？它們不就是跟我們一樣有大愛，所以才會付出無所求啊？

風和日麗的清晨，一打開車窗，草香味便撲鼻而來，奧莫克大愛村與奧莫克市車程距離不到半小時，空氣大不同；人多吵雜的奧莫克市總是烏煙瘴氣，而奧莫克大愛村這兒的空氣，卻清涼帶著花甜草香。

莉婭（Lea De La Peña）與阿爾貝托（Alberto Monteves）夫妻倆，一早載了一大袋白菜來奧莫克慈濟辦公室分享，他倆從

I see a fire tree through the car window. The blooming red flowers represent joy, hope, and bountiful harvest. Trees can live longer than any human being and can see a wider world than what humans can. They quietly watch over people's lives, sometimes nodding, sometimes shaking their heads, saying nothing. Regardless, they do not hesitate to provide service to humans! They know love as much as people do. Trees serve but never ask for anything in return. On a windy morning, when the window is open, the smell of grass drifts into the car. Ormoc Great Love Village and Ormoc City are only half an hour away from each other, but the air in each place is very different. Ormoc City is always plagued with noise and air pollution, but Ormoc Great Love Village is cool and smells of sweet flowers.

Couple Lea De La Peña and Alberto Monteves delivered a huge bag of cabbage to Ormoc Tzu Chi office to share with the villagers. They used to be neighbors and their families are two generations of farmers. In Leyte, the children take over their father's jobs and because of poverty, many are having

前是鄰居，兩家世代務農。

　　在萊特島，大半的人家都是子承父業，因為貧窮，沒能力讓子女好好受教育，是此地父母普遍的遺憾。

　　海燕風災發生時，強風摧毀了他們的家產，莉婭有四個孩子，阿爾貝托也有四個孩子，他們一起住進了政府的收容所，相互照顧而日久生情，之後兩人又有兩個孩子，最大的孩子十三歲，最小的才兩歲。也許是大自然反撲的恐懼，加上十二口人的沈重生活壓力，又望不見未來，阿爾貝托生病了。

　　阿爾貝托雙耳下的淋巴結、頭上、肩膀……長出一顆顆腫瘤，經醫師診斷為急性淋巴性白血病。這個病讓阿爾貝托的眼睛幾近失明，他看不清任何人，只能用聲音辨識。阿爾貝托的心情沈到谷底，恐懼、憂慮……各種情緒爬滿心靈寸土。

　　住在收容所未生病前，阿爾貝托還回卡賓坦（Carbintan）的土地去耕種，莉婭留在收容所照顧十個孩子。他在田裏種了各種蔬菜、甜椒、馬拉巴爾菠菜、秋葵、白菜、甘藍菜、番茄、洋蔥、茄子、豆類、佛手瓜……土地很大，阿爾貝托為了一家子人很勤奮地工作。尤其是白菜，需要種植在比較涼爽不炎熱的地方，他們有四公頃的土地可種植，因此種了很多。

　　阿爾貝托開始接受化療，從二〇一六年二月到十月，奧莫克和宿霧兩地奔波，總共接受九個月的療程。期間，他的身體虛弱痛苦，莉婭要照顧年幼的孩子又要照顧先生，那是一段艱辛難熬的歲月。

　　化療進入第八個月時，正是秋涼時節，大地上植物葉子漸漸變色，斑斑落落紛紛。這時，他們一家十二口終於盼到入住

difficulty sending their children to school to get an education. This is very common here. When Typhoon Haiyan happened, storm surge washed away the couple's property. Leah and Alberto each had four children from their previous unions. They lived in a government shelter and took care of each other for a long time, and later settled down together. Then they had two more children together. Their eldest is now thirteen years old while the youngest is only two years old. Perhaps it is the fear of nature's wrath and life's hardships that made the couple feel insecure about the future.

Alberto is sick. Tumors grow on his lymph nodes, head, and shoulders. He was diagnosed with acute lymphocytic leukemia. The disease rendered Alberto almost blind. Unable to see, he could only recognize people with their voices. Alberto's mood sank. His mind was filled with negative thoughts. Before he fell ill, while they were staying in the temporary shelters, Alberto even returned to Barangay Cabintan to cultivate crops, while Leah stayed in the shelter to take care of their ten children. Alberto planted various vegetables: sweet peppers, Malabar spinach, okra, cabbage, kale, tomato, onion, eggplant, beans, chayote... Alberto works very hard to support his family by tilling a four-hectare land.

From February to October 2016, Alberto underwent chemotherapy. For nine months, he traveled between Ormoc and Cebu City for the treament. Throughout this period, his body ached and weakened. Lea had to take care of the children. It was a difficult time. In the eight month of his chemotherapy, the weather begins to cool. And while the plants gradually wilt, the cold weather inevitably brings comfort; as if to say that something good is about to happen for Alberto and Lea's family. It was during this time that the family of twelve moved into the Ormoc Great Love Village.

The clean, white walls of the house has water and electricity supply. Everything is convenient and comfortable. There are two small yards in the front and back where flowers can be planted. The children run in a safe and worry-free environment, almost as if they were in heaven. It is like holding a

奧莫克大愛村。

潔白清爽的屋子，有水有電，一切都好方便又舒適，還有前後兩片小院子可種花樹。孩子們在大愛村的巷弄裏安全無憂地奔跑，彷若置身於天堂。

他們感到一股希望竄流過心田！好比拿著一臺相機，調整焦距、快門、光圈，稍稍轉折、慢慢靠近，終於找到一個美好的風景！

阿爾貝托治病時用盡存款，他不想把土地全賣掉，必須為妻兒打算，於是不得不停止治療。

莉婭勸他回醫院治療，他不肯。在這新的生活環境，慈濟每個月提供他們兩大袋大米和雜貨，莉婭不離不棄，把孩子照顧得很好，阿爾貝托想到這些，就覺得自己要堅強起來，帶著妻兒在這裏安居樂業，讓十個孩子都能接受良好的教育。

他從床上爬起來，到僅剩的兩公頃土地上繼續種菜。莉婭勸不動，只好帶著未上學的孩子一起下田，陪伴阿爾貝托。

秋天正午的陽光織著千絲萬縷的金線，燦爛、溫情，聽著妻兒的朗朗笑聲，丘陵吹來的微風習習，天地這麼大，什麼才是他真正要重視的事情？阿爾貝托在忙碌中，內心不斷湧現希望，沸騰不已！

一開始他們使用摩托車，從奧莫克大愛村到卡賓坦去種菜，並騎車到獨魯萬去賣，因為那裏買家較多。抵達獨魯萬，莉婭讓阿爾貝托休息，自己到超市出售作物，省去中間被剝削。

阿爾貝托滿心想著工作和妻兒，忘了自己的病，菜收成了，除了自家食用，也回饋給大愛村辦公室。

camera, adjusting the focus, shutter, aperture, slightly turning; and then slowly the resounding click captures a beautiful scenery - a picture that paints a happy family with hearts filled with hope. Alberto had used up his entire life savings when he was ill. He didn't want to sell his land but he had to think of his wife and children, so he decided to stop his treatment. Lea prostested but he stuck with his decision. At their new living environment, Tzu Chi provided them with two large bags of rice and groceries every month. Lea takes good care of their children. Every time Alberto thinks of these, he tells himself that he must remain strong so he can take care of his wife, and give their ten children a chance to receive a good education.

Every morning, he still rises up from bed and continues to plant vegetables on the two hectares that remain of his land. Lea cannot convince him to change his mind. Instead, she took her other children to work with Alberto. The midday sun is woven with thousands of golden lines, splendid and warm. Listening to the laughter of his wife and children, and feeling the breeze blowing from the hills, Alberto knows that his heart is at peace. The world is so big. Alberto is busy, but his heart continues to hope for the best for his family. At first, they used motorcycles from Ormoc Great Love Village to Cabintan to plant vegetables, and then drive to Tacloban City to sell their produce. There would normally be a lot of buyers in the city, and Alberto would let Lea do the selling. This way, they won't be exploited by the middlemen. Alberto is often filled with thoughts of his work, his wife and children that he sometimes forgets that he is sick. He continues to plant and harvest vegetables to support his family. In addition to cooking and eating these vegetables at home, he also gives a portion of his harvest to the office of the Great Love Village.

Hard work pays off. Eventually, the family receives more vegetable orders, especially from the tourist areas of northwest Leyte. After depositing a sum of money, they replaced their motorcycle with a multicab (a vehicle similar to a jeep) that could carry more vegetables. Last year, the cab had been replaced by a truck. The husband and wife are inseparable – both in sweet and

後來，他們得到萊特島西北部一些旅遊勝地的訂單，存到一筆錢，便將摩托車換成 multicab（類似吉普車的車輛），多功能用途可以載更多蔬菜去賣。近一年又換成卡車，夫妻同心，短短三年時間，生意愈做愈成功。

　　大家都說他們夫妻倆是「綠手指」，莉婭卻謙虛說不是，因為他們在卡賓坦種番茄長得非常好，在奧莫克自家庭院卻種不活！

　　慈濟志工好奇去他們卡賓坦的農場瞧瞧，放眼望去肥沃的土地，已由兩公頃又變回原來的四公頃了。

　　那片土地靠近奧拓峰（Alto Peak），是明杜穩（Mindowin Volcano）火山的土壤，含有二氧化碳、硫化物及微量元素，是植物重要的營養源，加上栽種的人懷著虔誠與愛心，難怪種出來的菜特別好吃。

　　恩典一點一滴匯聚，他們有時雙雙站立在豐收的綠田上，有如向陽植物，望著太陽的方向，感恩上帝的垂憐！

　　莉婭與阿爾貝托都會參與奧莫克大愛村的活動，特別是浴佛大典。每天下午三點，辦公室開始播放《人間菩提》節目時，只要他們工作回來得早，都會來聽證嚴法師說話。他們也逐漸茹素，翻轉人生！

　　世間道路歷經波折，一念之差，使人自春天走入冬天，而莉婭與阿爾貝托卻是一路自冬天走到春天。這一路有著太多凹痕、受損而顯得黯淡的影子，然而，傷口像山坳起了美麗的雲霧，層層疊疊掩去了傷痕。

　　愛，是最好的良藥！

bitter circumstances. In just three years, their business has grown even more successful. Everyone agrees that the husband and wife have "green thumbs", but Lea politely begged to disagree because the tomatoes are growing well in Cabintan but not in their home in Ormoc.

Tzu Chi volunteers got curious about what she said, and went to visit their farm in Cabintan to see it for themselves. Looking at the fertile land, which was bought back to become its initial four hectares, they saw that Alberto and Lea are cultivating it well. It looked immaculately healthy. Their land is close to Alto Peak. It is the soil of the Mindowin Volcano. It contains carbon dioxide, sulfides and trace elements which are nutrients needed by plants to flourish. It is no wonder then that people who cultivate this land diligently will bring home some of the best and delicious vegetables worthy of other peoples' praise. Grace gathers bit by bit, and sometimes grows on the harvests of green fields, like a sunny plant, looking at the direction of the sun, thanking God for His mercy! In Alberto and Lea's hearts, they hold gratitude not only towards God but also towards the Master Cheng Yen. Both of them participate in the activities of the Ormoc Great Love Village, especially the Buddha Day Ceremony.

Every day at 3 pm, when the office starts to broadcast the "*Life Wisdom*" program, they will come if they are back early so they can listen to Master Cheng Yen teach. They will become vegetarians gradually, and their lives are turning around. In life, people experience twists and turns and the difference between the two makes people walk into winter from spring. But Lea and Alberto went to the opposite direction of the seasons. The road they have traveled may be paved with many bumps, but they walk through it with grace and courage. And like clouds with silver linings, their pains gradually turn into healing and peace.

Love is indeed the best medicine!

(Translated by BT Lin)

潔拉丁姊弟 Geraldine and Romeo Casila

有志一同

Aspiring Together

羅米歐跟著姊姊潔拉丁加入慈青而改掉惡習，目前姊弟倆均是大學犯罪防治科學生。

Romeo Casila followed his sister Geraldine in joining the Tzu Ching and avoiding ill vices. They both took up criminology in the university and dreamed of becoming policemen in the near future.

車子在時光流裏穿梭奧莫克市街頭，連著好幾輛吉普尼自車側滑過，湧入車流，慢動作的我總捕捉不到它完美特殊的身型。吉普尼是由美軍二戰後留下的吉普車改造而成，我喜歡它們紅、綠、黃、藍交織的流線，有時黑色線條點綴其間，好像卡通裏的車樣，它們的用途類似小巴士，比三輪車載更多人。

菲利士把車開往奧莫克大愛村時，總不忘讓我們買些水果分享給大愛村的志工們。我在臺灣看過波羅蜜，但未曾嘗過它的美味，還有一種叫做 guyabano 的水果，長得像臺東太麻里的鳳梨釋迦，但更大一些，綠皮薄容易撞壞，據說可以抗癌，吃起來酸酸甜甜，是我在菲律賓最喜歡的兩種水果。

往奧莫克大愛村的路，剛開始覺得好長好長，天空好大，夾道的灌木叢一路綠往遠方山谷，人彷彿飄浮在綠色空中。及

Cars filled the streets of Ormoc City in a steady stream, while jeepneys threaded in and out of the traffic. As someone who moves slowly, I always fail to capture its unique appearance in my photos. Jeepneys are modified based on the World War II jeeps with body and chassis colorfully decorated. My favorite colors are the combination of red, green, yellow and blue lines. Sometimes, black lines highlight the vehicle, like a car in a cartoon. They resemble small buses and can carry more people than the tricycle. Jeepneys are the ubiquitous taxi cabs in the Philippines.

As Felix Cascara drives our car to Ormoc Great Love Village, I always remember to buy fruits to share with the volunteers. Although I had seen jackfruits in Taiwan, I had never tasted it. There is another fruit called guyabano, which resembles a pineapple custard from Taimari, Taitung, Taiwan, only it is bigger, with a thin green skin that easily breaks. It is said that this fruit can fight and even prevent cancer. It is both sweet and sour. They are my two favorite fruits in the Philippines.

至到了大愛村，看到活潑的慈青們，自己似乎也回到學生時代……

短髮的潔拉丁目光炯炯，乍看以為是個男孩，她大學畢業了，正準備警察執照考試，是個內心堅強的女孩。她的弟弟羅米歐個子修長，濃眉大眼帥氣無比，姊弟倆大學讀的都是犯罪防治學科，但羅米歐入學晚了好幾年，因為他曾經遺失自己一段時間。

他們的父親是三輪車夫，為了一家十口人，辛苦工作，完全沒有假日。從前他們住在奧莫克市邦帝格（Bantigue），那兒出入的人龍蛇混雜，父母親限制他們外出，擔心孩子們沾染惡習。即便如此，羅米歐上高中後還是結識了損友，開始抽菸、喝酒、打架，讓父母親心碎。他們擔心羅米歐一直錯下去，再也走不回來。

拮据的家境，為了讓潔拉丁上大學，母親甚至不惜借高利貸。潔拉丁為了緩和家中經濟，加入學校的籃球隊好取得獎學金。懂事又富正義感的她，會幫著母親規勸弟弟，但當時的羅米歐像是著了魔，還會惡煞似地反擊父母，傷盡家人的心！

海燕風災發生後，他們住進政府收容所，潔拉丁在那兒遇見慈濟。慈濟幫助受災的學子們繼續受教育，那時潔拉丁就讀大學一年級，慈濟每個月給她助學金。

這是她有生以來遇見最美好的事情，一個遠在她不認識的地方，有一位證嚴法師創立了慈濟，抱持著對世界與眾生的大愛，馳援許多受災的國家，予以慈善、教育、醫療救助與環保人文的教養。

On my first visit to Ormoc Great Love Village, it felt very far away from the city. The sky is vast, and the green bushes stretch to the distant valley. It seems like people float in the green sky. When we arrived at the Great Love Village, it felt like I was brought back to my childhood when I saw the Tzu Chings were there. Geraldine Casila looks like a boy with the short hair that she wears. She has a pair of bright eyes. Having graduated from college, Geraldine is now preparing to get her police license. She is a lady with a strong determination. Her younger brother, Romeo Casila, is slender with thick eyebrows. Both siblings studied criminology in college. However, Romeo has yet to finish college because he lost direction for a while.

Their father is a pedicab driver who works even on holidays to support his family of ten. He was quite strict with allowing his children to hang out with other kids out of fear that they may pick up bad habits. Even so, in his high school days, Romeo still got acquainted with other young people who have bad habits such as smoking, drinking and fighting...It was enough to break his parents' hearts. They were afraid that Romeo may have wandered off the wrong path and might never find his way back.

Their life was one of poverty...Their mother was forced to borrow money to send Geraldine to college. Aware that her parents were struggling to put her to school, Geraldine joined the school's basketball team for the free tuition. Geraldine also tried to help her mother bring back some sense into Romeo but he seemed to be possessed by a demon and had broken his family's heart!

After Typhoon Haiyan struck, the family moved into a government shelter. It was there that Geraldine became acquainted with Tzu Chi. Tzu Chi helped the children of typhoon-stricken families to continue their education. Geraldine was in her first year at the university when Tzu Chi granted her scholarship. It was the best thing that have ever happened to her. She found that there is a faraway place that she did not know of before, and that there is a person like Master Cheng Yen who founded the Tzu Chi Foundation out

潔拉丁非常喜歡法師的開示，雖然宗教不同，但她深愛著法師說的一句話：「萬般帶不走，只有業隨身。」過去，她認為人生只是為了生活與回饋父母恩情，如今她發現生命有無限可能，幫助與付出，讓生命開出芬芳的花朵。

　　四年前，他們一家入住大愛村，羅米歐看著姊姊從大學畢業，心裏很是羨慕。從小他便渴望穿上那一身看起來英勇無比的警察制服，還記得兒時與兄弟姊妹玩射擊遊戲，自己就是扮演那英勇的警員！

　　羅米歐沈淪三年，其實內心很欣羨同齡去上學的人，大愛村的靜謐環境早已搖撼出他遠離損友的想法，他決定續讀高中課程。但是母親不相信他會改變，不肯給他學費，羅米歐只好一邊上課，一邊去球場當撿球員，打工支持自己的學業。

　　直到他拿到畢業證書，母親才相信他真的回頭了。經年累月的憂慮，化為金黃的蜜糖，又如風乾的果實，凝結了甜美。欣慰之餘，她想到了慈濟，覺得孩子們都是因為在慈濟接受證嚴法師的教導薰陶，才學會擁有一顆慈悲心，真正去尊重、善解他人。

　　羅米歐上了大學，選擇了與姊姊同樣的科系——犯罪防治。

　　問姊弟倆為何都選擇了犯罪防治科？姊姊說：「我叔叔曾經被一名警官陷害為肇事逃逸者，因而死亡。因此我認為一個忠誠且善良的警察，才能真正保護人民。」弟弟說：「我孩提時便夢想自己能穿上警察制服，長大後更意識到身為警察，能保護我們的國家。」

　　一位懷仁，一位懷勇，真是一對有仁且勇的模範姊弟。

of her great love for the world and all sentient beings. She loves the Master's teaching very much, and even though she is of different religion, Geraldine likes these words by the Master: "Nothing follows us when we die except our Karma." Geraldine used to think that in life, she needs to give back only to her parents. But she has discovered an entirely new meaning in life. Helping others, who are not related to us in an anyway, enriches our lives, like blooming flowers.

Four years ago, the family moved into the Great Love Village. Romeo watched with envy as his sister graduate from college. Since he was young, Romeo had dreamt of wearing a police uniform. He imagined himself as a hero. He remembered playing with his brothers and sisters in their childhood. In the game, they would pretend to be heroic policemen, shooting guns.

Romeo lost his tracks in life for three years. He would feel envious every time he sees his batch mates go to school. The peaceful environment at the Great Love Village shook him to consider avoiding friends with bad influence. He decided to finish his secondary education but his mother refused to believe that he would change. Romeo was determined. To put himself to school, Romeo worked as a caddie.

Eventually, he graduated from high school. His mother was finally convinced that he was serious about straightening his life out. The mother knew that her children changed after being immersed in the teachings of Master Cheng Yen through Tzu Chi. This is where they learned to be compassionate and thoughtful of others as well as to respect all living beings.

When Romeo went to college, he chose the same path as his sister: Criminology. When I asked why the two of them had chosen this path, Geraldine shared: "My uncle was set up by a police officer and got killed. I want to be a policewoman to prove that not every police is corrupt. I want to show that they could be kind and honest too, protecting everyone." Romeo added: "When I was a child, I used to believe that I could wear a police

把夢想想得太簡單時，夢想是不會服氣的；通常要耗費時間甚或受傷，才能深刻體會它的不可或缺與存在，才會使勁抓著它不放。用心看時，它也像一場慢慢痊癒的病症，細細的灰塵透過安靜的呼吸，讓混濁的血液漸漸澄明；破碎、日常的一切，需要耐心等待它的改變。

　　很多時候，我們有話想說但沒有人懂，枝條藏在葉子背後，故事藏在灰濛無知的過去式裏。潔拉丁兒時的痛，轉化成往後志願的動力；羅米歐則是脫胎換骨，找回兒時遺落的星星，自黑暗中勇敢跳脫，努力發出微光，兩者均是難能可貴的金石試煉與琢磨。

　　羅米歐曾與我一起造訪大愛村裏的醫療關懷個案，哭鬧中的孩童喜歡他的氣味，願意讓他抱抱，連小狗也搖著友善的尾巴跟隨著他。深刻體解《慈悲三昧水懺》後的他，散發一股柔波，相信經歷沈淪，他已記取羞辱以及每一次信念考驗，現在的他比任何人都謙遜。

　　他感謝慈濟能接納曾經學壞的自己，願意給他一個成長機會去追夢。如果此刻人生是他的第二次旅行，相信市容已與幾年前大不相同，而記憶或許也被修改過了。

　　綠色山谷環抱的奧莫克大愛村開放了另一處幽靜，一條敘事軸線穿越過不同人事，記述不同風景，在乎不同感情。有什麼是姊弟倆共同擁有的呢？

　　縮小一點自我，多了幾分大愛，如飛鳥放膽去散播善良，如魚穿過藻荇與泥土，充滿覺悟的心，誠心實意守護生命的翻轉與希望。

uniform if I want to. But when I grew up, I realized that it takes a kind and brave person to become a policeman and to serve and protect our country." One is benevolent; the other, brave. This pair of siblings is truly a role model for the youth.

If our dreams are thought of so simply, it may never come true. Often times, we need to spend a lot of time and may even get hurt in our pursuit of our dreams in order to realize and cherish its value. If we observe it mindfully, it is like an illness that gradually heals; like fine dusts that slowly settles with each silent breathing; like blood particles in different densities precipitating in layers after centrifugation. Damages, and everything around us need patience in awaiting its transformation.

Many times, we have something to say, but it feels like nobody would understand. Just as the branches of a tree are hidden by the leaves, our story is concealed in the past. The painful experiences in her childhood have become Geraldine's motivation to volunteer. After Romeo turned his life around and escaped from his dark past, he bravely strives forward every day toward the light. Romeo once accompanied me on a follow-up visit to several medical patients at the Great Love Village. A crying child liked his smell and wanted to hug him. A small puppy followed him around. His understanding of "*The Compassionate Samadhi Water Repentance*" seem to make him radiate with softness. His past mistakes have taught him faith, and humility. He appreciates that Tzu Chi has given him a chance to pursue his dreams despite his past.

Surrounded by green valleys, Ormoc Great Love Village is rich with stories on different subjects and views. So what do these stories have in common? Reduce yourself a little bit, increase love a bit more. Be like flying birds who spread goodness, a fish swimming through the algae and the muddy water. With enlightened hearts, they diligently seize every chance to turn their lives around.

(Translated by BT Lin)

成就夢想

Achieving the Dream

慈濟為貧困的村民進行眼科義診，學護理的瑞秋正檢查一位老奶奶的眼睛。
Tzu Chi conducted an eye surgical mission for poor villagers. Rachel, who is studying Nursing, is checking the eyes of an old lady.

秋分，奧莫克大愛村堤防旁土地上，常可見殷實的身影，捧起一顆大南瓜割下，仔細拍淨它身上的泥土；或是摘下翠綠的秋葵，兜攏了收成。

對岸平鋪直去的綠田與丘陵，似近又遠，我始終沒有走向它的時間。

陽光帶著輕輕甜味，透過玻璃，寬容地照著瑞秋（Rachel Mae Costelo）早熟的臉龐。

瑞秋的母親年輕時反覆幾次走過情感的冬天，像練習彈鋼琴，反覆出錯、反覆再彈，真實的人在生活裏離開又靠近，不只是琴聲消佚與一成不變的曲調。

因著這些情感的變換，瑞秋的童年就像扎在草垛裏被蚊蟲咬了一身疙瘩的孩子，對父愛與呵護的渴望，癢在心底，隱忍

In the autumnal equinox, on the land next to the embankment of Ormoc's Great Love Village, a figure is often seen. Take a large pumpkin, cut it and carefully pat the dirt off it, or pick the green okra and gather the harvest. The green fields and hills that stretched on from the other side of the village seemed so close. But in truth, there were far away. Sadly, I never got a chance to visit them.

The sweet sunlight faithfully follows Rachel Mae Costelo's precocious face as she moves about. When Rachel's mother was young, she walked through the winter in her love affairs several times, like practicing the piano. She repeatedly made the same mistakes. Real people in her life left and came again, until the melody was lost in the repetition of the tunes.

Because of this, Rachel spent her childhood like a child hiding in a haystack, bitten by mosquitos. Hungry for a father's love and care, Rachel constantly felt an itch on the bottom of her heart.

不發。

母親的前兩段婚姻裏，瑞秋從未感受到父愛，即便是自己的親生父親，從她初萌的幼年，父親便不接受她。

是何原因呢？小小的心靈不明白，她懷疑而膽怯地度過飽受父親冷落的歲月。

夫妻就像一棵樹，風雨飄搖一起度過。丈夫對女兒無以名狀的情緒，瑞秋的母親看在眼裏，卻不知該怎麼解開，如果只是一條繩子繫住那麼簡單，不知多好！

十月懷胎辛苦生下女兒，得不到丈夫認可的苦楚，她能彌補給瑞秋的就是滿滿的母愛，並且讓瑞秋有正常上學的機會，希望同窗情誼，可以沖刷掉部分心底的失落。

生活中總有許多瑣碎的細節需要磨合，瑞秋父母間的距離，時間長了就無法追補或忍受，終至離婚。

一段情感消逝，彷彿斷了線的風箏，從夢中醒來，卻再度失去方向。

瑞秋的母親再婚，繼父對瑞秋有更多負面情緒的宣洩，和瑞秋的母親也有許多衝突。

悲劇有時會重複發生，順著因緣走到這裏，卻是事與願違，加深悲傷。

她不想像初婚時那般衝動，還存著一些盼望，想給對方多一些時間來接受瑞秋，於是不得不把瑞秋送到外婆那兒生活，辛苦工作供給瑞秋念書，想彌補女兒因為她所受的種種委屈。

瑞秋喜歡與外婆一起生活，她穿制服上學，像小麻雀小小跳步，繞過盆栽與盆栽，制服底下變換著細瑣的腳步。親生父

Unfortunately, Rachel never got a chance to receive love from a father. Neither her biological father nor the two other men that her mother had subsequently married accepted her. Why? Her little heart could not understand. She suffered from her father's coldness. As a result, she doubted her capability and spent her childhood in timidity.

A couple is like a tree being constantly blown by a storm. Her mother and her step-father are never lacking in arguments, especially when it comes to Rachel. Rachel's mother sees the absence of love between her husband and her daughter. And yet, she does not know how to solve it. A knotted up rope would be much easier to fix. She gave birth to her daughter, yet she could not get any of her husband's comfort and approval. The only thing she could do was give Rachel her full maternal love and the opportunity to be educated. She hoped that in school, Rachel would make many friends who will fill up the empty parts of her heart with love.

There are always many trivial details in life that need to be run in. Rachel's biological parents were unable to settle their differences and none of them wanted to endure it for a long time so they separated. The love that bound them together at first suddenly disappeared, like a kite that was blown by the wind after the string broke.

After the separation, Rachel's mother met a new man. Rachel's stepfather cannot accept Rachel, which resulted to fights with her mother. Tragedy sometimes repeats itself. Rachel's mother have learned not to be as impulsive as she was when she first got married. To give her new husband more time to accept Rachel, she sent her daughter to live with her grandmother. She worked hard to provide for Rachel and to atone for her daughter's grievances towards her for accepting another man. Rachel likes living with her grandmother.

Wearing her school uniform, she looks like a small sparrow that walks along the garden with subtle steps that seem to change every minute. The coldness of her biological father and the rejection of her step-father made her

親與繼父對她的冷落，雖讓她因此自卑，卻也使她更想努力求表現，希望藉此得到認可與愛。

母親與繼父為她添了一雙弟妹，她沈默地接受了。她在學業上認真耕耘，制服在風裏輕輕飄搖，她像植物一樣順著光的方向，記著太陽給她的指引，她願自己有一顆溫暖的心，能點燈照亮外海，讓巨大的輪船慢慢靠近港灣，不受巨浪驚擾。

瑞秋的母親維持著婚姻，她工作、牽掛瑞秋，和第二任丈夫生下一兒一女，她努力想挽住身邊的男人，他卻出了軌，離開了家庭。

明明早晨還盛開在枝頭的美麗花朵，天空的雲彩卻瞬間變成灰色，下起傾盆大雨，不知從哪個方向吹來的風，使勁把花枝搖晃著，花朵就離枝隨風飄散了。

然而，黑暗的夜總還是會退去，天亮的時候，潮溼的路面在霧裏緩慢伸展，陰霾心緒漸漸淡化，消失在遠方。

路上一個行人走向瑞秋的母親，挽起她的手，再度走入她的生命。

雖然這男人之前有過一段婚姻，他卻是唯一接受並愛護瑞秋的好男人，他包容瑞秋的母親與她所有的孩子。

人生，常常在你覺得路上一個行人也沒有，沒有花朵、沒有風、沒有草時，告訴你不要急，只要像摺疊一件舊衣裳那般，把哀傷的事情慢慢理平就好。

瑞秋重新回到母親身邊，但她也常念著外婆。

初中時，瑞秋曾在路上遇見一位斷了腿的乞丐，她憐憫地給了他麵包，並問他為何斷了腿？

feel inferior, but it also pushed her to study even harder to excel, hoping that through this, she will catch their attention and eventually, their love. Rachel's mother had two more children with her stepfather. Rachel quietly accepted her new siblings. She also takes her studies seriously. Her uniforms seem to sway with the wind. Like a sunflower, she remembers the direction of the sun and follows it. Rachel longs to have a brightly shining loving heart. She wants to be the lighthouse that guides ships to dock smoothly.

Rachel's mother worked hard to keep her new husband. However, he had an affair and subsequently left the family. While the beautiful flowers on the branches are still blooming in the morning, the clouds in the sky suddenly turned to gray. Under the heavy rain, the wind blows from all directions, causing the branches to sway violently and the flowers to drift away. However, the dark night always retreats. When dawn comes, the road gradually appears through the mist; the haze gradually fades and disappears.

One day, a man walked into Rachel's mother's life again and took her hand. Although he had been married before, he is a good man. He accepted and loved Rachel and was tolerant of all her siblings. Most of the time when you felt you're all alone on the road, with no flowers, no wind, and no grass, life will tell you to slow down. It is like folding old clothes, you just have to straighten things up.

Rachel returned home to her mother. But she often remembers her grandmother. In junior high school, Rachel met a beggar who had a broken leg. Out of compassion, she gave him bread and asked how he broke his leg. He said that when his granddaughter was sick and was brought to the hospital, she did not receive treatment because she did not have money. So, he rushed out, intending to raise money but got hit by a car. The driver had fled, leaving him there with a broken leg....

Rachel could not bear to ask further details of the accident because he was ragged and was nursing a broken leg. But her desire to care for injured

乞丐說，他的孫女生病送醫時，因為他付不出錢而得不到救治，他急著出來籌錢卻又被車撞，撞他的人肇事逃逸，他失去了腿……

瑞秋不忍再問後來結果，看他斷腿又衣衫襤褸，一股想幫助、照護受傷者的欲望不斷在她胸臆蠢動，想當一名護理師的念頭開始滋長。

繼父與母親要籌措三個孩子的教育基金和生活費，生活非常拮据。高中畢業的瑞秋聽說慈濟有獎助學金的面試機會，她鼓起勇氣前來。她說著自身的故事，淚水不斷自眼角滴下。

「這對我來說非常重要，因為這個獎學金給了我實現夢想的機會，這個夢想不僅對我一人，同時也能利益其他人；這個夢想能讓我擁有照護別人的能力，它才有了意義。」

從小孤單地長大，還期望自己能足夠強壯去照護那些弱勢族群的瑞秋，這一股大愛精神正好契合了慈濟理念，志工們上前擁抱瑞秋。

拍著孩子的背，李偉嵩告訴瑞秋：「慈濟每一位志工都有自己的家庭和事業，但是當全球有地方或人群受難需要我們時，我們便把私事先放一旁，不分宗教信仰地去救助，為同一個大愛信念齊心努力。」

晴好的秋天，風裏搖曳的成串枝葉漸漸變了顏色。

人生中每一分波折，都不與另一分相同，光影閃爍，美好而難以形容。時光彷彿是不歇的，它安寧、穩定，瑞秋的夢想此刻像流瀉的瀑布，能聽見輕輕的風吹與水漩，她踏上慈青的步履，向理想邁開腳步，堅定而沒有猶豫！

people was strong, so she continued to help. It was in that moment when the thought of becoming a nurse entered her mind and began to grow.

Rachel's mother and stepfather are paying for the children's education as well as their daily living expenses so life was difficult and money was very tight. After graduating from high school, Rachel heard that Tzu Chi is opening its scholarship program to Ormoc students. She mustered all her courage to apply and attend the interview. She told them her story as tears formed in the corners of her eyes: "Getting this scholarship is very important to me because this will give me the opportunity to realize my dream, which is not only going to benefit myself but other people as well. My dream is meaningful as it will give me the chance to care for others."

She added: "Growing up alone, I have hoped to be strong enough to care for the disadvantaged groups." This spirit of love is in line with Tzu Chi's ideologies. Hearing this, Tzu Chi volunteers embraced Rachel. Patting Rachel on the back, Alfredo Li said: "Every volunteer in Tzu Chi has their own family and career, but when there are places or people around the world who need us, we will set our personal needs aside to help. Regardless of the differences in our religions, we go to them in good faith, working together to spread great love."

In the fine autumn breeze, the leaves gradually change their colors as they dance with the wind.

Each obstacle in life is never the same from one person to another. It flickers like the light and shadow, and you just cannot describe its beauty. Time keeps moving on, quietly and unfailingly. Rachel's dream is like a waterfall. You'll hear the gentle blow of the wind and the twirl of the water. She embarks on her Tzu Ching journey toward her goals with firm steps and without hesitation!

(Translated by Joanne Lee)

【跋】暗夜星光

蘇芳霈

　　寫此書有許多困難點需突破，第一個考驗是語言。菲律賓當地以英文為主，萊特島又以米沙鄢方言為主，到了奧莫克大愛村，我的中文只能跟少數的華人說，其他人就要「練習英文」了。所以過程中錄音很重要，用心聽，沒聽懂先錄了再說，錄音筆、手機齊來，就擔心有所遺漏。

　　錄回來的聲音檔要化成文字，得反覆聽，騎單車上下班、在家裏抹地板、做瑜伽、澆花，一遍又一遍重複聽。一有不解，立即找筆記下來，有時是一個人名，有時是一個地名或風土民情，記錄以後再查詢。

　　奧莫克大愛村的慈青瑪恬（Marithel Valiente）、爾文（Ervin John Lagahit）、馬克（Mark Mendoza）、安娜莉亞（Annarea Camielle Impas）、潔拉丁（Geraldine Casila）、萊卡（Lyka Joy Aseo）、耶羅（Erold Quinto）、詹姆斯（James Anthony Anasco）、瑞秋（Rachel Mae Costelo）、艾莉莎（Alyssa Candela）等人，協助把米沙鄢方言譯成英文給我，仔細不遺漏任何蛛絲馬跡。

　　第二個考驗是時間與耐力的比賽。寫文章，真像入禪定，靈感來時，一發不可收拾；偶爾在一個字上斤斤計較好久。一年裏，火力集中為完成一本書或畫集，熬夜一季總有的；這時，我會補充一顆含有朝鮮薊、西洋蔘、兒茶酚、五種身體需要的重要胺基酸、九種 B 群維生素的保健食品，或是將羅漢果半顆、黃耆三片、杭菊十朵、澎大海三顆、枸杞十顆，以五百毫升熱

— Postscript Starlight in the Dark Night —

By Fang-Pei Su

There were so many difficulties to break through while writing this book. The first of which is language barrier. English is the main language used in the Philippines, and the main dialect being used in Leyte is Visayan. In Ormoc Great Love Village, I can only speak in Chinese Mandarin to a few Chinese. Others would tell me that they are "practicing my English". When we did the interviews, sound recording became very important. We have to record everything before anything else. I used recording pen and hand phone at the same time, for good measure. In case we miss out a part of the interview in the first recording equipment, we can go through it again in the other.

To convert these recorded audio files into text, I had to listen to it over and over again. While riding the bicycle to and from work, while mopping the floor at home, while doing yoga exercises and while watering the flowers, I had to listen to the recordings repeatedly. Whenever a question came to mind, I would immediately take note of it. At times, it might just be a person's name, a location or some traditional culture. After listening to the recording, I would have to check and inquire.

The Tzu Ching Group in Ormoc Great Love Village comprised of Marithel Valiente, Ervin John Lagahit, Mark Mendoza, Annarea Camielle Impas, Geraldine Casila, Lyka Joy Aseo, Erold Quinto, James Anthony Anasco, Rachel Mae Costelo, Alyssa Candela, among others helped translate the interviews from the Visayan dialect into English. They were so thorough that they did not miss a single important detail.

Every day, save from the four to five hours of sleep, I was busy listening to the recordings, translations and writing articles. What remained of my time, I spent on my profession as a pharmacist.

水沖泡飲用，養肝、排毒、養肺、增加抵抗力，第二次沖三百毫升，第三次一百毫升，這樣算一日量。然而，心的快樂才是最佳良藥，能治百病。

第三個考驗是飲食。菲律賓當地少人食素，我們在萊特島要茹素，每日早餐只能出入麥當勞，吃些薯餅、薯條、咖啡及可可。中午、晚上大多在奧莫克大愛村廚房用餐，那時彷若置身天堂。偶爾假日廚房沒開伙，就在披薩店裏將披薩去肉，好不容易有餐廳，也一定把肉換成蘑菇。

接受過考驗，我所收穫的是美麗的風土人情。為書籍配圖找照片時，發現前奧莫克市長艾德華寇迪拉永遠是一身紅上衣，不知是同樣式衣服買了好幾件，還是菲律賓氣候炎熱，當天洗立刻乾，隔日又可再穿？總之，艾德華市長給人的感覺就是那麼樸實、親民又節儉，待人卻一點也不吝嗇，他有一顆寬闊與慈悲的心。

傑里醫師跟我們一起探勘奧莫克大愛村時，經常輕快地吟唱英文歌，歌聲美好耐聽。當我們請他把維希的夫人送的香蕉捧回家時，他的腳步由慢轉快把我們都拋在腦後，我們開始笑著對他唱「Oh My Love My Darling」那首老歌，結果走在兩岸菅芒小路上，手負沈重香蕉的背影，也不斷回首望著我們笑……

英文主編美國的鄭茹菁也是幽默風趣的人物，每每詞窮總說要去請教 YY（湯耀洋），一開始我以為 YY 是茹菁的女兒，但茹菁立馬回答我：「我跟我女兒不熟！」噗噗……

另一位英文翻譯林碧桃，她的先生是老布希總統的發言撰稿人。每次林碧桃用心在體會蘇式散文，她的先生便挑戰句子

Writing is pretty much like entering into meditative concentration. Whenever an inspiration comes up, it could hardly be contained. Occasionally, I would have a long internal debate over the choice of a word. For over a year, I concentrated my full energy and frequently stayed up late in the night to complete the book. I would take one tablet of vitamins that contains five important amino acids such as artichoke, citronella and catechol as well as nine kinds of vitamin B as my health care supplement. Alternatively, I would brew a half piece of Luo Han Guo, three slices of Scutellaria baicalensis, ten chrysanthemums, three pieces of malva nuts, and ten wolfberries in 500 ml of hot water to nourish my liver, detoxify, nourish the lungs and strengthen my immune system. After that I would brew it again for the second time in 300 ml of water and for the third time in 100 ml of water. Nevertheless, a happy mind is still the best medicine against all diseases.

The second challenge is food. Very few Filipinos are vegetarian. To follow a vegetarian diet in Leyte, we go to McDonald's for breakfast and order hash brown, French fries, coffee and cocoa. For lunch and dinner, Ormoc Great Love Village's kitchen prepares our meals. Angelique and Myra's cooking skills are exquisite. We seemed to be living in paradise. Occasionally, during the holidays when the kitchen is closed, we would go to pizza shops and remove meat from the pizza before eating. It was very difficult to find a restaurant that is vegetarian-friendly but we still need to replace meat with mushrooms.

Overcoming such challenges, what I reaped were the beautiful local cultures and customs. While browsing through the photos we took, looking for images that will match the book, I noticed that the former mayor of Ormoc, Edward Cordilla, is always wearing a red shirt. I wondered if he had bought several clothes with the same pattern or was it because the climate in the Philippines is so hot that after washing, clothes can dry up on the same day, making it possible for him to wear the same shirt the next day. In short, Mayor Edward gave people the impression that he is simple, friendly and frugal yet generous to others. He has a broad and compassionate heart.

的「主詞＋動詞＋形容詞＋名詞」，夫妻倆各執一詞，曾為了某句翻譯打起冷戰，三天不講話！這是個意外篇。

　　茹菁總是一路翻譯一路校正，她還負責美國醫療志業的Newsletter，十分忙碌。她總是叨念「蘇蘇的散文超難翻譯，很難用英文描述」，曾經有段時間，她的美國同事都叫她「鐵樹身上的行雲流水」，因為她逢人便提問。噗噗！茹菁啊，真對不起！

　　翻譯校正過程漫長，我們（英文主編鄭茹菁、中文主編陳玫君與我）的群組，常常看她倆一句來一句去：「笑容如何了？」「笑容改好了，有兩個地方無法修整，我請YY幫我看一下。」噗噗！篇名〈每一個笑容都值得紀念〉字數特長，譯成英文更不得了，我像是個麻煩製造者！

　　還有，我寫菅芒，群組裏討論英文翻譯時，她倆都寫官芒，我很擔心再次查了字典確認無誤，卻捏了一把冷汗！

　　中文於二○一九年九月底完成，陸續經由鄭茹菁（Andrey Cheng）、張麗雲（Celia Chang）、林碧桃（BT Lin）、黃時好（Si Ho Ooi）、楊大蓉（Christine Fisk）、譚瑞欽（Danny Tam）、李慧瓊（Joanne Lee）、周晶婷（Gloria Chou）、林妤（Erin Lin）、林婕（Jane Lin）、蔡碧清（Carmen Sy）、簡婉平（Emily Chu）、林秀雲（Helena Lin）等志工將中文譯成英文。菲律賓方面另有一個英文總校正群組，直到全書完成已是年底。幾個月來，大家都辛苦了！

　　我像一隻誤闖叢林的粉蝶，衝撞出奧莫克大愛村專書，但願不辱使命，融入菲律賓的風土民情，將人人堅定信念共譜大愛、翻轉人生的故事，傳達給更多人，因感動而心蓮朵朵相連，

When Jery joined us in surveying the Ormoc Great Love Village, he often delightfully burst into singing English songs. He has a beautiful voice. When we asked him to carry the bananas, which were given by Vergelio's wife, to the office, his footsteps quickened, leaving us all behind. We laughed and sang the old song, "Oh My Love, My Darling". Walking on the narrow road lined with silver grass on both sides, we watched Jery carry the heavy bananas with both of his hands while he kept looking back at us, smiling.

My English editor-in-chief from the United States, Audrey Cheng, also has a good sense of humor. Every time she runs out of vocabulary words, she would consult "YY" (Yau-Yang Tang). At first, I thought YY was the name of her daughter but Audrey immediately said, "I am not familiar with my daughter!" Huh Huh ....

Another English translator is BT Lin whose husband used to write President Bush's speeches. Every time BT Lin has mindfully translated in my writing style, her husband would challenge her on the "subject + verb + adjective + noun" structure of the sentences. Each would insist on using their respective choice of words. Once, after disagreeing in the translation of certain sentences, they refused to talk to each other for three days! This was truly unexpected!

Audrey translated as well as proofread the materials. Since she also handles the US medical team's newsletter, she is extremely busy. She always grumbled, "Susu's prose poems are extremely difficult to translate. They are very difficult to describe in English." For a time, her American colleagues had described her as "so natural and spontaneous like the moving clouds and flowing water on the iron tree" because she raised questions whenever she came across anyone... Huh Huh! Audrey, I am really sorry!

The translation and proofreading process took very long. In our Line group, I would often saw Audrey and my Chinese editor-in-chief Milly Chen arguing: "How about the smile?" "The smile has already been corrected, there

於暗夜星光下續續綻放。

　　豐收而飛越阡陌無數，講最多英文，認識最單純可愛的一村人，我與維希牽著艾菲達一起在稻田裏散步閒聊，與前奧莫克市長、夫人、伊薩卡尼神父、本土人醫會醫師長談，及至關懷他們在村裏的病患狀況，甚至衛教、藝術治療、到拜訪平價披薩店英文老師艾德溫；與潘信成陪著傑里赴這有著美麗晚霞的國度探勘，在雨中跳著坑疤泥地，口裏依然苦中作樂哼著歌……好似一場美夢。

　　為重度憂鬱的喬娜琳藝術治療時，我們事先買好六支白色蠟燭，藉著這聖潔的白色，在藝術治療後，點燃鐵盤上的蠟燭，關了燈，墨色中我與潘信成、傑里、羅米歐、喬娜琳及其雙親坐著，手牽手圍個圓，英文不怎麼溜的我竟能如神父一般為喬娜琳禱告十分鐘！艾莉莎竟也能聽懂，為我譯成萊特島語。不得不讚歎我自己，噗噗……尤其她重展美麗笑顏那一刻，她的父母也轉愁容為笑顏，大夥兒又哼起歌來了……

　　二〇一九年底，奧莫克大愛村有十九人來臺於慈濟板橋園區受證。我買了手帕、蓮花琉璃掛飾、鑰匙布包送給他們。我告訴他們：「手帕是願落實環保於生活，少用衛生紙便能減少伐木救地球；蓮花琉璃於默中能展亮，願奧莫克大愛村點點心燈相連；至於鑰匙布包，則願大家如鑰匙成串永不散去！」

　　世界一家親，讓我們無藩籬，緊繫菩薩行。

are two lines which cannot be corrected. I asked YY to have a look." Huh Huh! The article entitled "Save Each Smile in My Mind" has a long word count, and to translate this into English is even worse. I am like a troublemaker!

Also, when I wrote the word "silver grass," they were discussing its English translation in the group and both of them wrote "Guan Mang". I was worried and so I checked the dictionary again to reconfirm whether it is correct but I broke out into a cold sweat!

The Chinese version was completed by the end of September 2019. One after another, the articles were translated from Chinese into English by these volunteers: "Audrey Cheng, Celia Chang, BT Lin, Si Hoo Ooi, Christine Fisk, Danny Tam, Joanne Lee, Gloria Chou, Erin Lin, Jane Lin, Carmen Sy, Emily Chu and Helena Lin".

Over in the Philippines, another group did the final English proofreading. When the book was finally completed, it was already the end of the year. Over these few months, everyone has really worked hard.

I was like a butterfly that was flying around the forest when it accidentally crashed into a book about the Ormoc Great Love Village. Yet, I hope that I have not discredited my mission, presented the local traditions and customs of the Philippines accurately, and let the stories of everyone's resolute conviction that collectively brings out the spirit of Great Love and the stories of transformation of the villagers be passed on to more people. May these touch and inspire the lotus flower in each and every heart, and may these lotus flowers continually bloom under the starlight in the dark night.

(Translated by Si Ho Ooi)

慈濟國際援助系列001·菲律賓

奧莫克 看見希望
Tzu Chi Village of Hope

作者／蘇芳霈Fang-Pei Su
翻譯／鄭茹菁Audrey Cheng、張麗雲Celia Chang、林碧桃BT Lin
　　　黃時好Si Ho Ooi、楊大蓉Christine Fisk、譚瑞欽Danny Tam
　　　李慧瓊Joanne Lee、周晶婷Gloria Chou、林妤Erin Lin、林婕Jane Lin
　　　蔡碧清Carmen Sy、簡婉平Emily Chu、林秀雲Helena Lin
攝影／潘信成、陳玉萍、李佳美、娜彼安、鍾文英、Jonas Trinidad、曾永忠、徐金生
校對／高怡蘋、Bill Lockhart、Jerry Olson、David Rojas、Alfredo Li

創辦人／釋證嚴
發行人／王端正
平面總監／王志宏
英文主編／鄭茹菁
英文編輯／Michael Siao、Jonas Trinidad、Jamaica Mae Digo、Erika Vizcarra
　　　　　Lineth Brondial、Camille Nepomuceno、Erika Vizcarra、Laddee Li
　　　　　Kalam Chan、Erin Lin、Mary Angeli Adviento
中文主編／陳玟君
特約編輯／吟詩賦
企畫編輯／邱淑絹
執行編輯／涂慶鐘
美術指導／邱宇陞
美術編輯／金魚
出版者／慈濟傳播人文志業基金會
　　　　11259臺北市北投區立德路2號
編輯部電話／02-28989000分機2065
客服專線／02-28989991
傳真專線／02-28989993
劃撥帳號／19924552　　戶名／經典雜誌
製版印刷／新豪華製版印刷股份有限公司
出版日期／2020年1月初版一刷
定價／新臺幣400元

國家圖書館出版品預行編目（CIP）資料

奧莫克 看見希望／蘇芳霈作
初版.一臺北市：慈濟傳播人文志業基金會，2020.01
376面；15×21公分 — （慈濟國際援助系列；1）
ISBN 978-986-5726-80-5（平裝）中英對照
1.佛教慈濟慈善事業基金會 2.社會福利 3.菲律賓
548.126　　　　　　　　　　　　　　109000072